God Gave Us the Right

God Gave Us the Right

Conservative Catholic, Evangelical Protestant, and Orthodox Jewish Women Grapple with Feminism

CHRISTEL J. MANNING

RUTGERS UNIVERSITY PRESS
New Brunswick, New Jersey, and London

Library of Congress Cataloging-in-Publication Data

Manning, Christel.
  God gave us the right : conservative Catholic, Evangelical
Protestant, and Orthodox Jewish women grapple with feminism /
Christel J. Manning.
      p. cm.
  Includes bibliographical references and index.
  ISBN 0-8135-2598-5 (hardcover : alk. paper). — ISBN 0-8135-2599-3
(pbk. : alk. paper)
    1. Feminism—Religious aspects—Christianity. 2. Conservatism—
Religious aspects—Christianity. 3. Christian women—Religious
life—United States. 4. Feminism—Religious aspects—Judaism.
5. Conservatism—Religious aspects—Judaism. 6. Jewish women—
Religious life—United States. I. Title.
BT704.M355 1999
305.48'6'0973—dc21   98-8500
                                                                        CIP

British Cataloging-in-Publication data for this book is available from the British
Library

Manufactured in the United States of America

For my Parents, Anita and John Manning

Contents

Acknowledgments

THIS BOOK EXAMINES what it means to be a religious conservative in secular America at the end of the second millennium. Using feminism as a symbol of secular liberalism, I sought to understand the different ways in which conservative Protestant, Catholic, and Jewish women negotiate the often conflicting demands and rewards of membership in their religious community and the larger society. I focused on three communities in southern California as case studies of broader developments in three very different conservative traditions—Evangelicalism, Catholicism, and Orthodox Judaism—and employed an ethnographic approach, involving study of the groups' literature, extensive fieldwork, and over seventy-five personal interviews. Because of the personal nature of many of the narratives recorded here, I have changed the names of all individuals, organizations, and locations, and have altered many identifying details. I am deeply grateful to the women in these communities who so generously shared a piece of their lives with me, and to the religious leaders who facilitated my entry into their congregations. Although they may not agree with all aspects of my interpretation, I hope they will sense the respect and empathy in my attempt to tell their stories.

Numerous individuals and institutions supported the research for this book. Many thanks to my mentor, Clark Roof, for his encouragement of my initial research idea, his unfailing faith in my ability to carry it out, and his consistent support through all stages of research and writing. Thanks also to Julie Ingersoll, Father Virgil, and Tamar Frankiel, who helped me locate appropriate communities, and to Mark Thoburn for letting me crash on his couch on so many of my trips to Los Angeles. And thanks to the Society for the Scientific Study of Religion for a grant that allowed me to hire a typist to transcribe the many hours of interviews I had taped, as well as the two transcribers, Richard Merkel and Dinah Crawford, who ended up doing the work.

As this research took on written form, many individuals offered helpful suggestions. I would like to give particular thanks to Julie Ingersoll, Debra Kaufman, and an anonymous reader at Indiana University Press who gave valuable pointers to assist my analysis of Evangelicalism, Orthodox Judaism, and conservative Catholicism respectively. Thanks also to Patrick Foster who helped me think through the problem of "consistency" vs. "coherence," and to Mark Chaves who referred me to the literature on the "new institutionalism." I have had numerous opportunities to present some of this material at the national meetings of the Association for the Sociology of Religion and the Scientific Study of Religion, and I thank all those who responded. I also appreciate Bradley Hertel's invitation to present my research to a faculty seminar at Virginia Polytechnic Institute in Blacksburg, and Claire Marrone's invitation to do the same at Sacred Heart University in Fairfield, as well as the comments of faculty who participated. Others who have reviewed my writing include Catherine Albanese, Richard Hecht, Celia Rumsey, Elisa Vandernoot, Stewart Hutchings, and Stephanie Toise. I thank them all for their interest and insight.

In moving from manuscript to published book, I am deeply indebted to several people. Special thanks to Martha Heller, my editor at Rutgers University Press, for her enthusiastic support, patience, and practical advice throughout the revision process, and to my father, John Manning, who read and commented on the many drafts that never made it to my editor. Thanks also to Lynn Davidman whose critical comments motivated me to completely rewrite an earlier draft of this book, and to Margaret Bendroth, whose constructive suggestions shaped the final work. Last but not least I thank Sacred Heart University for a grant to pay for the index and the staff at Rutgers (especially Brigitte Goldstein) for putting the finishing touches on the volume you now have in front of you.

I dedicate this work to my mother and father, Anita and John Manning, whose love and support made it possible. It was my mother's spirituality and latent feminism that first sparked my interest in women and religion, and it was my father who encouraged me to pursue that interest academically. For the last five years, my father provided intellectual and practical advice on my research and writing, and my mother gave emotional support when, as so often happens, personal life interfered with the completion of this project. As I write this description of my parents, I notice how easily gender stereotypes (male professional, female nurturer) obscure the much more complex reality of who these individuals are and our relationship to each other (e.g., that my parents are of different nationalities and religions, divorced, or that my mother raised three children by herself). I feel fortunate to have been born to such unique and loving persons who have helped me to question surface perceptions of gender, family, and religion. I hope that this book may stimulate the reader to do the same.

God Gave Us the Right

Part I

Who Are We Talking to?

Chapter 1	Stories of Ordinary Women

As we approach the millennium, Americans are returning to conservative religion. In stadiums across the country, tens of thousands of Promise Keepers meet not to watch football but to commit their lives to Jesus and traditional family values. Teenagers are being born again at Christian rock concerts, and the conservative Christian political lobby group Concerned Women for America has more members than the feminist National Organization for Women. For the last thirty years, membership in conservative Protestant denominations has risen at an average five-year rate of 8 percent, at the same time that membership in mainline churches has fallen at an average five-year rate of 4.6 percent. Methodists and Episcopalians, for example, have decreased by 38 percent and 44 percent respectively as a proportion of the U.S. population, while Southern Baptists, Assemblies of God, and Churches of God in Christ have increased by 8, 211, and 863 percent respectively (Hunter 1987; Short 1997). What is new is that the resurgence of conservative religion has now spread beyond Protestantism. Beginning in the 1980s, journalists and scholars noted a revival of traditional Judaism and conservative Catholicism.[1] James Davidson Hunter, sociologist and author of *Culture Wars*, argued in 1991 that religious conservatives are overcoming their differences as they discover common concerns. The rest of the decade seems to be proving him right. The Christian Coalition, the most prominent religious-right lobby, is reaching out beyond its traditional Protestant base. In November 1993, *Newsweek* reported that "Robertson's Christian Coalition—heretofore a political engine for evangelical Protestants—is openly courting conservative Catholics." Two years later, the Christian Coalition had established the Catholic Alliance, an outreach program designed to bring Catholics into the fold of the religious right. The religious right's presidential candidate in the 1980s was Evangelical Pat Robertson; in the 1990s it is Catholic Pat Buchanan. Evangelicals are also courting Orthodox Jews. Orthodox Jewish film critic Michael Medved has been a guest on James Dobson's *Focus on the Family* radio show. And one of the most popular speakers at Christian Coalition events is Daniel Lapin, an Orthodox rabbi and founder of Toward Tradition, a conservative lobby group. If these trends are any indication, the conservative wave is not just rising up but spreading out in all directions.

Why? It is often thought that people are "returning" to conservative religion because they are fed up with the excesses of liberalism. Liberalism today is associated with big government that wastes money and discourages individual responsibility; with a therapeutic mentality that blames the social environment for individual behavior; and with an ideology of cultural and religious pluralism that has resulted in an absence of standards and in moral relativism. Even long-time supporters of liberalism (women, minorities, labor) are inclined to say that liberalism has created a welfare state that makes people dependent and lazy, a justice system that coddles criminals, affirmative action laws that allow underqualified applicants to get jobs, and a permissive morality that has destroyed the family. Liberalism today has become a dirty word, so much so that even the Democratic Party hesitates to associate with it. Conservative religion, on the other hand, has risen in prestige at least in part because it represents an antidote to liberalism. Conservative religion, its leaders tell us, provides a strict moral code that makes for intact families and good citizens; it encourages self-discipline, responsibility to community, and respect for authority. Conservative religion explicitly links social decline to the demise of the traditional family model that was dominant in the 1950s. If women stay home, so the argument goes, there will be more jobs for men, unemployment will fall, and wages will rise. If kids are taught good religious values, then they won't get pregnant or become criminals. Conservative religion promises the restoration of a golden age when life was simpler than today.

But what exactly are conservatives returning to? The 1990s are not the 1950s. The traditional family in particular does not seem a realistic destination. Less than 10 percent of families today fit the 1950s ideal (male breadwinner, female homemaker, and dependent children) and the majority of women (including married women with preschool children) work outside the home. More importantly, the decline in real income that most Americans have experienced in the last two decades means that women's employment is no longer a choice but a necessity to support a family (Coontz 1992). When both spouses work, chores must be done on weekends, leaving less time for religious observance, and children are cared for by nannies or day-care centers that may or may not share the parents' religious commitment. What then does it mean to be religiously conservative in the 1990s? How can religious conservatives function in a secular world? How do they resolve the tensions produced by conflicting economic and religious needs, and how do their solutions change what it means to be "religious"? How are conservative Catholics and Orthodox Jews different from conservative Protestants, and how do those differences affect the impact that the return to conservative religion will have on American society?

One way to answer these questions is to look at women who have returned to conservative religion. This book is a comparative study of women who have converted or returned to conservative Protestant, Catholic, and Jewish communities and the way they negotiate modern secular ideas—feminism in particular—with the demands and rewards of traditional religious participation. I chose to focus on converts (people who were raised in a more liberal religious community) and returnees (people raised in a conservative community who left and later rejoined) because their decision to switch represents a clear choice for conservative religion and against liberalism. My focus is on women because women are at the center of the cultural currents that are transforming American society. Because the privatization of religion in America means that the family is one, perhaps the only, area where religion has significant influence (and where most people consider that influence appropriate), conservative religious leaders have given disproportionate attention to what they call family values, especially to gender roles (hot-button political issues such as abortion or gay rights are directly linked to a concern that we are not abiding by God-ordained roles). Women are still the heart of most families. When parents divorce, mothers usually get primary custody. When Christian families homeschool their children, it is almost always the mother who does the educating. It is the mother who determines how closely a Jewish family will observe the kosher laws. And it is women who, by joining the labor force, are challenging traditional religious gender roles. Women therefore have a powerful influence both on what it means to be a religious conservative today and what it will mean for the next generation.

I focus on feminism because feminism has become a powerful symbol for the secular liberalism that religious conservatives are supposedly revolting against. By feminism I mean the liberal feminist movement that is represented politically by organizations such as NOW (unless otherwise indicated, the terms "feminism" and "feminist" will be used in this sense throughout the book). In an effort to secure equal treatment for women, liberal feminists have tended to downplay gender differences, arguing that they are largely a product of socialization and should not be the basis of differential rights and responsibilities. By pushing for government solutions to problems of inequality (e.g., legislation supporting reproductive choice, gay marriage, welfare, affirmative action) and by explicitly criticizing traditional religion as sexist, the feminist movement has become a powerful symbol for what religious conservatives reject. Thus feminism has in many circles become just as dirty a word as liberalism (just ask a group of college-age women if any would call themselves feminists). There are of course, many different kinds of feminism, some of which (e.g., the special rights feminists of the nineteenth century or the new difference feminists of the 1980s) disagree with liberal feminist assumptions about gender and methods of achieving equality (these distinctions will be discussed in more detail in the next chapter). But liberal feminism is the most visible, and more importantly, it is what religious conservatives associate with the term feminism.

Finally, I decided to focus on Protestants, Catholics, and Jews because, in America at least, these traditions are where the conservative upswing is most visible. The rise of conservative religion has made scholars increasingly interested in what some see as a worldwide fundamentalist revolution, but it has been difficult to define what exactly that means (these difficulties will be discussed in detail in the next chapter). Most fundamentalists are theologically conservative, but not all are socially or politically conservative; some fundamentalists separate themselves from society and some seek to change it; and there are denominational differences. Because fundamentalism first emerged within Protestantism, there has been a tendency to assume that characteristics of conservative Protestants (e.g., taking the Bible literally, seeking to reform society) apply to all religious conservatives when conservative Catholics and Orthodox Jews may be quite different. Looking at Catholic and Jewish, as well as Protestant, communities gives us a more inclusive understanding of conservative religion.

A comparative study of women in conservative religion and the way they come to terms with feminism is a powerful lens through which we can understand what it means to be conservatively religious at the turn of the century. Let us begin to look through that lens and listen to the stories of three of the women I met.

Three Women

KATRINA

Katrina is a woman in her late thirties who belongs to Victory Church, a charismatic, Evangelical Protestant congregation in Beachside, one of many ocean-side communities that make up greater Los Angeles.[2] A member for more than fifteen years, Katrina rejects such labels, preferring to call herself a "spirit-filled Christian." She is active in her church, attending both Sunday services and Wednesday evening praise meetings, as well as a weekly Bible-study fellowship. All of her four children attend Victory Christian School. I arranged to meet Katrina at her home on a Sunday afternoon in late March of 1993. Like most of the houses in Beachside, hers was small but well kept, the tiny yard filled with flowers and shaded by a large avocado tree. It was a warm, sunny day, and Katrina greeted me at the door wearing baggy shorts and a big, loose T-shirt. She is tall and slim, fair-skinned and freckle-faced with short curly red hair. "You must be Christel," she grinned, and invited me in. The decor was yuppie-rustic: white walls, door and window

frames and beams on the ceiling in unfinished pine, gray carpet, black
leather couch, lots of indoor ferns and palms. On a shelf next to the
impressive stereo system, I noticed several Bibles and success-tapes. We
sat down on the couch and plugged in the tape recorder. She talked
assertively, laughed easily. "So you want to know what it's like to be a
Christian woman . . . well, that's me!"

Like many other women at Victory, Katrina was raised in a liberal
Protestant home and, after a rebellious adolescence, met an Evangelical Christian man and was "born again" in her early twenties. She married young, had children, and stayed at home while they were infants.
She now works as a registered nurse who runs the emergency room at a
nearby hospital. Her husband, Jeff, is a contractor. She has been working part-time, but lately his business hasn't been doing so well, so they
have begun to rely more and more on her income.

The gender roles promoted by Katrina's church are very traditional:
women should stay home and submit to male authority. If returning to
tradition is a rejection of feminist values—and the secular liberalism
they represent—we would expect her to express discomfort about working, perhaps to explain how nursing is really just an extension of motherhood. Yet Katrina talked about her job and the role she plays there
in highly egalitarian terms that seem to contradict traditional gender
norms. She strongly rejected the notion that women should not have
authority over men. "If a leader is a leader, God's given us talents. I
run the emergency room, and I do a good job," she said proudly. "I've
got men under me. If you treat persons fairly and with respect and love,
and you're honest and not hypocritical, you're straight, have integrity,
then that's what's going to show through—whether you're a man or a
woman—in a leadership role. It's not your sex that's gonna show
through, it's your integrity as a person." Unapologetic about women's
employment, Katrina supports legislation prohibiting gender discrimination and sexual harassment. She is confident in her own abilities and
seems to enjoy her work. She even suggested that Jeff should stay home,
watch the kids, and start work on adding a second level to their home
while she brought in the income. "It's a job I absolutely love, you know.
I just love it, and it's excellent, excellent money!"

By contrast, when she talked about her role in the church, Katrina
defended traditional gender norms. Women's leadership "is just not

scriptural," she explained, citing the familiar arguments about male headship. She believes that women can teach other women or children, and they can be missionaries, but they cannot pastor a congregation. "I think a lot of ministry is not on the forefront. I think ministry is to people on the block, or . . . women who are at home with their kids can be, ministry is to your kids, or people at work. It doesn't have to be in front of a pulpit. Ministry is an everyday thing, and I think women that are hung up on having to be a minister, having to be in the limelight, that's a problem. There's plenty of ministry that happens on a day-to-day level that is equally if not more effective." Women should be content with the role that God has given them. Those who fight for ordination are, in her view, simply power hungry.

Katrina's interpretation of her role at work can be identified as feminist in the sense that she accepts and supports liberal feminist assumptions about gender equality: gender differences should not be the basis of differential rights or responsibilities. Her interpretation of her role in church is traditionalist in the sense that she embraces patriarchal notions of complementarity: gender differences mean that men and women have different roles to play. The apparent contradiction between these two interpretations is avoided by a strict separation of the secular and religious contexts of her life: work and church. The two interpretations come into conflict, however, when she considers her role in the home.

There is tension over who is responsible for home and childcare. When I asked her how she would define women's role, she asserted that women's primary responsibility is to care for home and children. "It's the most valuable thing you can ever do," she said, smiling, as we watched her two youngest romp around in the yard. "I used to think when I was home, I can always go back to work, I can always pay the bills, there's always going to be work, but there's not always going to be kids. They're not here for very long." In stark contrast to her earlier assertion that she loves her job and wants to be the breadwinner of the family, she now told me that "it's not my choice, to work. I love being at home. I love it." She now felt the need to justify her decision to work: "I think the way I've resolved it is, the way we've resolved it is, is that me working means that we can . . . live. Jeff isn't making enough money, there's really no other option right now. If I was working to support three

cars, or more cars, or more things, I think that's wrong, to support a
lavish lifestyle . . . but, you know, we live in a real world. Sometimes
women have to work. It just so happens that I can make really good
money, and Jeff—we need that right now. That's when you come alongside your husband and support him in that way. It's not what I want to
be doing, not at all. I want to be home with my kids, but it's what I
have to do right now." Like many Evangelical churches, Victory
encourages couples to live more modestly on one income, connecting
acceptance of traditional gender roles with a rejection of materialism
and consumerism. Yet Katrina builds on that connection to explain why
she has chosen not to be a full-time homemaker.

There is also tension over who has family authority. In contrast to
what she said about the workplace, Katrina claimed that men should
have authority in the home and affirmed that women should submit to
their husbands. But she then went on to define submission so as to set
clear limits on male authority.

> Submission, horrible thought, really. Submission does not mean
> you become a floor mat to your husband. What submission
> really means—you've got to take that whole piece of scripture
> as an entirety—it means, it says, wives submit to your husbands
> as Christ does for the church. And you think about it, what
> Christ did for the church? He died for the church. So the
> husband has to do it as Christ did, it's a mutual thing. See, you
> submit and come under leadership 'cause the male is the
> stronger vessel, you know. Somebody's got to be in charge.
> Whether you run an emergency room or you run an office, or
> you run a house, somebody has to be ultimately in charge. It's
> not that they're any better than you are or worse, it's just that
> somebody has to be in charge. Now, if the submission thing is
> working right, you're both in charge really.

Indeed they are. Jeff clearly does not have the authority over his family that Katrina has over the emergency room, since all family decisions
are made by her and Jeff together. As a good Evangelical, Katrina takes
the Bible literally, but she interprets it with a feminist twist.

What does it mean when conservative Christians contrast traditional gender roles with "the real world" or reinterpret them from a feminist perspective? Fundamentalist communities are often seen as a haven

from the uncertainty and relativism of secular society, a place where biblical norms are applied absolutely without regard for changing times and places. Yet this does not seem to be the case at Victory Church. Katrina does feel that conservative Protestantism gives her a structure that she was lacking before she became a Christian. She talked about how "there's an underlying set of rules" she is accountable to that non-Christians don't have. "When you don't have the Bible, you don't have direction, and you don't know where you're going." Yet she rejects the notion of biblical gender roles that are fixed and unchanging. "That's why you have a relationship with God," she explained. "Christianity is not a bunch of rules, it's a changing thing. The boundaries don't change, but what's right for me is not necessarily right for someone else. There are absolutes: you don't do adultery, you don't cuss and swear, you don't lie, cheat, and steal. Those are the absolutes, but within the relationship with God there's a lot of flexibility. Like a good marriage, within a good marriage, there's a lot of flexibility . . . and that's like the relationship with God, there's flexibility, there's freedom, and there's change. Nothing ever stays." Katrina seems well aware of what she wants out of her church: a sense of direction, of structure that is flexible enough to allow her to experiment with her role as a woman. When asked what attracted her to Victory Church, she gave a rather pragmatic response. She told me that she initially joined only because her husband happened to be a member. "I was real skeptical about church, I never saw it working. And that's what's kept me in this church. It works. If it didn't work, I wouldn't be here." She laughed. "I really wouldn't. Life's too short to stay with something that isn't working. If it didn't work for my marriage, I wouldn't be in it. If Christianity and having a relationship with God didn't save my marriage, which it did, I wouldn't be doing it. I wouldn't be telling my girlfriends that I'm saved and that, hey, you guys need God." Religion to Katrina is not just a matter of truth and meaning; it must also work to structure her particular situation and meet her personal needs. While her independence and her love for her career could create potential tension with the traditional norm of submissive homemaker that is promoted by Victory Church, she resolves that tension quite gracefully by creatively reconstructing Evangelical gender norms to incorporate feminist values.

Her acceptance of feminist values does not mean, however, that

Katrina supports the feminist movement. Though she acknowledges that feminism "grew out of a lot of frustration in women" and that the movement "has done some good," she believes feminism ultimately has a destructive impact on society. By denying the differences between the sexes, the movement has caused men to abdicate their responsibilities as providers and encouraged homosexuality. The movement has also harmed women, many of whom postponed marriage and children and are now "lonely and bitter." According to Katrina, "there's a lot of selfishness in movements like that. Like, I want to do my own thing, forget about you. I'm more important than you." It is this attitude that leads women to forget their natural maternal inclinations and support "the right to have abortions," which she believes is currently the main concern of the feminist movement. "The NOW movement is really quite dead. It's really just a pro-abortion movement now."

Katrina's rejection of the feminist movement is a metaphor for the tension between all religious conservatives and secular society. What may be unique to Evangelicals is how she seeks to reduce that tension. Political activism is not enough. Though she has signed petitions seeking to outlaw abortion and has called her congressional representative urging him to vote against letting gays into the military, she argued that "what we have to dwell on as Christians is not [political issues]. . . but it's the people. If people have a relationship with God, they're not going to be promiscuous or get an abortion. That's what we have to deal with . . . we need to get these people saved." Legislation alone will not change the selfish attitudes that feminism has promoted; the real solution is to "bring people to Christ." In other words, the way to resolve the tension between Evangelical norms and those of the larger culture is to expand Christian values to the rest of America. Because Evangelicals like Katrina constitute the majority of religious conservatives in America, it is easy to assume that they are representative of all conservatives. But are they? Let us turn for a point of comparison to Orthodox Jews, the smallest contingent in America's conservative revolution.

MIRIAM

Miriam is a woman in her mid-thirties. She belongs to Beth Israel, a Modern Orthodox Jewish community in the Los Angeles area. Miriam, too, rejects labels and prefers to call herself an observant Jew. She observes the Sabbath, keeps a kosher home, and follows the family purity laws, but she does not cover her hair.[3] She is active in her synagogue, regularly attending Sabbath services and frequently catering food for events organized by Beth Israel. Once a week she attends an evening Talmud-study class where she practices translating Hebrew text and interpreting rabbinical commentaries. While she works as a public school teacher, all of her three children attend a private Hebrew day school in the neighborhood.

I arranged to meet Miriam on a Thursday evening in early September of 1993. It was already dark when I arrived at her apartment, the ground floor unit of a two-family house located on a quiet, tree-lined street in the heart of the city's Orthodox neighborhood. Looking through the screen door as I rang the bell, I could see Miriam approaching. Medium height, her thick dark hair tied up in a pony tail, she was wearing a red dress and an apron covered with flour. She seemed to be counting, repeating the number six, over and over again. "Six, six, six . . . come right in and have a seat, I'll be done in a minute . . . six, six, six. . . . " I followed her into the kitchen where she was measuring cups of flour into a large bowl. "Seven, eight, nine, ten—I'm making challah bread for the holidays, and I didn't want to get the proportions wrong." She was preparing about ten loaves to be frozen for *Rosh HaShanah* (Jewish New Year) the following week, eight plain and two with raisins. "My husband hates raisin challah, so I never make it, but I love it, and since I'm making so many there will be enough of the plain kind that I can make some with raisins for me." I sat down and looked around. The kitchen was long and narrow with wooden cupboards painted white, a big gas stove and linoleum floor. The counters were covered with bags of flour, sugar, yeast, raisins, and spices, and there were several bowls and a pile of dirty dishes in the sink. Four loaves of challah sat on the table cooling off, filling the air with the yeasty scent of just-baked bread. I chatted a bit with Miriam's husband, Leonard, who was loading the washing machine in the next room. Finally, after about half an hour, Miriam was done kneading the dough. She placed it in the oven to rise, and we sat down to begin our talk.

Like many women at Beth Israel, Miriam was not raised Orthodox. "We identified ethnically as Jews, but my family was not religious." She became more interested in Judaism in college after attending a Jewish summer camp. They had a "very intellectual approach to Judaism, like why you do the *mitzvot* [commandments], and the ethics, the reasons behind everything . . . I was very excited about it. I felt very much that this is me, this is what I believe in, and it's already what I am but I didn't know it was what I was." She decided to begin observing the Sabbath, but she was not very strict about it. "We used to have like Shabbes dinners and invite people over, but we'd drive and we used lights." After a few years, she decided to go to Israel to learn Hebrew. It was there that she met Leonard who had become Orthodox several years earlier. Miriam further increased her level of observance until "by the time I came back from Israel, I was *shomer mitzvot* [observant of the commandments]."

Miriam's perception of her role in the synagogue initially struck me as less traditionalist than Katrina's. She explained to me that one of the reasons she and her husband came to Beth Israel was its progressive rabbi. "I didn't like the synagogue we went to before because the *mechitzah* [partition separating the men's from the women's section], it was, the men were in the front and the women were in back, and there was a curtain in between." At Beth Israel, the two sections are side by side, separated by a fence that you can see through. By contrast, at the other synagogue, "you couldn't see, you couldn't see through that curtain. And that didn't even bother me so much, 'cause many synagogues in Israel were set up that way, but what I found very offensive here was that you also couldn't hear." Her voice was distraught. "I mean, when I can't see, I don't know how critical that is to your praying. But hearing is critical! There are certain parts of the *tefillah* [prayer] that you have to respond to. If you're listening to the *Torah* [Pentateuch; Jewish Bible] being read and you can't hear the Torah being read, you really feel like a non-entity." Similarly, Miriam rejects what she calls "a very dual standard in the area of education of girls and women that exists in many Orthodox circles." She complained that the school her daughter attends "doesn't teach *Gemara* [part of the Talmud] to girls" and that the quality of girls' education declines after boys and girls are split in fifth grade. "Even if the contents of what they're learning is different, I would expect her to learn at a high level . . . and that she feels—I think the problem is those people who denigrate women's education." She strongly disagrees with "the whole concept that women shouldn't learn Gemara, that girls don't really need to be that well educated. They just need to know *halacha la ma'aseh*, the *halacha* [Jewish law] of what you do, how to keep a kosher kitchen, how to keep Shabbes, how to raise the children, and other than that not really much. That's really the only thing in Orthodoxy that offends me." What offends her is not that women are given different roles, but that they are not fully included in the religious community. "Not only am I insulted by [that exclusion], I think it's very harmful to Judaism, because you take girls and women who are very bright and very intellectual and open them up to university and the highest challenges of secular education, and don't open up Jewish education at a high level to them. And I'm afraid that the best and the brightest will turn to secularism and not be involved in Judaism, and to me that's a terrible loss." Compared to Katrina's enthusiastic defense of traditional gender roles in her church, Miriam seems to have a lot to gripe about.

Yet Miriam's gripes do not indicate a rejection of tradition. While she sets clear limits to Orthodox restrictions on women, her criticism of women's exclusion is motivated by her desire to maintain the tradition—including that tradition's separation of gender roles. Her insistence on a permeable mechitzah and on girls' Gemara classes suggest that, so long as she is allowed to participate, she can accept a role that is separate. Miriam does not think women should be ordained because "there's too many *halachic* [legal, according to Jewish law] problems with that", and she believes that sitting separately from her husband, behind the mechitzah, actually helps her concentrate on her prayers. If both she and Leonard want to go to *shul* [synagogue], she will stay home to watch the children. "If one of us has to stay home, I mean there's a halachic issue, I mean he's obligated as a body of the *minyan* [quorum of ten men needed for Jewish communal prayer] and I'm not. So if only one of us could do it, I think the person who is obligated should do it, 'cause he has the *mitzvah* [commandment] and I don't." She does not question why she is not counted in the minyan or has fewer religious obligations than her husband.

By contrast, she does question differential treatment of men and women on the job. While she asserted that the Orthodox distinction between male and female roles is "in a lot of ways accurate—accurate to nature," she also insisted that "just because men and women are different, I don't know if that means that they necessarily perform roles with unequal ability. Just because they approach it in a different way doesn't mean the job won't ultimately get done. If you ask me, I would be chauvinist the other way: I think that women are superior to men." She laughed. "OK, that's because I'm a woman and I like my sex, but really, as far as management and getting things done, women's approach is generally better, being cooperative and involving people and getting feedback and stuff like that." Miriam believes that "women are as capable as men in professions or jobs, there's no question that is true, and that women deserve the same pay as men for the same job, there's no question that that's true. She feels "it's awful that women didn't have those options in the past," and that we need legislation prohibiting gender discrimination and sexual harassment in order to maintain those options.

Like Katrina, Miriam avoids tension between two contradictory interpretations of women's role by compartmentalizing her life. But she too struggles to define her role in the home. Like Evangelicalism, Orthodox Judaism teaches that the man is the head of the family, but Miriam strongly rejects any notion of male authority in the home. "My husband would laugh if he heard you asking that. No, I don't [submit to my husband], and I don't think there's that much halachic interpretation that you necessarily should." Like Evangelicalism, Orthodox Judaism assigns domestic responsibilities to the woman. Miriam agrees that this is natural. "Women are much more attuned to the small details of child rearing," she asserted, "all the ins and outs. I mean if I were going to do something with our kids, I would think about the different ramifications and moods and this and that, while my husband would probably say, 'OK, we're going to do this now.' It's not that he wouldn't find an activity, but his approach would be much more like, this is the activity and everybody should just go along with it, that's it. Whereas I would say, what does this one like? what does that one like?" Yet she qualified her acceptance of tradition by noting that this role does not come naturally to everyone. "I'm really a big advocate of mothers of young children staying at home and spending all their time on young children. However, if you hate being at home and you're depressed and yelling at your children all the time, then I think you should put the children in day care and go to work, and then everybody can be a little bit more sane. . . . Besides, one income families aren't doing so well anymore, so I don't know that [staying at home] is an option, and I don't know what should or shouldn't be. You have to work out how you're going to be happy." Miriam clearly does not see financial need as the only valid reason for women to work. As I watch her husband fold the laundry, I realize that for Miriam, whether or not to adopt traditional gender roles is not a religious decision but a practical choice.

What does it mean when religious conservatives, especially Jews, see traditional norms as a choice? Whereas conservative Christians emphasize belief in religious teachings (e.g., the resurrection of Christ, the millennium) to distinguish themselves from liberals, Orthodox Jews emphasize observance of religious practice (e.g., dietary laws, the prohibition of work on the Sabbath, the requirement that married women cover their hair). Because some of these practices are visibly different from the habits of mainstream culture, Orthodox Judaism appears even more antimodern than fundamentalist Christianity. Yet, like Katrina, Miriam does not see traditional gender roles as fixed and unchanging. She told me that "one of the standard misconceptions of Orthodoxy, even perpetuated by some Orthodox Jewish people, is that halacha is unbending, it doesn't change and it doesn't move. It just is, and you either take it or you don't take it, and if you can't take it, get out. And that just isn't true! That just isn't true! I mean we've studied so many things [in her Talmud class] over the years . . . and clearly halacha does change. And it changes according to the times, it changes according to what people are doing and not doing." Not only do gender roles change but it is perfectly appropriate to disagree on what they are. "I have a halachic lifestyle, so I mean when you have a halachic lifestyle, you base a lot of your life's decisions on halacha, and anybody who knows halacha knows that there are a variety of halachic decisions that can be reached on certain questions." Disagreement, according to Miriam, is built into the Orthodox Jewish tradition. "If there's a question about whether—if there's a halachic question about something, we ask a rabbi . . . but no Jewish people follow the same halachic interpretation." Yet despite that flexibility, Orthodoxy provides Miriam with a sense of structure that she feels she needs. Thus she appreciates traditional roles because "it takes a lot of pressure off relationships when a certain part of the relationship is accepted as given." She believes that the structure provided by Orthodox Judaism "is very good for family life, I think it's a great way to raise children, I think it's a great way to build a marriage." She also values the strong sense of community at Beth Israel. "I felt very disconnected from my whole environment when I was growing up. That was the amazing thing about Israel, it was the only place I've ever lived in where I felt part of the society, I really felt like part of the majority there." Her synagogue and the Orthodox neighborhood surrounding it replicates that experience. Like Katrina, Miriam has chosen a religious community that provides her with what she needs: structure and community coupled with the flexibility to explore who she is. Miriam, too, is able to resolve potential tensions between the traditional gender norms of Orthodoxy and the roles she wants to play by drawing on resources within her tradition that are compatible with feminist values.

Yet Miriam does not embrace feminism as a movement. Like Katrina, she acknowledges that women have benefitted, but Miriam, too, has reservations about feminism's impact. "A lot of women, certainly my generation—I'm forty—got screwed up by the women's movement, totally screwed up. A lot of women never married and never had families because they were so into being women and not being subservient to men . . . they didn't form any relationships, and I think they got screwed. It was awful for them." Though she does not fault feminists for making men irresponsible or turning them into homosexuals, she would agree with Katrina that feminism has encouraged selfishness in women, which has led to callousness toward others. Recalling feminist opposition to legislation mandating a twenty-four-hour waiting period before getting an abortion, she is outraged at the women's movement. "That was one of the things where the women's movement has corrupted American values . . . if you can't wait and think about it for twenty-four hours, that's really sick!" However, Miriam differs significantly from Katrina in that she has no interest in fighting feminism's influence on the larger culture. This difference is most apparent in her attitude toward the abortion issue. Miriam believes that "potential life" begins at conception and that abortion on demand is a violation of Jewish law. But she does not believe that this norm should extend to anyone outside the Jewish community. "Judaism is for Jews, it's not necessarily for non-Jews. Most of American society is not Jewish, and I don't think that they need to be bound by halacha. I think I need to be bound by halacha, and open abortion on demand is not halachic, but that doesn't mean that whoever, Sally Rodriguez in East LA, has to be bound by my religious commitment." For Miriam, the way to resolve the tension between Orthodox Jewish norms and those of the larger culture is not to expand her values to the rest of America—as Katrina does—but to separate herself from mainstream society.

Miriam's response to feminism—and the liberalism of secular society—is different from Katrina's. On the one hand, her calls to make the synagogue more inclusive of women and girls and her argument that Jewish law does not require female submission contrast with Katrina's defense of tradition in church and home and suggest that Miriam is more inclined to embrace feminist values and adapt to secular society. On the other hand, her refusal to be the custodian for the rest of society with respect to political issues such as abortion is a much more separatist position than that taken by Katrina. As we shall see, these differences are no coincidence. Both Evangelicalism and Orthodox Judaism have endorsed patriarchal gender norms, but their theological traditions and their historical relationships to the larger society make for a very different interpretation of those norms.

What about conservative Catholic women? Though conservative Catholic women share the traditional gender norms of Evangelicals and Orthodox Jews, their situation is different in that they do not have the option of joining a separate, *conservative* Catholic community. Most of the members of an Evangelical church are likely to be conservative Protestants, just as most of the members of an Orthodox synagogue are likely to be observant Jews. A Catholic church, by contrast, is likely to include both liberals and conservatives, feminists and traditionalists, in the same congregation. Conservative Catholics therefore often find themselves in the minority within their own church. Moreover, while many of the Evangelical and Orthodox Jewish women were raised in liberal Protestant or Reform Jewish communities, most conservative Catholics, even if they made their commitment to traditionalism as adults, were raised Catholic. Thus a Catholic woman who rejects feminism is unlikely to make that rejection visible—as her Evangelical or Jewish counterparts might—by joining a different church. Keeping these differences in mind, let us turn to the life of one of the Catholic women in this study.

BARBARA

Barbara is a woman in her early forties who belongs to St. Joseph's Church, a conservative Catholic congregation in Altura, one of many Los Angeles suburbs in the San Fernando Valley. Born and raised in the church, Barbara is active in her congregation, attending Mass regularly and leading a support group for teenage girls. She has participated in a cursillo (an intense, encounter-type three-day weekend) and marital retreats and has had several mystical experiences.[4] Both of her older children attend St. Joseph's School; her youngest is still an infant.

I arranged to meet Barbara on a hot July day in 1993. She runs a day-care center out of her home, so we scheduled to meet during nap time, from noon to two o'clock in the afternoon. Her house is virtually indistinguishable from the myriad of tract homes that make up new development areas like Altura: pink stucco with blue trim, a small strip of green lawn, a Honda Civic parked in the driveway. Barbara greeted me at the door. "The kids are asleep, thank God." She is a small woman, a little plump, with curly brown hair and a warm smile. She led me into a hallway decorated with small framed pictures of waves or rolling hills with sayings such as "Where he leadeth, I shall go" superimposed in fancy white script. The living room had been transformed into a nursery. A big wooden bookshelf was stuffed with children's books, games and plastic toys; dolls and trucks littered the floor. A playpen in one corner held a little boy, fast asleep. On a cot near the window were two older children, also napping. Barbara and I sat down on two well-worn couches in front of a white Formica coffee table strewn with copies of *Catholic Digest.* I plugged in the tape recorder next to the baby-noise transmitter that monitored the infant in the next room, and we began our interview.

Unlike Katrina and Miriam who switched from more liberal to more conservative denominations, Barbara never officially left the Catholic church. She chose St. Joseph's because "I live in Altura and there is no other Catholic church here" but also because she grew up here "and I know a lot of people." She says her faith has always been strong, but admits that she was not always as committed a Catholic as she is now.

"When I was nineteen . . . I got pregnant and I married a man who had no faith at all." She had a second child and was divorced by the age of twenty-two (her marriage was annulled a year later). Yet it was her faith in God that pulled her through difficult times. She related a mystical experience she had during a retreat for single women soon after her divorce.

> It was real easy to find a place alone, and I was sitting there—
> they had this little stream running through this land—and I
> remember hearing noise. I was just sitting there with my eyes
> closed, praying, and I remember feeling angry that somebody
> had the nerve to intrude on my quiet time, and I looked up and
> I saw a crowd of people, and I was really scared . . . and all of a
> sudden two men started walking from the crowd, and the fear
> was gone instantaneously. And I saw Jesus, and he just sat there
> and smiled at me, and he kept saying, "Things are going to get
> tough, but keep your faith and let people know that other
> things may be unhappy in your life but you're happy because of
> your faith." And it was the most overwhelming sense of peace I
> ever felt.

Barbara's religious experience led her to intensify her commitment to her church. Committed to raising her children as Catholics, she worked full-time to pay the tuition at St. Joseph's School. After twelve years as a single mother she met her current husband, Ben, a computer programmer with a local company. Also divorced and raised Lutheran, he eventually converted to Catholicism.

Although conservative Catholic leaders promote traditional gender norms similar to those found in Evangelical and Orthodox Jewish communities, Barbara's position as a single mother has instilled her with strong feminist attitudes about women's role in society. Like Katrina and Miriam, she insists that women are capable of anything men can do and strongly supports equal rights legislation, but her arguments are more passionate because they are grounded in her personal experiences of discrimination.

> I worked for a company and I didn't get paid as much as a man
> who was there less time. We had . . . there was a printout that
> said who was the most viable employee, who did the most work,

and I was double his! But he made more money. And I talked
to my supervisor who suggested the pay raises, and she told me,
"Well, he has a family to support." And I was a single mom at
this time, and she knew I had two kids! I—I was just flabber-
gasted. And I did have the right, even then, to sue but I didn't
have the knowledge or . . . I would have been too scared
anyway. I wouldn't have sued anyway, even if I'd known I
could. But I think we need those laws, 'cause there's still a lot of
belief within this society that it's OK to pay a man more, and
not just pay a man more, it's OK to promote men and not
women. And I don't think that's OK! I don't think women
should choose a career over family, but if they choose a career,
nobody has the right to keep them at a certain level.

Barbara's encounter with gender discrimination provides an explanation for why religiously conservative women support feminist values in
the workplace: they know what it is like without them. Barbara has gone
through what feminists would call a "consciousness-raising" experience.
She recognizes that women's domestic work is not valued as highly as
men's jobs, and that even when women are engaged in paid employment, they are often not taken as seriously as men. Her present position as a day-care provider is an example. Working five days a week, "I
take weekends off. I do this until . . . the children usually come in around
eight . . . and I do it until five-thirty. It is definitely a job! The hard
part about this job is that a lot of people, my husband included, keep
forgetting that it is a job. He really does expect a lot out of me. I think
if I was gone, like if I worked at a preschool, if I was gone out of this
house, I don't think he would expect as much as he does [regarding]
taking care of the house and family and everything else that I do." Because she recognizes the double standard that is applied to women, she
supports feminist efforts to pass comparable worth and affirmative action legislation. In her view, society still has a long way to go before
sexism is eliminated.

By contrast, Barbara takes a more traditional view of women's role
in the church, resisting recent feminist attempts to get women ordained
as priests. "I think the women's movement has pushed too hard to get
women ordained. . . . I don't see that as one of the major issues facing
women because I don't think this world is ready for it yet." She defends

her church against charges of sexism. "I think women need to see that they already have a stronger role in the church than most people believe. I'm lucky. Most people I know at church are very, very involved, so they don't have any delusions that their voice doesn't count because they're female. They know that's ridiculous. They know that good priests listen to the women of their parish." Barbara is not particularly concerned with the theological reasons against women's ordination, but opposes it on practical grounds. "I don't think they should be [priests] because I don't think the church is ready for it yet. And I don't think it's an issue important enough to split the church over. Because I really think there would be a major split like there was back at the Reformation if women became priests." Since women already have plenty of power in the church, she feels that risking such a split is simply not worth it.

Like Miriam and Katrina, Barbara struggles to balance traditional and feminist conceptions of her role in the home. When I asked her if she thinks there are divinely ordained natural roles for men and women, she responded: "I don't know. That's really hard for me because . . . women can and should be able to do lots of different things. I just don't think it's fair to have children and then have somebody else raise them. You can do both [work and raise children] to a point, but you can't immerse yourself in your job at the expense of your children. I really honestly believe the most important thing any woman can do is raise happy healthy children, and you can't do that if you never interact with them." While Barbara supports a woman's right to have a career, she feels that most women underestimate the impact they can make by staying home, raising their children. "A nanny is not going to give them the morals they need. . . . You can't depend on people like me [day-care providers] to do it for you. You can use people like me to supplement that, but it's your job." When I asked if moral education is mainly the woman's responsibility, she answered, "No, but it usually falls on the woman. I don't think it should, but it is. That's just the way the world is. With very few exceptions, the woman does it. I've thought about that. I don't know if it's genetic or not. I don't know if women are naturally more nurturing or if it's just a role we've always assumed. I don't think it necessarily should be like that. It just is. I don't think people should necessarily be greedy and obnoxious, but people often are." While Barbara questions the idea that women *should* be the primary caretakers of home and children, she accepts the reality that in practice they often are.

She is similarly "realistic" about male headship of the family. While Katrina claimed to embrace male authority in the home and Miriam flatly rejected it, Barbara openly expressed her ambivalence. She admits that "I get upset" every time the priest discusses biblical passages relating to female submission. "Submit is a hard word. I couldn't submit to something I felt was morally wrong. I think husbands and wives need to work together." On the other hand, she sees submission as one of the necessary consequences of married life. "I also think [that] in any relationship, I don't care how much you say it's fifty-fifty, one of the people is going to dominate more than the other. Not all the time, but that's just human nature." Submission, like staying home with her children, can be a practical decision. "In my marriage, it's usually my husband [who is dominant] because he's stronger than I am . . . no, I shouldn't even say stronger than I am. I really think I'm stronger than he is, but I'm strong enough to think more and say: 'Is this really important to me?' I do that a lot more than he does, he'd be the first to admit that, that when it comes to a disagreement, I have the ability to stand back and really be objective about it and say: 'Now how important is this? Should I continue with an argument that's really going nowhere or should I give in?' " Like Katrina, Barbara sees strength in submission. Yet unlike Katrina, Barbara does not believe her husband is the spiritual head of the family.

> I see it as the opposite. Not in all cases, but in the families I
> know the women are really the spiritual leaders. Somebody, I
> don't remember where I heard it, said women are more capable
> of spiritual depth. I don't believe that, but I think in many
> cases they have more opportunity to be. I have a lot more
> chances and time to read the Bible, and not just read, I have a
> lot more opportunity to think about it. During the day when
> I'm working, the things I do, in my case childcare, naturally
> lend themselves to thinking about God. I put up a picture in
> the playroom of Jesus and children. I put that there on purpose
> because I want to remind myself that these are his children. So
> that just lends itself to thinking about it. My husband works on
> computers all day, and I don't see how you can connect that
> real easily . . . with God.

To Barbara, who takes on the position of headship, just as who takes on primary responsibility for childcare, is determined not by feminist or traditionalist ideology but by the context of a particular relationship.

Barbara sees Catholic gender roles as flexible, ever evolving to meet the needs of the times. She questions some of the church's rules, particularly those on divorce, birth control, and women's relationship to men. "If I could go back in time and talk to anybody, I would talk to him, to St. Paul. I really have a feeling that we'd argue a lot, but I kind of like that. I like debating with people. I really would like to know what he really meant." Yet she also sees the wisdom in church doctrine, even in some of the rules she has trouble following. "A lot of people think the church wants Catholics to have as many babies as possible so the church gets bigger. That's not the reason they don't want you to use contraception. They don't want you to use it because they want you to put it in God's hands." She acknowledges that "I use it. I don't like using it . . . I like the idea that I have faith in God to leave that in his hands . . . but that's where my faith is a little bit weak at this point." And she is convinced that those rules which she experiences as excessively restrictive of women will change in due time, "perhaps when we get a new pope." In the meantime, being Catholic provides her with a sense of order and community that has "pulled me through every difficulty in my life." Even though she has misgivings about the church, Barbara "like[s] being Catholic." The church to her is "like family— you don't just up and leave just because you're upset at someone. You try to work it out."

Like Katrina and Miriam, Barbara affirms some feminist values and struggles to reconcile these with the more traditionalist norms of her religion. Yet like her Evangelical and Jewish counterparts, this conservative Catholic woman is critical of the feminist movement. Feminists, she feels, have devalued motherhood, and she is convinced that many women at her previous job looked down on her when she decided to quit and run a day-care center out of her home. "Raising my family and being a good wife is my number one, no matter what job I have . . . but in their eyes, all women for the sake of sisterhood should want to climb the corporate ladder. I think that's wrong!" Barbara's willingness to take action against the feminist movement falls somewhere in between that of Miriam and Katrina. While she does not endorse the separatism of the Orthodox Jew, neither would she make common cause with the Evangelical. Unlike Katrina, Barbara's antifeminism is not connected to antihomosexual sentiment. "God made [gays] that way, and I don't think it's fair to discriminate against them." Barbara is critical of feminist support for abortion, but unlike Katrina she does not equate feminism with abortion. "Pro-life women who are speaking out, I think one of the reasons they feel they *can* speak out now is because of the women's movement." In Barbara's view, it is "women [who] are going to do more to end abortion than men." When each woman begins to think that "my voice is important," she will stand up for what she sees as a real women's issue, the concern for life. That concern includes not only abortion, but "the death penalty . . . the health care issue. There's so many things involved with being pro-life, and to me being a good Catholic means being pro-life in everything, not just abortion. . . . if we're not willing to use our resources, time, money, whatever it takes, to give an equal life to all people, then you can't say you're pro-life." Barbara does not support the kind of anti-abortion politics promoted by Evangelicals like Katrina because an alliance with Evangelicals would require her to support issues she opposes. Calling herself a "pro-life Democrat," she insists that "what's gonna end abortion is prayer, is people realizing that this is a holocaust . . . politics isn't going to end any of the evils of the world. Prayer and faith is going to end that." Neither does she support evangelization to convert others to a Christian pro-life perspective. Opposing abortion means "making your voice heard against what every human being, regardless of their faith, should naturally know is wrong—killing another human being." In short, although Barbara does not separate herself from the larger culture in the way that Miriam does, she is at best a reluctant participant in the culture war.

Feminist Values and the Feminist Movement

Barbara, Miriam, and Katrina, all belong to conservative religious communities, churches and synagogues that have been considered part of the so-called religious right, the conservative revolution that rejects the feminist movement as a symbol of the excesses of liberalism. Yet what is striking is that all of these women have also been influenced by feminist norms and manage to integrate the two seemingly opposing value systems in rather pragmatic ways. Official gender norms in Orthodox Judaism, Roman Catholicism, and much of Evangelical Protestantism define a woman's role by her biological function as mother: abortion and in some cases any form of birth control is prohibited; woman's place is in the home raising the children and caring for her husband, while religious leadership is reserved for men. Yet none of these women fully accept that line: biology alone is not sufficient to confine women to a particular role. A woman's role, in their view, is also defined by the choices of the individual.

Within their individual lives, these conservative women of Catholic, Evangelical, and Orthodox Jewish background integrate feminist values in a similar manner: by compartmentalizing their lives into work, where feminist norms prevail, and church or synagogue, where they do not. These women choose to work, despite the fact that they have small children, because they want to maintain a middle-class standard of living in a high-cost area, but also because they enjoy it. Work, they feel, should be governed by feminist norms: complete equality for men and women. Yet they have also chosen to be part of a traditional religious community that is governed by traditional religious norms: men and women have different though complementary roles and male authority prevails. They balance these seemingly contradictory choices by supporting traditional gender roles within the symbolic boundaries of that community—the church or synagogue—but embracing feminist roles outside those boundaries—on the job or in the wider society.

That strategy fails, however, when it comes to the home. In this context, each woman develops a unique method of reconciling traditionalism and feminism by drawing on the particular resources of her religion. Katrina's literal interpretation of scripture does not allow for much variation in interpretation of women's submissive, homebound role. Yet Katrina finds that her personal relationship with Jesus allows her to interpret that role in new ways. In any given situation, God may want her to do something other than stay at home or do as her husband tells her to. Miriam, on the other hand, finds that the halachic tradition allows for multiple interpretations of Jewish law. At issue for her is the denial of equal religious education for women, which is based on the assumption that women's primary responsibility is homemaking and that the man is the head of the household. Since halachic disagreement is an integral part of Judaism, the fact that some rabbis prohibit equal education is irrelevant so long as *her* rabbi permits it. Barbara's case is different still. The Catholic Church has been ambiguous on women's role in the home, calling for women's equality while prohibiting contraception. For conservative Catholics, who distinguish themselves from liberals by their insistence on obedience to the magisterium, it is this prohibition that creates a potential conflict with modern gender roles. The hierarchical structure of the church does not allow for the kind of disagreement found in Judaism, nor is there much emphasis on the personal relationship with Jesus promoted by Evangelicals. Instead, Barbara counts on the fact that church doctrine has changed in the past to predict that it will do so again in the future. In the meantime, she can ignore the prohibition on artificial birth control by attributing it to her weak faith and hoping that God will forgive her. Modern gender roles, then, create different conflicts in the lives of conservative Catholic, Evangelical, and Orthodox Jewish women, and they deal with these conflicts in different ways.

The women also differ in their views of the feminist movement and their relationship to the larger culture. Despite their embrace of some feminist values, Katrina, Miriam, and Barbara oppose feminism as a political movement and are critical of its impact on American society. They all see abortion as a reflection of feminism's negative influence: it devalues motherhood and undermines women's natural inclinations to care for others. But they differ significantly in what they are prepared to do about that. For Katrina, the feminist movement is a problem because it has secularized society. Thus she seeks to reshape the culture according to the values of her tradition, or, as Evangelical leaders have put it, to Christianize America. For Miriam, by contrast, feminism's influence on non-Jewish America is, by and large, not a problem. Concerned with preserving the values of her own community, she has no interest at all in shaping the larger culture, much less allying herself with Evangelicals. Barbara is somewhere in between. She is concerned that the feminist movement promotes abortion in America, but she is even more concerned that feminism threatens to divide her church. Reflecting the dilemma faced by American bishops, she wants to keep her church together without compromising principles. Her broader understanding of "pro-life" as including support for poor women and op-position to the death penalty reflects the bishops' teaching about a "Seamless Garment Ethic." As if to reach out to more liberal Catho-lics, she redefines the pro-life position as essentially feminist.

The reader may object that these individuals may not be typical of Evangelical, conservative Catholic, or Orthodox Jewish women in America. But that is precisely the point! There is no typical conserva-tive Christian or Orthodox Jewish woman.[5] Generalizing about reli-giously conservative women as antifeminist, and lumping together traditionalist Protestant, Catholic, and Jewish women into the same religious-right camp distorts who these women are and the ways in which they participate in the transformation of gender roles in America. Moreover, the lives of these "atypical" women do reflect more general characteristics of their respective communities, characteristics that are essential for comprehending the conservative revolution.

First, the experience of Katrina, Miriam, and Barbara reflects the broader reality that feminist values have penetrated conservative reli-gious communities. The Catholic Church, for example, has long been involved in the promotion of traditional gender norms through its ac-tive opposition to reproductive choice. Yet most Catholic women vir-tually ignore the church's teaching on birth control, and Catholics have abortions at almost the same rate as non-Catholic women (Francome and Francome 1979; Westoff and Jones 1977). A majority of Catholic women have expressed concern over their lack of a role in church ser-vices (Brown and Lukes 1988; Forman 1988; Greeley and Durkin 1984), and organized attempts to fight for women's ordination, such as Womenchurch, have existed since the mid-seventies (Trebbi 1990). While such efforts have been firmly rebuffed, the shortage of priests has meant that a growing number of parishes are pastored by women.[6] This policy undermines arguments against women's ordination and has led increasing numbers of Catholics to support it (Wallace 1992).

Evangelicals are perhaps most closely associated with the promo-tion of antifeminist attitudes. Within the conservative coalition of re-ligious groups that mobilized political opposition to the ERA and abortion, fundamentalist and Evangelical Protestants have been the most vocal in espousing traditional gender roles: wifely submission to her husband's authority and women's duty to stay home and raise the children (Brown 1984). Yet there is mounting evidence that such norms do not necessarily reflect the experience of ordinary women. Studies show that even among fundamentalist Protestants, most wives do work outside the home (Ammerman 1987) and that younger Evangelicals support such work even if it is not necessary to support the family (Hunter 1987). While many Evangelical women are willing to assume a traditional role for themselves, they reject the traditional role for their husbands, insisting on greater male involvement in house holding and child rearing (Hunter 1987; Rose 1987; Stacey 1990).[7] Ironically, it is Pentecostal churches, who are among the most conservative on gender norms, where women preachers appear to be most prominent (Lawless 1988). Increasing numbers of Evangelicals, particularly younger ones, support women's ordination (Hunter 1987), and their concerns have led to organizations such as Christians for Biblical Equality and a growing body of popular literature debating the issue (e.g., Gundry 1977; Karssen 1987; Malcolm 1982).

Orthodox Jews too have experienced tension with patriarchal gender norms. Alone among all major Jewish denominations, Orthodox Judaism rejects women's ordination, continues separate seating in the synagogue, and excludes women from the minyan. However, like their Catholic and Evangelical counterparts, some Orthodox Jewish women in America have organized to fight for gender equality in the synagogue. Due to such efforts, women in some Orthodox synagogues now participate in rituals previously reserved for men. There are women's *tefillot* (prayer groups), women sit in the *sukkah* (booth) during the *Sukkot* holiday (festival of booths or tabernacles), they dance with a Torah scroll on *Simchat Torah* (festival celebrating the conclusion of the annual cycle of Torah readings), and many women insist on celebrating a *bat mitzvah* (initiation into adulthood) for their daughters. While most of these changes remain highly controversial (and are officially opposed by some prominent rabbis), women's study of the Talmud, which had previously been considered only appropriate for men, has become increasingly accepted in Orthodox circles. With respect to women's role in the home, some studies show that contemporary women trying to commit to the patriarchal family structure experience significant role strain (Bunim 1986; Schwartz 1991); others find that Orthodox women avoid such stress by incorporating "proto-feminist principles" into their lives

(Kaufman 1991). While these women may not call themselves feminists, it is clear that they are not insulated from the impact of the feminist movement.

Secondly, the diverse experiences of Katrina, Miriam, and Barbara highlight long-standing theological and historical differences between Catholics, Protestants, and Jews. By theological differences I mean that specific beliefs about women and practices considered appropriate for women vary in each group. Emphasis on submission is strongest in the Evangelical tradition, which requires male headship in both home and church. Yet Evangelicals also stress each individual's personal relationship to Jesus, which can undermine doctrines of male authority over a woman (if both the male pastor and her husband oppose a woman's intent to attend a class at the local community college but Jesus tells her to go ahead, she has a very strong case for taking the course). In Orthodox Judaism, there is less emphasis on submission than on domestic responsibility. Women are exempt from most time-bound mitzvot, which frees them up for domestic work but also excludes them from synagogue leadership. Women in an Orthodox shul sit separately from men, do not wear special ritual clothing (yarmulke, prayer shawl) and do not publicly read the scripture. Yet women play a significant role in domestic rituals such as the Sabbath, a celebration considered as central, if not more so, as community worship in the synagogue (Frankiel 1990). There is also an emphasis on ritual purity that is not found in conservative Christian communities. Thus women are responsible for preparing food according to the laws of kashrut and must follow family purity laws during their menstrual period. Contemporary Catholicism, finally, emphasizes motherhood more than either submission or domestic responsibility. The veneration of Mary and a long list of female saints has generally been used to support traditional women's roles, but their existence also legitimates spiritual leadership roles for women (Weaver 1985). More than in Evangelicalism and Orthodox Judaism, restriction of women is tied to the female body: through the absolute prohibition of contraception and through the argument that priests must be male so that they can physically represent Christ. Traditional gender roles, then, mean something different for conservative Protestants, Catholics, and Orthodox Jews.

Other differences between these women have to do with the diverse historical experiences of Catholics, Protestants, and Jews in America. The Jewish experience is shaped by being a minority. Partly due to employment discrimination against Jewish males, Orthodox communities have put fewer restrictions on women obtaining secular education or working outside the home. Ironically, it is because Orthodox tradition has seen religious scholarship as a male prerogative that many Eastern European Jewish women worked outside the home to contribute to its economic support (Glenn 1990) and that upper-class women entered secular schools and universities before their male counterparts (Weissman 1976). In the American context, on the other hand, maintaining traditional gender norms became a way of perpetuating Jewish identity, while embracing feminist gender norms was seen as Americanization (Wertheimer 1987)—an interpretation strengthened by the trauma of the Nazi Holocaust and the resultant concern with the survival of Judaism and the Jewish people.

By contrast, the most striking fact in the history of Evangelicals is their identification with America as a whole. Because of the dominant role that Evangelical Protestantism has played in shaping American culture in the past, contemporary conservative Christians see their resurgence as a move to revive that past, to reestablish a "Christian America." Rejection of feminist gender norms can thus be perceived not as tension with the larger culture, but as expression of the values of a "silent majority" whose voice has been drowned out by a minority of secular humanists. The history of Catholic women, finally, is shaped by a growing division within their church. Like Judaism, Catholicism in the past was often fused with ethnic identity, and violation of traditional gender norms was equated with disloyalty to one's culture. But when Vatican II opened the door to potential transformation of patriarchal norms, the expectations of further liberalization led to a growing number of "angry Catholic women" (Greeley and Durkin 1984) while opposition to existing changes roused a conservative movement, creating a conflict that is yet to be resolved.

How do these differences shape the way in which ordinary women in each community come to terms with feminism and how they relate to the larger society? There are several fine case studies that may suggest some clues. Davidman's (1991) study of adult women in two Orthodox Jewish congregations in New York shows that the Lubavitcher

Hasidim insulated themselves from the larger society while the Modern Orthodox tended to compartmentalize their lives into home, where they submitted to male authority, and work, where they did not. Kaufman's (1991) study of women in a variety of Orthodox settings across the country found that women balanced patriarchal norms by emphasizing other traditions that elevate women and by insisting on the moral superiority of women. Klatch's (1990) study shows conservative Protestants actively engaged in reforming society so as to reduce feminist influence. By contrast, women in Ammerman's (1987) study of Fundamentalist Protestants insulated themselves from the rest of society and accepted submission as a means of saving their marriage. Such bargaining with patriarchy was also observed in Stacey's (1991) study of newly Evangelical Protestants, although these women relied on a doctrine of "mutual submission" that tended to require greater changes of their husbands than of themselves. Although Klatch's sample included Catholics, no case study focusing exclusively on conservative Catholic women exists as of this writing. The chapter on women in Weaver and Appleby's (1995) book on conservative Catholics suggests that these women actively oppose feminism both within the church and in the larger society. The essay is not a sociological study, however, but an insider's perspective written by Helen Hull Hitchcock, founder of Women for Faith and Family which outlines the goals and accomplishments of her organization. Neitz's (1987) study of charismatic Catholics found patterns similar to Ammerman's; however, since many conservative Catholics reject the charismatic movement, scholars are still debating whether or not it should be defined as part of conservative Catholicism.

These studies demonstrate that conservative Christian and Orthodox Jewish women come to terms with feminism and relate to the larger culture in a variety of ways: *insulation* from society, *reformation* of society, *compartmentalization* of life, *bargaining* with patriarchy, *balancing* patriarchal norms with quasi-feminist ones, and *reinterpreting* tradition. What these studies cannot tell us, however, is whether or not a particular way of responding to feminism and relating to the larger culture is characteristic of women in a particular tradition. While an answer to this question can be approximated by comparing the findings of these studies, any conclusions drawn from such a comparison are limited by the fact that these studies were done in different parts of the country, with different demographic populations, by different methods and with different objectives in mind.[8] It is to overcome these limits that this book was written.

Drawing on two years of ethnographic research in three conservative religious communities—one Protestant, one Catholic, and one Jewish—this book explores the diversity among women who have returned to tradition. In order to understand the larger cultural context they find themselves in, we need to examine the events of recent history: the emergence of modern feminism in the 1960s and the rise of the religious right in the 1970s and 1980s. This is the focus of the next chapter. We then turn to the narrower context of the particular religious communities that these women have joined and the research methods employed in this study. Chapters 4 through 6 show how these communities have been influenced by feminist values and describe the ways in which women who are members of these communities negotiate gender roles in three different environments: at work, at church or synagogue, and at home. The following chapter explains how women deal with the inconsistencies created by their attempt to integrate feminist and traditionalist norms. Chapter 8 discusses the women's attitudes toward the feminist movement and its impact on American culture. The extent to which the women seek to *resist* that impact is examined in chapter 9. Focusing on two issues commonly associated with the feminist agenda, abortion and gay rights, we learn that although women in all three groups experience tension with feminist ideology, they resolve that tension in very different ways. The final chapter of this book explains how these differences reflect the diverse theologies and historical experiences of the three communities and suggests ways in which this diversity continues to have an impact today.

Chapter 2

The Rhetoric of the Elite

*Much of the conflict in the modern family is caused
either by misunderstanding of or by the refusal to accept
the role each member was designed by God to fulfill. . . .
It is essential to family harmony that the wife submit to
her husband's leadership.*

—TIM LAHAYE

*A true partnership between the sexes demands a
different conception of marriage, an equitable sharing of
the responsibilities of home and children and of the
economic burden's of support.*

—NATIONAL ORGANIZATION FOR WOMEN[1]

IT IS EASY to think of feminism as the enemy of conservative religion,
and it seems obvious that women who join conservative Protestant,
Catholic, or Jewish communities have chosen sides in that enmity. Conservative religious leaders have referred to the women's liberation movement as a "disease" and a "philosophy of death." They have described
feminist women as "witches," man-hating lesbians, female chauvinists,
and self-destructive neurotics reacting to an unhappy childhood (Capps
1994; Lienesh 1993). Feminist leaders are no more sympathetic to conservatives. According to some feminist writers, Judaism is the original
patriarchal religion that drove out the goddess traditions of earlier times,
while the Christian church is a power hungry patriarchy conspiring to
keep women oppressed by forcing them to have unwanted children. As
a recent article in MS put it, the Catholic Church's anti-abortion
efforts are motivated by "a stubborn will to exercise authority and control, a determination made fiercer by . . . the deep contempt the hierarchy feels for women."[2] Both feminists and conservatives see the rise
in conservative religion as a reaction against changes wrought by the
feminist movement, but they interpret those changes and that reaction
very differently. While religious conservatives blame feminists for

destroying the traditional family, feminists take credit for freeing women from what they see as an oppressive patriarchal institution. And while feminists like Susan Faludi see the upswing in conservative religion as part of an antifeminist backlash that is threatening to undo all the progress that women have made, religious conservatives like Jerry Falwell argue that they are giving voice to a previously silent moral majority that has always rejected the excesses of liberalism.

Such rhetoric has led some observers to conclude that we are in the midst of a culture war, in which gender has become a central battleground. Sociologist James Hunter asserts that the cultural "cleavage is so deep that it cuts across the old lines of conflict, making distinctions that long divided Americans—those between Protestants, Catholics, and Jews—virtually irrelevant" (1991:43). According to Hunter, the culture war has created a new divide. On one side are the "orthodox," characterized by commitment to an external, definable, transcendent authority, who believe it essential for the "traditional family"—and patriarchal gender roles within it—to remain the dominant family form. On the other side are the "progressives," characterized by a tendency to resymbolize historic faiths according to prevailing assumptions of contemporary life, who are open to a variety of family models and seek to equalize gender roles. While the culture wars model is useful for mapping political rhetoric, it leads to a rather simplistic vision of who religious conservatives are. More specifically, the model lends credence to the arguments, made by both conservative and feminist ideologues, that (1) the feminist movement is responsible for transforming gender roles; (2) the rise of conservative religion is a reaction against this transformation; and (3) the only way to resolve this conflict is for one side to "win" the culture war. Since there is some evidence to support all three of these contentions, let us examine them in more detail.

Is the Feminist Movement Responsible for the Transformation of Women's Roles?

There is no question that women's roles have been transformed in the last quarter century. Most dramatic is the expansion of women's roles outside the home. Women have gained in political power, both as voters and as political officeholders. Prior to the 1980s, women's votes generally resembled those of men. However, beginning in the 1980s, a gender gap emerged with women favoring more liberal and men more conservative candidates. Although the gap has not been decisive in presidential elections (except for 1984), women's votes made a difference in several senate and gubernatorial races, tipping the balance in favor of the democratic candidate (Simon and Danziger 1991). There are also more women politicians. Pointing to large numbers of women running for political office, the media dubbed 1993 "the year of the woman," and the Clinton administration has appointed record numbers of women to high public office, including five at the cabinet level.

Women have also made more significant progress toward equality in educational attainment and in participation in the labor force. As Simon and Danziger have pointed out, in the 1990s "it is generally taken for granted that women have equal access to university educations and professional degrees" (1991:46) In 1995, more than half of all bachelors and masters degrees were awarded to women, compared to about 25 and 14 percent respectively in 1950. Higher education is accompanied by a rise in professional occupations. While the majority of women continue to do some type of clerical or administrative support work, about one-third of women now have managerial positions (up from one-fifth in 1970), and there are more women lawyers and doctors than ever before: women received 42.2 percent of law degrees and 34 percent of medical degrees in 1990, compared to 2.5 and 5.5 percent respectively in 1960. The more educated a woman is, the more likely she is to work full-time and year round. In 1992, 58 percent of all women were in the paid labor force (constituting 45 percent of the total), compared to 33.9 percent (29.6 percent of total) in 1950. Women are expected to constitute 65 percent of new labor force entrants between now and the year 2000. Although women, especially singles, have always worked, there has been a major shift in the record number of married women entering the labor force. The number of married women working outside the home has jumped from 25 percent in 1950 to over 56 percent in 1987. Since 1950, there has been more than a fivefold increase in the number of working women with preschool children (from 11.9 percent in 1950 to 56.9 percent in 1987). By 1992, more than half of women with children under age three and more than two-thirds of those with children under age eighteen were in the paid labor force.[3] As family researcher Stacey Coontz puts it, "the orderly progression from student to single jobholder to wife to mother to married older worker that prevailed from the 1920s to the 1960s is now gone. Modern women take on these functions in different orders or occupy all of them at once" (1991:186).

Not only have women expanded their roles outside the home; their roles within the home have also changed. As divorce rates rise and women postpone marriage and have fewer children, women spend less time being wives and mothers. Divorce rates tripled between 1960 and 1982 and then leveled off so that today 50 percent of first and 60 percent of second marriages are likely to end in divorce. The average age for marriage has risen by six years since 1950, and more than three-quarters of today's eighteen-to twenty-four-year-old men and women have never married. Most women still want children but are having them later and feel less pressure to get married first. Women in the baby-boom generation are two to three years older than their mothers were when they had their first child, and there has been a sharp increase in the number of women who do so after age thirty. Since 1960, the proportion of single teenage mothers has risen from 15 to 61 percent, and the total number of children raised by a single parent has doubled to 25 percent of all children under age eighteen. Finally, women are having fewer children (an average of 1.8 compared to more than 3 in the 1950s) and are spacing them closer together (Coontz 1992:181–187; McLaughlin 1988:123). Researchers, such as Coontz, conclude that being a wife and mother is less salient in a woman's life than in the past. "Marriage has ceased to be the main impetus into or out of other statuses, and it increasingly coexists for women, as it has long done for men, with several other roles" (186).

Many of these changes—both inside and outside the home—were actively promoted by the feminist movement, so it is not unreasonable to conclude that this movement is to blame or praise for the transformation of gender roles. Yet such a conclusion is problematic. The most serious problem is that there is no agreement on what exactly is feminism. If we just limit ourselves to secular feminism (I will discuss religious feminism later in this chapter), at least three distinctions need to be made.

To begin with, we must distinguish at least two women's movements in American history: "first wave" and "second wave" feminism. The first wave began in the 1830s and 1840s and focused on suffrage. This movement, which officially commenced with the 1848 Seneca Falls convention, eventually culminated in the passage of the nineteenth Amendment in 1920. Having achieved this goal, many women's groups disbanded, and the women's movement seemed to have dissipated until it reemerged in the 1960s. Second wave feminism, which is officially dated to the 1963 publication of Betty Friedan's *Feminine Mystique*, was primarily focused on educational and employment discrimination, abortion rights, and the passage of ERA. Although second wave feminists achieved significant gains in the 1970s, the failure to ratify ERA and the rise of the conservative religious opposition motivated continued feminist activism. Besides fighting to preserve their achievements of the past (especially with regard to abortion rights), they have added new issues, such as sexual harassment and lesbian rights, to their list of concerns (Simon and Danziger 1991). Some younger (under thirty) feminists, while grateful for the progress achieved by the second wave, have criticized the older generation for denying real differences between men and women and for failing to include women of color. These young feminists have begun to call themselves "the third wave," though it is not yet clear whether they constitute a separate movement.

Within these waves of feminism, there are ideological differences. First, we must distinguish between "equality" and "difference" feminists. The former movement, also often labeled "liberal feminism," has its roots in the eighteenth century when discrimination was justified by the argument that women are by nature inferior. In order to gain equal rights for women, early feminists had to minimize male-female differences and demonstrate that if differences did exist they were due to nurture not nature. Difference feminism, by contrast, emerged in the nineteenth-century labor movement when women factory workers fought for recognition of their child rearing responsibilities. This movement, sometimes identified as "special rights feminism," emphasizes gender differences and uses these differences to justify that women be granted exceptional treatment (Tong 1989). The women's movement of the 1970s was dominated by equality feminists who continue to wield influence in political organizations such as NOW. Beginning in the 1980s, however, there has been a resurgence of difference feminism, this time not among labor but in the halls of academia. The new difference feminism draws on the postmodern critique, which argues that norms, theories—indeed, knowledge itself—are always based in the subjective experience of those who created them and therefore distort the experiences of others who live in a multicultural, multigendered society. Since Western patriarchy was created by white men, it distorts and ignores the different needs of women and/or ethnic minorities. The goal of feminism must go beyond legislating equality—which merely allows disadvantaged groups to succeed according to white male norms—to create a society that celebrates these differences.

Another ideological distinction should be made between what I'll call "women-focused" and "race/class-focused" feminists. In both waves of feminism, there has been a split between working-and middle-class women and between white women and women of color. White and/or middle class women feel oppressed primarily because they are women, and their focus is on improving their status as women. Black and/or working-class women are also members of other oppressed groups— the working class, the black community—and may be just as, or more, concerned with improving the status of these groups than improving the status of women. Many race/class-focused feminists feel that the dominant feminist organizations are dominated by women-focused feminists who promote policies that do not benefit, and may even harm, the former.

Clearly, not all of these various feminists would applaud the changes we have seen in women's roles. Yet even if we limited our discussion to one type of feminism (second wave, liberal, women-focused), we cannot conclude that it has transformed gender roles. The fact that more women are rejecting or at least postponing marriage and motherhood in favor of education and careers could also be attributed to demographic trends (declining fertility) and economic changes (the shift from a manufacturing-based to an information or service economy).

Women may be leaving home and working in larger numbers because they are having fewer children. In *The Way We Never Were*, Stephanie Coontz convincingly argues that the 1950s family that is idealized as "traditional" is not demographically typical of America's past. The 1950s were aberrant in their reversal of long-term declining fertility trends and rising marriage age. The median age for women's first marriage was twenty-two in 1890 and did not change much until after World War II when it fell to an all-time low of 20.1 in 1956. The average number of children a woman had fell from 7–8 in 1800 to 2.6 in the early twentieth century, but rose to over 3 in the 1950s. More than feminism, it was the widespread availability of the birth control pill that returned these trends to their prewar directions by reducing the need for shot-gun weddings and giving women more control over the number of children they had (Coontz 1992:183–184; McLaughlin 1988:56, 123).

Women are also leaving home and working because they have to. As Parsons (1953) has shown, family structure is shaped less by ideology than by economic necessity. As the base of the American economy shifted from agriculture in colonial times, to industry in the nineteenth and early twentieth centuries, to information/service in the late twentieth century, family structure changed from the premodern "Godly family" (patriarch presides over integrated economic/domestic life) to the modern family of the 1950s (male breadwinner/female homemaker) to the postmodern family of today (both men and women work and negotiate relationships in "blended" families). As the economy shifted employment from heavy industry to the non-unionized service and information sectors, men began to lose well-paying union jobs and more women had to supplement family income. At the same time, employers were more willing to hire women, including married ones, because they were a cheaper source of labor. As Stacey's *Brave New Families* illustrates, what propelled women out of the home and into the paid labor force was not so much feminism as economic necessity and opportunity.

I think it is fair to conclude, however, that even if it did not cause the transformation in women's roles, the feminist movement helped accelerate the pace of change. Feminists created organizations and pushed for legislation that made many of these changes possible. One of the first and definitely the best-known is the National Organization for Women (NOW) which, since its establishment in 1966, has lobbied Congress and filed class action suits on behalf of a wide variety of women's concerns. To expand women's participation in politics, feminists established the National Women's Political Caucus (a bipartisan organization working to persuade parties to give women and women's issues more attention) in 1971, the National Women's Education Fund (which uses tax-deductible funds to train women for campaign work and for holding elective or appointive office) in 1973, and Emily's List (which raises funds and offers training to Democratic women candidates) in 1986. Feminists also worked to end educational and employment discrimination. As late as the 1960s, quotas limiting women's entry to higher education were still common. Law and medical schools restricted admissions so that only 10 percent of law students and 11 percent of medical students were women. Such practices were outlawed in 1972 by Title IX which bars sex discrimination in educational programs receiving federal funds. Although Congress passed Title VII of the Civil Rights Act (which prohibits sex-based employment discrimination) in 1964, the law was not enforced until 1972 after NOW brought suit against the Equal Employment Commission (Simon and Danziger 1991).

Feminists also pushed hard for laws that impacted women's role as wife and mother. They supported no-fault divorce laws because women were often found "guilty" and denied alimony if they initiated divorce. Feminist activism resulted in the liberalization of abortion laws in many states which eventually culminated in Roe v. Wade in 1973, the Supreme Court decision that declared abortion a woman's choice. Although feminists failed in their effort to pass the Equal Rights Amendment, their activism on its behalf undoubtedly contributed to the passage of much of the legislation listed above. Beyond legislation, feminist "consciousness-raising" also contributed to the demise of the traditional family. In their enthusiasm for female autonomy, feminists "encouraged women's massive entry into the post-industrial labor market" (which in turn abetted corporate de-unionization strategies) and provided ideological support for divorce and female-headed households (Stacey 1990:13). In short, feminists did not set the match to the house of the Leave-It-to-Beaver family, but they definitely fanned the flames.

Is the Rise of Conservative Religion a Reaction against Feminism and the Changes It Has Wrought?

Religious conservatives have worked hard to put out this fire and preserve traditional gender roles. If feminism started gaining a mass following in the 1960s, the ranks of conservative religion began to swell in the 1970s. The most visible growth occurred among Evangelicals (Hunter 1987; Roof and McKinney 1987). Since 1965, membership in conservative Protestant churches has increased at the same time that membership in liberal denominations has declined. Yet Evangelical growth goes beyond church membership. There has been considerable expansion in Evangelical publishing and religious broadcasting through which the conservative Protestant message reaches millions of people, including many who do not belong to Evangelical churches. Television preachers Jerry Falwell and Pat Robertson, radio talk show host James Dobson, magazines like *Christianity Today* or *Focus on the Family*, and books published by Zondervan, Intervarsity, or Eerdmans have an influence far beyond Protestantism (e.g., many of the Catholic women I interviewed listened to Dobson's show). Equally important is the growth in Christian schools. While publication and broadcasting provides visibility, education is invaluable because of its socializing influence on future generations. At a time of overall declining enrollment in U.S. schools, there has been a significant increase in both numbers and enrollment of private Evangelical elementary and secondary schools. In the 1970s alone, the number of Christian schools increased by 47 percent and student enrollment rose by 95 percent. By 1985, the total number of Christian schools was estimated to be seventeen to eighteen thousand, with about two and a half million students attending (Hunter 1987:6–7). Finally, and perhaps most important, is the increase in Evangelical political activism, much of which is directed against changes associated with feminism such as abortion or gay rights. Evangelicals not only mobilized voters through organizations like the Moral Majority, but ran their own candidate, Pat Robertson, in several presidential elections. While conservative Protestant political influence reached a peak during the Reagan years, their influence has not so much waned as shifted. Concentrating more heavily on local elections, such as school boards, they are considered a core constituency of the Republican party whose voting power must be acknowledged.

Less well-publicized than the rise of Evangelicalism has been the resurgence of Orthodox Judaism. The high visibility of the *ba'al teshuvah* movement, due to both scholars (Danzger 1989; Davidman 1991; Kaufman 1991) and the media (e.g., Gittleson 1984) have induced much speculation about an Orthodox resurgence. While its size is often exaggerated, there are signs of growth.[4] For the first time in fifty years, Orthodox Judaism is not declining, and is gaining—rather than merely losing—younger members. Although Orthodox Jews remain a minority (6 percent of the U.S. Jewish population), they have high fertility rates and large numbers of young people (there are more eighteen- to thirty-four-year-olds than middle-aged Orthodox Jews), many of whom are more observant than their parents. Moreover, the Orthodox are more involved than either Reform or Conservative Jews in terms of synagogue membership. If Jews were counted by synagogue membership, as Christians are, then the Orthodox would constitute 11 percent of the Jewish population (Wertheimer 1993:52–55). More important perhaps than numbers is the rising prestige of Orthodoxy within religious Judaism. Publishers of Orthodox books (such as Ktav and Aronson Press) and journals (such as *Tradition*) have prospered, and Jewish communities have seen a proliferation of businesses that cater to Orthodox needs, ranging from stores that sell prayer books and *yarmulkes* to kosher Chinese restaurants. As in the case of Evangelicals, the future growth of Orthodox Judaism is ensured by an expansion in the number of educational institutions, particularly Orthodox day schools. In 1961, there were 278 Hebrew day schools in North America, 90 percent of them in New York City. By 1981, there were 546 day schools in thirty-six states and five Canadian provinces (Raphael 1984:167–168).[5] During the same period, enrollment jumped from sixty-seven thousand in the late 1960s to close to one hundred thousand by 1983 (Bulka 1983:8). There has also been increased political activity by Orthodox Jews, such as lobbying for funding of private schools or against sex education programs in public schools (Hunter 1991:202; Raphael 1984:165–170). Agudat Yisrael has been particularly vocal in representing Orthodox political interests. Most Orthodox Jews, however, are not active on religious right issues, partly because they associate conservative Christians with religious intolerance and partly because Orthodoxy, unlike Reform and Conservative Judaism, has been characterized by severe institutional and ideological fragmentation (Wertheimer 1993).

Religious conservatism within the Roman Catholic Church is more difficult to assess and has received much less attention than either Evangelicalism or Orthodox Judaism. Indeed, research on American Catholics usually emphasizes trends towards liberalization, especially among laity (D'Antonio 1989; Greeley 1990; Hegy 1993). Yet recent studies (e.g., Weaver and Appleby 1995; Cuneo 1988, 1989) have drawn attention to a growing conservative minority in the church. Although the nonsectarian nature of the Catholic Church makes it difficult to estimate the size of this conservative contingent, there is plenty of evidence that is exists. Weaver and Appleby have documented a wide variety of conservative Catholic lay groups, including movements imported from Europe (e.g., Opus Dei, followers of Marcel Lefebvre), traditionalist Catholic identity groups (e.g., the Marian movement, Catholics United for the Faith), antifeminist and anti-abortion groups, educational and intellectual groups, and liturgical groups. The significance of these groups depends on who is attracted to them. Although conservative Catholics tend to be older and less educated, they wield a disproportionate influence on their church's policy. Moreover, younger college-educated Catholics are well represented in the movement's most visible contingent: militant anti-abortion activists. And like their Protestant and Jewish counterparts, conservative Catholics have worked hard at increasing their visibility and influence. They have established conservative Catholic journals and newspapers, such as *Fidelity, The Wanderer*, and the *Catholic Register*, and computer networks, such as the Catholic Forum, established in 1993. Responding to increasing interest among Catholics, conservatives have set up organizations to assist parents in schooling their children at home in order to provide a more "orthodox" Catholic education. According to Weaver and Appleby (1995:300–324) they have also built "self-consciously countercultural" conservative Catholic educational alternatives to mainstream Catholic schools (e.g., Trinity High School in Indiana and Thomas Aquinas College in southern California) and conservative enclaves within Catholic universities (e.g., St. Ignatius Institute at the University of San Francisco). Conservative Catholics have also become politically active. The American bishops have expressed their opposition to abortion not only in pastoral letters but in the public condemnation of Catholic pro-choice candidates (Matthews 1989). Bishops such as Los Angeles' Roger Mahoney have supported activists blocking access to abortion clinics, and priests have encouraged parishioners to join forces with Protestants in the pro-life crusade. But conservative political activism is not limited to clergy.

Less visible but equally important is the conservative Catholic lay movement. Among their spokespersons are individuals—such as historian
James Hitchcock, his wife Helen Hull Hitchcock, and erstwhile presidential candidate Pat Buchanan—and organizations—such as Women
for Faith and Family (founded by Mrs. Hitchcock) which claims over
fifty thousand supporters, and the Catholic League for Civil and Religious rights which boasts approximately thirty thousand members.
While conservative Catholics have often complained about not being
taken seriously, they received a boost from the 1985 Ratzinger Report,
which indicated that their views had acquired legitimation in the highest echelons of the hierarchy (Cuneo 1988:352).[6]

Because of its timing and rhetoric, it is easy to conclude that the
rise of conservative religion is, in large part, a reaction against the
success of feminists in transforming gender roles. But there are serious
problems with this conclusion. First, it is not clear what counts as conservative religion. Both scholars and the media have paid a lot of attention to fundamentalism as a worldwide movement that crosses
denominational boundaries, but a definition that fits all these fundamentalisms has yet to be found (Marty and Appleby 1995). Even if we
limit ourselves to the American context, at least two distinctions need
to be made. One is between "isolationist" and "integrationist" religious
conservatives. If the latter try to maintain traditionalist beliefs and practices while at the same time being part of the larger society, the former
separate every aspect of their lives from mainstream society. They usually live in a separate part of town or state and limit all interactions—
including education of their children, employment, medical services—to
fellow believers. They may be recognizable by a different style of dress
and sometimes a different language. Hasidic Jews and Amish Christians
are examples of isolationist conservatives; Modern Orthodox Jews,
Evangelical Protestants, and conservative Catholics (the groups that are
the subject of this study) are integrationist conservatives.

Even more important is the distinction between social and theological conservatives. The former means being conservative relative to
the society one lives in. It means being conservative on social issues
(e.g., opposing abortion and homosexuality) and siding with "the right"
in politics. In the United States, being a social conservative usually correlates with support for the Republican Party. Being a theological con-

servative, on the other hand, means being conservative in one's interpretation of a particular theological tradition. It means being suspicious of new interpretations and preferring a close reading of texts or laws. For Protestants, this usually correlates with a more literal reading of the Bible, for Catholics with strict adherence to canon law, and for Jews with observance of halacha. Though many theological conservatives are also socially conservative, this need not be the case. The association appears to be strongest for conservative Protestants, whose support for conservative public policy is well known. Yet even among Evangelicals, there are social liberals, particularly within black or Hispanic congregations. The proportion of theological conservatives who are socially liberal is higher among Catholics. In contrast to Evangelical leaders such as Robertson or Falwell, American bishops have actively opposed the death penalty and supported welfare, and conservative Catholics have followed their lead. Theologically conservative Judaism, finally, is even more likely to be associated with social liberalism. Though Orthodox Jews are certainly more conservative on social issues than other Jews, their minority status and relatively high level of education mitigates that tendency. Moreover, even a conservative interpretation of Jewish law allows for a more liberal position on some social issues (e.g., abortion, divorce) than would be possible for conservative Christians.

Not all of these religious conservatives have opposed feminism. Yet even if we limited our discussion to one type of conservative (socially conservative and integrationist), it is not at all clear that the rise of conservative religion was caused by a reaction against secular feminism. Though the conservative resurgence coincides with feminist success in the 1970s, the reason why people turn to conservatism is different in different communities, and conservative religious communities have responded to feminism in different ways.

In Judaism, the resurgence of Orthodoxy is rooted in a concern for the survival of Jewish tradition. The rise in ethnic consciousness of the 1970s and the emerging ideology of multiculturalism created a new respectability for difference. The growing secularism and increasing rate of intermarriage in the Jewish population as a whole is accompanied by the rise of a passionate and vocal minority who see themselves as the only barrier to the threat of Jewish assimilation. Wertheimer (1993) convincingly argues that the Six-Day War, which increased concern with Jewish survival, hurt liberal (both Reform and Conservative) Judaism and legitimated Orthodoxy as the carrier of authentic Judaism. Though many Orthodox Jews are fairly adaptationist (the Hasidim are a small minority), they provide the exemplary model of authentic Judaism to non-Orthodox Jews.

Orthodox Jewish resistance to feminism is shaped by this concern for survival. According to Orthodox writers (Poupko 1983; Greenberg 1989), it is religious feminism that challenges the survival of Orthodoxy by challenging the boundaries of Jewish tradition (traditions that feminists seek to abolish, such as the mechitzah, are what makes Orthodoxy distinct) and by its demographic impact on Orthodox Jewish membership (because career women tend to have fewer children). Worse yet, the two effects reinforce each other: the looser the boundaries of Judaism, the greater its demographic decline (the rate of intermarriage is lowest for Orthodox Jews and highest for Reform Jews). It is therefore not surprising that, compared to Protestants and Catholics, Jews have organized the least resistance to secular feminism. To the extent that they have, Jews are more concerned with the impact of particular legislation on the Jewish community than with the role of women in American society.[7]

The resurgence of fundamentalism within Protestantism, on the other hand, is a reaction against the decline of Protestant hegemony in the United States in the twentieth century (Hunter 1987). Beginning in 1965, changes in immigration laws brought large numbers of non-Protestant immigrants to the United States. At the same time, Catholics and Jews were moving into the middle class and several Supreme Court decisions reduced Protestant influence on the public square. Conservative Protestants are trying to regain that influence and have organized impressive political structures to do this. Thus when Evangelicals speak about "bringing religion back" into public institutions, they usually mean Christianity, not Judaism; when they refer to a "Christian America," they mean Protestant, not Catholic.

Evangelical resistance to feminism reflects this concern with shaping the larger culture. In contrast to Orthodox Jews, conservative Protestants face no threat to their survival from feminism. Yet feminists do hinder the ability of Evangelicals to influence public policy. By insisting that opposition to abortion or gay rights reflects personal religious preference rather than broadly shared American values, feminists challenge the legitimacy of Evangelicals to speak for the rest of America. Predictably, Evangelicals demonstrate the highest level of organized resistance to secular feminism, and the most significant antifeminist organizations (including Concerned Women for America) are primarily Protestant.

Within the Catholic Church, finally, the rise of a conservative wing reflects a deep concern over the crisis in church authority. For Catholics, the watershed event of the 1960s was Vatican II, which potentially revolutionized the hierarchical structure of the church by defining it as "the people of God" and emphasizing the apostolate of the laity. While the council's changes in liturgy, ethics, and doctrines alienated many conservatives, it raised the hopes of Catholic liberals for still further progressivism. Greeley has argued that when Humane Vitae reaffirmed the church's traditional prohibition of contraception, many liberals were disappointed, which they expressed in lower rates of giving and church attendance. Trying to keep liberals in the fold, the bishops began to pay more attention to their concerns, including feminist issues. Thus in their 1988 pastoral letter the National Conference of Catholic Bishops decried the "sin of sexism" and urged more roles for women in the church. Even Cardinal Joseph Bernadin of Chicago—known as a staunch opponent of women's ordination—said that a rejected draft of the Bishops' Response to the Concerns of Women, which endorsed ordination, would be the basis of "further study and dialog" thus leaving the door open for change.[8] It is this kind of accommodation that galvanizes lay Catholic conservatives who feel that the American hierarchy is being taken over by a feminist conspiracy.

Conservative Catholics' opposition to feminism reflects their concern that the authority of their church is being watered down. Thus antifeminist activism is often directed at the church itself. Some conservatives have pulled their children out of Catholic schools because they believe too many of the teachers are feminist nuns. Conservative lay groups blocked the National Conference of Catholic Bishops from appointing a Jesuit theologian to head the committee on doctrine because he opposed the ban on women's ordination (Hyer 1986). Women for Faith and Family gathered fifty thousand signatures for a declaration of loyalty to Rome to let the hierarchy know that not all Catholic women have been converted to feminism. According to Greeley, one could make a persuasive case "that Catholic Conservatism is motivated largely by negative attitudes toward changing roles for women" (1991:160).[9] But the issue is not that simple. It is not the changes in women's roles per se that conservatives oppose, but the accommodationist stand that it represents. Fighting abortion, for example, has motivated many conservative Catholics to resist feminism. Yet, as Cuneo argues, this fight is symbolic of something deeper. For these Catholics, anti-abortion protest, while overtly directed to protect the unborn, has become "a medium for the crystallization of a contracultural Catholic identity at variance with the evolving denominational identity of mainstream Catholicism" (Cuneo 1989). The problem for conservative Catholics—unlike their Protestant and Jewish counterparts—is that their very conservatism also prevents these Catholics from leaving a church in which most members do not share their views. "Stuck" in an increasingly liberal church, Catholic conservatives oppose feminism in American culture but often lack the support of their leaders who are trying desperately to keep the Catholic Church together.

Are Feminism and Conservative Religion Incompatible?

If feminism is not entirely responsible for transforming gender roles, and if conservative religion did not arise to resist that transformation, the fact remains that feminism and conservative religion do appear to be at war. Even though conservative Protestants, Catholics, and Jews oppose feminism for different reasons, it seems reasonable to conclude that feminism and conservative religion are diametrically opposed to each other. Yet there are also reasons to doubt that conclusion. Contrary to what secular feminist and conservative religious leaders would have us believe, there is a feminist movement within conservative communities and many of the leaders of those communities have incorporated feminist ideas into their rhetoric.

The story of Evangelical feminism is confusing because of the changing use of the term "Evangelical." Until the late nineteenth century, beliefs and practices that are today associated with "Evangelicalism"— biblical literalism and the active effort to convert non-Protestants— were part of mainstream Protestantism. The question of how to adapt to an increasingly secular and pluralistic society split American Protestantism into modernists, who questioned biblical literalism and took a more ecumenical attitude toward other religions, and fundamentalists, who rejected such changes. As the majority of American Protestants moved toward modernism, scholars identified modernists and liberals as "mainstream" while fundamentalists and other conservatives retained the label "evangelical." Though feminism is usually associated with liberalism, the birth of the feminist movement preceded the fundamentalist-modernist spilt. Indeed, "nineteenth-century American feminism was deeply rooted in Evangelical revivalism" (Hardesty 1984:9), and some of the same women who worked for women's suffrage also provided a critique of sexism in religion and called for women's ordination. Among them were Frances Willard, who published *Women in the Pulpit* in 1888, and Elizabeth Cady Stanton, who wrote *The Woman's Bible* in 1895. Although such women had considerable influence on what were later dubbed "mainline" denominations, the secession of fundamentalists resulted in an expressly antifeminist Evangelical camp.[10]

It was not until the 1960s and 1970s that feminism began to make inroads into conservative Protestantism, when Evangelical writers like Lucille Sider Dayton, Nancy Hardesty, Virginia Mollenkott, and Letha Scanzoni, began to push for biblically based marital partnership (rather than male headship) and women's full participation in the church (including ordination).[11] Evangelical feminists began their activism in the late 1960s by persuading magazine editors to publish their articles, so that "many Evangelicals first encountered feminism while browsing unwarily through Christian periodicals" (Bendroth 1993:121). By the mid-1970s, Evangelical feminists had founded their own journal, *Daughters of Sarah*. At the initiative of Nancy Hardesty, a feminist plank (albeit a rather watered-down version calling on "both men and women to practice mutual submission and active discipleship") was inserted in the 1973 Chicago Declaration of Progressive Evangelicals.[12] This meeting also led to the formation of the Evangelical Women's Caucus (EWC) in 1974 which endorsed the ERA and women's ordination, and generated considerable controversy. In 1986, because of disagreements over homosexuality, a new Evangelical feminist organization, Christians for Biblical Equality, was established which has now taken up many of the causes previously championed by the EWC.[13]

For contemporary Evangelicals, feminism is hard to avoid: while the strict fundamentalists of the early twentieth century could insulate themselves from the feminism of their times, neo-Evangelicals have purposefully opened themselves up to dialogue with the intellectual culture of their society. Because Evangelicalism had an entrenched antifeminist ideology as part of their very identity, progress in accepting feminism has been slow. Nonetheless, there are some signs of Evangelical feminist success. When the Evangelical feminist handbook *All We're Meant to Be* was published in 1975, it was voted most influential book of the year by the subscribers of *Eternity*, an Evangelical magazine. *Christianity Today* publishes many articles addressing feminist concerns, and Evangelical feminist titles are now available in many Christian bookstores. Feminism has also made its way into the leading Evangelical seminaries. Though Paul Jewett's *Man as Male and Female* provoked bitter controversy at Fuller Theological Seminary when it was first published in 1975, the seminary now requires its students to use gender-neutral language when writing papers (Fowler 1985). Clearly, there are at least some Evangelicals who think feminism and conservative Protestantism are compatible.

Feminism has had a profound impact on the Catholic church as well, but the story of Catholic feminism is quite different from that of Protestants.[14] Although many Catholic women supported women's equality in the nineteenth and early twentieth century, a self-conscious Catholic feminism did not emerge until Vatican II. Since that time, Catholic feminists have revolutionized not only the Roman Catholic Church but religious feminism generally as several of the most prominent religious feminists in America have been Catholic.

In the mid-1960s, Mary Daly's book, *The Church and the Second Sex*, provided for religious feminism what *The Feminine Mystique* did for secular feminism: it raised consciousness of women's status and set off a debate over women's roles that continues to the present day. Among the most prolific of Catholic feminist contributors to this debate are Rosemary Radford Ruether and Elizabeth Schuessler Fiorenza whose work has become classic in the religious feminist canon. Like their Protestant counterparts, Catholic feminists have challenged the traditional role of women (although in addition to questioning male headship, Catholics also questioned the use of Mary as a role model for women)

and pushed for women's ordination.[15] The first national women's ordination conference was held in 1976 in Detroit, followed by another in
Baltimore in 1978 and a third in St. Louis in 1985. Frustrated by the
hierarchy's lack of response, Catholic feminists began to call for the
empowerment of women *as* church by establishing Womenchurch.[16]
The first Womenchurch conference was held in 1983 and drew four-
teen hundred women to attend workshops on women's spirituality, create inclusive liturgies, and help lobby the hierarchy. Since then
Womenchurch groups have proliferated, and some twenty-six of them
have formed a coalition, Womenchurch Convergence, which continues to sponsor conferences and other feminist activism.

While the push for women's ordination began at the initiative of a
Catholic laywoman, a significant factor in the development and progress
of Catholic feminism has been its appeal to women religious. Although
Catholic feminism did not originate in the convent, nuns have played
a central role in helping feminist ideas penetrate the Roman Catholic
Church (Weaver 1985).[17] Ironically, several Vatican actions actually
helped bring Catholic sisters to feminism. In the 1950s, Rome's push
for higher education of sisters to make them a more effective apostolic
force exposed them to a wide range of ideas, including feminism.[18] In
the 1960s Rome's decision to send women missionaries to Latin America
was a radicalizing experience for many nuns. About twenty thousand
sisters went to work there, and many of them became converts to liberation theology. Gradually sisters became aware of their outsider status in the hierarchy and began to challenge Vatican authority which
had previously set the rules for how they ran their lives. In the mid-
1960s the Conference of Major Superiors of Women sent a unanimous
petition to Rome asking to be represented on commissions dealing with
the lives of sisters, but received no reply. In 1971 they changed their
name to Leadership Conference of Women Religious (LCWR), signal-
ing a change in their thinking about authority. During the 1970s,
LCWR endorsed the ERA and supported Network, a Washington-based
lobbying group for Third World liberation and feminist issues. Other
organizations of feminist nuns include the National Assembly of Religious Women, founded in 1968 as an attempt to give ordinary sisters
(not eligible as members of LCWR) a national voice, and the National
Coalition of American Nuns, which publicly opposed the Hatch

Amendment against abortion and drew Vatican opprobrium. Feminist nuns have also been active in the ordination conferences and in Womenchurch.

Feminist consciousness among Catholic nuns is important for several reasons. The large proportion of nuns who teach at Catholic schools means that feminist views, to the dismay of conservatives, are likely to be passed on to future generations of Catholics. Moreover, feminist nuns highlight the crisis in the American Catholic church. Until their radicalization, nuns were such a paradigm of loyalty to Catholic teachings that the term "feminist nun" still has the ring of an oxymoron. The fact that nuns, the paragons of obedience and virginity, have gone feminist in a church that refuses to ordain women and continues to prohibit birth control underscores the deep divisions that seem to be tearing the church apart. That division itself is a sign of Catholic feminist success.

The story of Jewish feminism is different still. The liberal orientation of most Jews has made them particularly receptive to feminism, more so than other Americans.[19] Although Jews are well represented among the ranks of secular feminists (e.g., Gloria Steinem, Betty Friedan, Bella Abzug), a self-conscious Jewish feminist movement became distinct from the broader women's movement in the 1960s and 1970s. It originated in part in the ethnic consciousness of that time, and its growth was helped by antisemitism in the secular feminist movement.[20] Some of the concerns of Jewish feminists reflected those of the larger feminist movement, such as fighting discrimination against women and their restriction to the family. These concerns were usually voiced by secular feminists who happened to be Jews. Other efforts reflected specifically Jewish concerns, such as divorce or women's role in communal worship; these were expressed by religious Jews who felt alienated by what they perceived to be a sexist tradition. It is these religious feminists that interest me here.

Among the most influential Jewish feminist religious writers are Aviva Cantor, Rachel Adler, and Judith Plaskow, who, like their Christian counterparts, engaged first in feminist critique and later in reconstruction of Judaism. Like Catholic and Protestant feminists, these Jewish writers have both challenged traditional roles for women and called for women's ordination. But the goals of their activism are also uniquely Jewish. Partly because of Judaism's emphasis on ritual practice and partly because the position of rabbi has a different meaning than that of pastor or priest in Christianity, there are many issues (such as being counted in a minyan, being called to the Torah, or celebrating life-cycle events for girls) that are just as important to Jewish feminists as ordination, if not more so. However, because of the symbolic significance of ordination, the progress of Jewish feminism is usually measured by that achievement.

Jewish feminism has had the most visible impact on Reform Judaism but has gradually made its way into Conservative and even Orthodox circles. Although Reform Judaism had no theological barriers to women's ordination, it was not until 1972 that the first female rabbi, Sally Priesand, was ordained. Conservative Jewish women's push for ordination began in 1971 with the formation of Ezrat Nashim which expressed women's concerns at the convention of the Conservative Rabbinical Assembly the following year. But Conservative Jews did not ordain a woman rabbi until 1985. The National Conference on Jewish Women, first held in 1973, discussed not only ordination but the creation of rituals such as the now widely accepted bat mitzvah for girls. *Lillith*, a glossy Jewish feminist magazine, was begun in 1976. By 1977, an *American Jewish Yearbook* article on Jewish feminism provided striking evidence of legitimation by the Jewish establishment. By the 1980s, feminism was also penetrating Orthodox Judaism. In 1981 Blu Greenberg published *Women in Judaism: A View from Tradition,* in which she tried to integrate Orthodoxy and feminism. Orthodox women's prayer groups became popular in New York, despite criticism by the Union of Orthodox Rabbis. By 1984, about one hundred and fifty such groups existed in the United States.[21] Condemnation from several prominent rabbis failed to intimidate these women; instead they formed the Women's Tefillah Network to support such groups (Haut 1992). In 1984, a whole issue of the journal *Judaism* was devoted to the topic of women's ordination; it included several Orthodox writers who suggested at least the possibility of change. In 1993, a cover story in *Moment* again addressed the problem with a report on an Orthodox woman who applied to Yeshiva University despite the fact that the institution does not admit women.[22] Though Orthodox Jewish feminism is clearly a minority position, the fact that it exists at all demonstrates that the two are not entirely incompatible.

Feminism is a minority position within conservative religious communities, but it is beginning to have an impact. While religious conservatives resist feminism, they cannot escape its influence. Though they officially condemn feminism as heretical—declaring it outside the boundaries of orthodoxy—many conservative religious leaders have begun to incorporate feminist language into their rhetoric, thus implicitly acknowledging its compatibility with conservative religion. They coopt feminism by acknowledging as valid the feminist complaint that women in American society are undervalued or that men often oppress them. Such problems are attributed to the secular society while a return to religious tradition is touted as the solution to the very problems feminists are trying to resolve. Characteristic of this kind of apologetic are the arguments that (1) religious tradition considers women to be equal, if not superior, to men; (2) American society does indeed undervalue women's work, but feminism intensifies that problem while conservative religion solves it; (3) men often are emotionally inexpressive and insufficiently involved with child rearing, but conservative religious communities encourage greater male sensitivity and involvement with children; (4) religious tradition celebrates sexuality; and (5) religious tradition provides strong role models for women. Let us examine these arguments in turn.

Conservative Christians and Orthodox Jews insist that their tradition considers women to be equal, if not superior to men. Thus Orthodox Jews like to argue that "women hold a higher position in Judaism than in other societies" and that Jewish marriage imposes duties on the man, while giving rights to the woman (Kaufman 1993:xxv, 37). In an article otherwise devoted to affirming that women have a special affinity for child rearing, and, were it not for feminism, would choose to be homemakers, an Orthodox rabbi argues that "there is no reason why a woman who is gifted with a particular skill or talent or fascinated by a certain subject or discipline should not be given the opportunity to pursue and achieve excellence in that field" (Butman 1984). And many rabbis have devoted countless pages to explaining why the men's prayer "Blessed art Thou, Lord our G-d, king of the universe, who hast not made me a woman" is not degrading to women.[23]

Catholics have made the same argument. Thus the pope asserts that the "equal dignity of men and women fully justifies women's access to public functions" and rejects the familiar scriptural justification for the subordination of women by arguing that "he shall rule over you" is a curse, not a model (Pope John Paul 1981). At the same time, he continues to emphasize that "virginity and motherhood" are the two particular dimensions of the fulfillment of the female personality" (Pope John Paul 1988:sec. 17). Evangelical Protestants, too, are eager to demonstrate that they are not sexist. James Dobson argues that "the decision to have a career or to be a homemaker is an intensely personal choice that can only be made by a woman and her husband." To those who argue that being a housewife is boring and monotonous, he answers that "they are right—but we should recognize that practically every other occupation is boring too" while "no job can compete with the responsibility of shaping and molding a new human being" (1982:47–49).

The conservative camp acknowledges that women's work is undervalued, but argues that feminism has intensified that problem while religious traditionalism has helped resolve it. On the Evangelical side, both Dobson (1982) and LaHaye (in Lienesh 1993:64) argue that the women's movement has scorned mothers and homemakers, while conservative Christianity values that role and realizes how hard it is. "Just as Friedan was tired of reading about the happy energetic housewife, so I am wearing of magazine articles about the successful, dynamic, mother-wife-career wonderwoman" (Dobson 1982:64). The pope argues that "true advancement of women requires that clear recognition be given to the value of the maternal and family role" and that "the mentality which honors women more for their work outside the home than for their work within the family must be overcome" (Pope John Paul 1981:21). Meanwhile, American Catholic conservatives assert that if feminism were true to the nature of women, it would recognize that "the worst injustice done to women is the undervaluation of the values of motherhood" (Smith 1991:44). Orthodox Jews, also, complain about American society's disrespect for motherhood. Strangely reminiscent of some feminist arguments, one rabbi asserts that women's interests are not advanced by "accepting a male-oriented system of values and trying to compete in that sphere" (Butman 1984).

Perhaps the best example of cooptation is the conservative admission that men are often emotionally inexpressive and not sufficiently involved with child rearing combined with the insistence that a return to religious tradition can help resolve this problem. Pope John Paul II (1981:23) asserts that the "absence of a father causes psychological and moral imbalance and notable difficulties in family relationships, as does, in contrary circumstances, the oppressive presence of a father, especially where there still prevails the phenomenon of "machismo" or a wrong superiority of male prerogatives which humiliates women and inhibits the development of healthy family relationships." The pope then goes on to encourage men to be more involved with their wives and children. Similar arguments have been made by Evangelicals, some of whom, such as Jerry Falwell, have pointed out that husbands who "spend little time at home and who take no interest in their wives and children" may actually induce women to become feminists. They articulate traditional models of masculinity that are strong but also sensitive and explicitly reject the macho standard of earlier generations. Thus Charles Stanley—an Atlanta pastor, TV preacher, and former president of the Southern Baptist Convention—admits that many Evangelicals grew up in families where "men did not hug each other, dads did not hug their sons, and people were not very expressive emotionally" (Lienesh 1993:59, 61), and Dobson concludes that "it is important for men to be able to cry and love" (1982:95). Such talk is also characteristic of the Promise Keepers movement whose efforts to involve men in childcare while maintaining male headship of the family are another example of the cooptation of feminist values.

Religious conservatives are also sensitive to the feminist claim that religion has served to suppress female sexuality and take pains to emphasize that sex is celebrated as positive—so long as it occurs within the confines of marriage. Evangelical writers acknowledge that many Christians are the products of religiously conservative homes where they have been victimized by Victorian sexual standards. To counter that problem, Tim and Beverly LaHaye's bestselling sex manual, *The Act of Marriage*, is touted as "fully biblical and highly practical" and provides detailed descriptions of male and female reproductive systems, discussion of sexual techniques and equipment, and suggestions for sexual activity (Lienesh 1993:56, 67). The Catholic Church, too, is trying hard to overcome its image as antisexuality. Conservative Catholic writers like to emphasize that sexuality (so long as it takes place in marriage) is considered holy, a sacrament, and quote John Paul II as seeing "in the simultaneous orgasm of loving spouses a uniquely intense moment of the communion of persons." The pope sees in that action "not only the epitome of married love, but a kind of model of what all human life should be—ecstatic and passionate reciprocal self-abandon" (Rousseau 1991:19). Orthodox Jews, for their part, have jumped at the opportunity to demonstrate that the sexual asceticism that has plagued Christianity since Paul is completely foreign to Judaism and that women's sexuality has always been positively acknowledged. They point out that because Judaism considers a woman's sex drive to be more powerful than the man's, the married woman has greater rights to fulfillment. Thus one of the fundamental marital duties of the husband (besides providing food and shelter) is *onah*, the duty to have conjugal relations with his wife, while the woman has no obligation to sexually satisfy the man (Kaufman 1993:128).

Finally, traditionalist Protestants, Catholics, and Jews all insist that their tradition provides strong female role models to women. On the Orthodox Jewish side, Frankiel (1990) points out that the biblical mothers (Sarah, Rebecca, Rachel, and Leah) were prophetic figures concerned not only with children but with the future of Israel. Michael Kaufman's book *The Woman in Jewish Law and Tradition* has an entire chapter on strong women, including not only biblical leaders like Deborah, but European and American women such as Emma Lazarus and Sara Schenirer. Similarly, conservative Christian women writers, while insisting on traditional roles for women, choose as models strong women like Deborah, Frances Willard, Joan of Arc, or Queen Brigitte of Scandinavia, whom Beverly LaHaye calls a "Viking warrior who became a Christian heroine." In short, the traditionalist camp acknowledges the problems, but sees itself as the solution. As LaHaye puts it, it is up to Christian conservative women to "save our society", transmitting "civilization and humanity to the 21st century. . . . Make no mistake. It is the women who will do it" (Lienesh 1993:75).

Although conservative religious leaders co-opt feminist language in order to prevent change, such use also implicitly places feminism inside the boundaries of orthodoxy. This may facilitate the efforts of genuine feminists who, though still a minority in conservative Christian and Orthodox Jewish communities, are becoming a strong and vocal one.

Feminism and conservative religion, then, are not entirely incompatible. Women in conservative religious communities therefore find themselves in a situation that is much more complex than either secular feminist or conservative religious leaders acknowledge. The notion that shared opposition to feminism can overcome past divisions between conservative Protestants, Catholics, and Jews serves the political purposes of both feminist and religious right leaders, but does not correspond to the reality faced by ordinary women. Ordinary women in conservative religious communities must make sense of their lives in a context that is shaped by both orthodoxy and feminism. How they navigate between these two will vary depending on which religious community they belong to—Protestant, Catholic, or Jewish—and what kind of social context (religious or secular) they find themselves in. In order to understand how women respond to these contexts, let us now visit the three communities that are the focus of this book.

| | Three Conservative |
| Chapter 3 | Religious Communities |

THE MISPERCEPTIONS that many of us have about women in conservative religious communities result in part from a lack of interaction with
them. We listen to their leaders and (in an attempt to get a balanced
picture) we listen to feminists—and come away with a highly polarized and distorted view of who these women are. If we want to understand these women, we must talk to them directly, on their own turf.
This takes time and effort. Getting to know a community is much like
building a relationship. Looking back at my fieldnotes, it is remarkable
how many of the defining characteristics of each community I studied
were evident at my first visit; but it wasn't until later that I realized
their significance.

Victory Church

My first introduction to Victory Church came on a Sunday in January
1993. The church is located on a corner lot, at the intersection of two
very busy streets in downtown Beachside. The sanctuary is a modest,
single-story building painted white with blue trim. The church school
next door is similar in style but is surrounded by a wire fence to keep
the children from running out into the traffic. As I parked my car in
the adjacent lot, I noticed many "Jesus loves me" and Bush/Quayle
bumper stickers.

I was greeted warmly at the door by a dark-haired woman in her thirties. When I inquired, she showed me to the staff bathrooms, the "nice ones," as she put it. Everyone seemed very warm and friendly. I took a seat in the back, next to a tall, red-haired woman and her teen-age daughter. Not knowing anybody, I took in the scenery. The room was long and square, white walls, no pictures. Across the ceiling were wooden beams from which hung the California flag and another flag in what seemed to be the colors of some Central American country. Instead of an organ, they had a band set up behind the pulpit, com-plete with piano, percussion, saxophone, and two guitars.

People milled around talking to each other until about 10:40 when the service began. Three men went up behind the pulpit. One of them announced, "Let's worship the Lord," and began singing. The music was very rhythmic, more like rock 'n roll than traditional church hymns, and people swayed and clapped their hands in time. Lyrics were pro-jected onto a big screen that hung from the ceiling, so it was easy to participate. I was struck by the militancy of the lyrics: God portrayed as glorious king who leads us into battle and defeats our enemies. I was also struck by the energy of the songs, their emotional power to pull me in to join the congregation in singing and clapping. The singing went on for almost an hour, during which the church, initially only half full, completely filled up, with people sitting along the sides as well as filling up all the pews. Most people seemed to be young (under forty) and there were many children. Their attire was festive, but not formal. Many women wore dresses, the men jeans and jackets. Most congregants were white; about a third were Hispanic and black.

It was unclear to me who was the pastor of the church; there were so many people behind the pulpit. It must be one of the three men sing-ing, I thought. Eventually, two of them left, and the one remaining, a tall thin man dressed in a dark suit, began to make announcements about upcoming events: a Valentine retreat, a lecture on homeschooling, a pro-life rally, the women's fellowship dinner, and so on. He also wel-comed newcomers and asked them to raise their hands. "Good to have you here," people said as they turned to me and smiled. "And now let's welcome Pastor Bill," the thin man continued, as the pastor finally stepped behind the pulpit.

Pastor Bill Jordan is a tall, athletic man with a deep voice; he too wore a dark suit. After calling the congregation to prayer, he began his sermon. The sermon was about Satan and the conspiracy of evil that is "out there to deceive good Christians." The pastor related this theme to teen pregnancy, drugs, and other problems which liberals are deceived into trying to solve the wrong way. "There are no teen pregnancies in our school . . . but the public schools are not the enemy, your spouse is not the enemy, Bill Clinton is not the enemy. The enemy is Satan." Drawing on the Bible and several recent Christian books (mostly of the self-help and political variety), he encouraged congregants to take responsibility for their actions and turn to Jesus for help.

After the pastor's sermon, a woman stepped up to the pulpit and took the microphone. "I want to give you a testimony," she said, and proceeded to relate how her husband had recovered from cancer after the church had prayed for him. "He has decided to become a Christian," she concluded, and everybody clapped. Next, Pastor Jordan asked us to form circles of three or four people and express our needs to each other and pray over them. Newcomers were encouraged: "It might feel awkward, but that's OK." I joined hands with the woman next to me and her daughter. The woman talked about her desire for her husband, who is Jewish, to come to Christ. The girl discussed a school science project. Then it was my turn. I told them that I hoped to find a job next year. Then the woman said, "I pray to the Lord that Christel finds the kind of job she wants, and that her boss is a Christian . . . and that Amy successfully completes her project." Next, Amy prayed over everyone's wishes, and I did the same. Finally, the pastor called the church to order. He asked all who wanted to repent their sins and drive out the devil to come to the front of the church and kneel down before the altar. One by one, about fifteen people followed his call. As the pastor waved his arms, the band began to play, first softly and then louder and louder, and the congregation joined in a final song.

Victory Church has several characteristics typical of modern Evangelicalism: the simplicity of church decor, the informality of people's attire, the triumphalist songs, the long and very political sermon, and the call to individuals to publicly commit their lives to Jesus. Like the majority of conservative Protestant churches in this country, Victory is Evangelical, but not fundamentalist; it is also charismatic. Evangelicals share much of fundamentalist theology (the emphasis on the born-again experience, the belief that the Bible is inerrant and should therefore be interpreted literally, and the active effort to evangelize) but have softened it in order to integrate into society. What distinguishes charismatics from other Evangelicals is their belief that the events of the Pentecost described in the Bible (Acts 2 and 19) apply equally to Christians today. Since anyone who has been born again can receive the gifts of the Holy Spirit, including healing, prophesying and speaking in tongues, charismatic worship tends to be more lively and emotional than that of other conservative Protestant churches.[1] Victory's contemporary music, informal style, and "touchy-feely" prayer service reflect the charismatic influence but are also an attempt to appeal to the baby-boom generation, or, as the pastor puts it, to render a "Bible-based Christianity relevant to this world." The approach seems to be succeeding. Many of Victory's congregants were unaffiliated individuals who came to Evangelicalism as adults and are now raising their children as Christians; many of the children attend the school run by the church. Although church members do not all live in the same neighborhood, most participate in so many church-sponsored events (Bible studies, home-fellowships, midweek Praise service) that they spend much of their time with each other. In a city like Los Angeles where neighborhood connections are often lacking, Victory provides its members with a real sense of community.

St. Joseph's Church

That sense of community was also evident at St. Joseph's Catholic Church. Finding a conservative Catholic church turned out to be much more difficult than finding a conservative Protestant church. Since they do not constitute a separate denomination, conservative Catholics must be located within existing churches. Depending on the size of the conservative contingent and on how vocal that contingent is, a church may or may not have a reputation for being conservative. I selected St. Joseph's because various conservative Catholic organizations had recommended it to me. Once there, I categorized the women I interviewed as conservative based on their self-identification and on where they located moral authority: a conservative Catholic is one who accepts the authority of the magisterium and feels that a good Catholic should be obedient to all church teachings (in contrast to a liberal who questions the church, locates authority in herself, and only selectively adheres to church doctrine).[2] Despite St. Joseph's reputation as a conservative community, only about half the women I talked to either identified as or fit my definition of conservative.

I started doing research at St. Joseph's in the summer of 1993. I had been invited by the pastor to come to the St. Joseph's carnival, an annual event held to bring the community together and raise funds for the church and school. So, on a hot day in mid-July I drove down to Altura, one of Los Angeles' sprawling suburbs in the San Fernando valley. I arrived at St. Joseph's a little after 10 A.M., parking beneath a huge red and white banner advertising the fair. As I got out of the car, I could smell the hot dogs and could clearly visualize a large, ice-cold diet Pepsi—but first I had to go to church.

St. Joseph's is a modern, sixties-style church building with simple lines and long stained-glass windows. The sanctuary is large, about twice the size of Victory Church, with high ceilings and long wooden pews and cushioned prayer benches. When I came in, the service had already begun, though much to my relief other late church-goers continued to arrive. I took a seat next to a woman and three little boys, ranging in age from about five to ten. There were many families, all dressed in their Sunday best, often with four or more children, all very close in age. Babies were wailing throughout the service, but no one seemed to mind. Most of the congregation seemed to be white, but I learned later that many Mexican American parishioners attend the Spanish-language Mass held later in the day.

Having just completed more than six months of participant-observation at Victory Church, I was struck by the contrast between the Evangelical worship service and the Catholic Mass. To begin with, it was much easier for me to identify the pastor at St. Joseph's. The priest was a pale, dark-haired older man wearing a long, white robe under a green vestment embroidered with gold. He was flanked by two altar boys, about twelve years old, wearing white robes under black tunics. Because St. Joseph's had been recommended to me as a conservative parish, I was surprised to see that the hymns were led by a female cantor standing at the front of the church to the right of the priest, while a female lector to his left did the readings. Both women stood below the altar and wore average clothes which clearly differentiated them from the priests and altar boys. The atmosphere at the St. Joseph's service was more solemn and formal than at Victory Church; compared to the latter, the speakers here seemed less spontaneous and more serious. While the Evangelical service had gone on for more than two and a half hours, much of which was taken up by singing and what to me seemed like a very long sermon, the Catholic Mass lasted just under an hour. The sermon was short, focusing on the importance of reaching out to those in need, and there were several Bible readings and many prayers. As in all Catholic Masses, the central event occurred toward the end of the hour in the celebration of the Eucharist. The priest brought out the host and chalice, consecrated them, and lifted them up for all to see. "Do this in remembrance of me. . . . We remember, we do this to commemorate you. . . . " Following the Eucharistic prayer, everyone lined up to take Communion. "The body of Christ," a middle-aged man intoned as he placed the bread in each parishioner's mouth; "the blood of Christ" a heavy-set Mexican American woman echoed as she gave each person a sip of wine, carefully wiping off the glass with a piece of cloth after each use. When all were back in their seats, the priest spoke a final blessing, and the sacred vessels were cleansed and put away. The organ began a final hymn and the Mass was over.

Following the lead of the crowd, I ambled over to the grounds of St. Joseph's School where the carnival was being held. The classrooms had been transformed into cafes offering cookies and donuts and gift shops selling trinkets, pencils, key rings, scarves, and many hand-crafted items made by women and children of the parish. The school yard was where the action was. You could buy raffle tickets from teenagers standing in red and yellow booths, ride a merry-go-round, or throw balls into nets or rings around sticks and win huge pink and blue stuffed animals. Laughter and screeching of children punctuated the general chatter of people milling around. The spicy aroma of salsa, hot dogs, popcorn, and pizza, all mixed together, filled the air. Staffed by volunteers, with food and prizes donated by local businesses, the carnival seemed to be achieving both its financial and public relations goals. This really was fun!

The carnival is only one of many efforts St. Joseph's has made to bring its parishioners together. As in many American Catholic parishes, the shortage of priests means that one church must serve a large number of people. St. Joseph's is the only Catholic church in this suburb, as well as the adjoining one, and has about two thousand registered members, though only about a quarter of those are active Catholics. Like other large churches, St. Joseph's must make a conscious effort to prevent members from feeling anonymous and alienated. Besides a huge variety of ministries, committees, and support groups—including Bible study, charismatic prayer, families anonymous, marriage encounter, peace and justice, prison ministry, respect life, and youth ministry—that cater to the needs of its diverse community, the church has recently begun to organize small groups that meet in people's homes so that they can get to know each other. St. Joseph's has a strong Hispanic outreach program and holds Spanish Masses. However, most of its members are white and middle-class. Among the active parishioners are a large number of families with children, many of whom attend the parochial school that is run by the church. Many felt that the church community was like an extended family that provided direction and support in an increasingly chaotic world.

Congregation Beth Israel

Shelter from chaos was also provided at Congregation Beth Israel. My introduction to this Modern Orthodox Jewish congregation was more gradual than at the other two communities. Though I had been raised in an independent, "New Age" Christian denomination, I felt confident that I could participate to some extent in the Evangelical and Catholic churches. In an Orthodox Jewish synagogue, I knew I could not. Upon advice of the rabbi, I began my research by attending the women's Gemara class, a Talmud-study group held weekly at his house.

On a Tuesday evening in March 1993, I went to my first class. Rabbi Feldman's apartment is on the second floor of a modest brick apartment building in West Los Angeles. From the street, I could see his wife and two children against the light of the kitchen window. When I rang, a little girl came to the door to greet me. Coming up behind her was the rabbi, a short, stout man with curly hair and a thick graying beard. He asked me to take a seat in the living room and went back into the kitchen to help his wife with the dishes. The room was modestly furnished with a sofa, two chairs, and a coffee table on an oriental rug. I looked at the bookshelves lining the walls. There were a surprising number of contemporary titles by or about women (including controversial writers such as Camille Paglia), as well as the expected religious books in both Hebrew and English.

The first person to show up was a woman about my age, in jeans and a big loose UCLA sweatshirt. "Hi, I'm Sarah," she said, and turned to greet the children, whom she apparently knew quite well. As we helped the rabbi set up more chairs around the dining room table, six more women gradually dribbled in. Most wore dresses, but only one covered her hair with a *tichel*. Rabbi Feldman introduced me and then handed me a leather-bound *Talmud Bavli* (Babylonian Talmud) with English translation opened up to the section we were to discuss. I noticed that all but two of the other women brought all-Hebrew editions. The procedure of the class was for one person to read a paragraph aloud in Hebrew and then translate it into English. The rabbi would comment and the group would discuss it. Then another woman would read, and so forth. The passage under study debated whether marriage can be initiated (rather than completed) by the *chuppah* ritual.[3] The central question was: how is the chuppah different from the three mechanisms (sex, money, contract) of initiating marriage? Though the topic had initially seemed abstruse and legalistic to an outsider like me, Rabbi Feldman's analysis was down to earth and often humorous. "Marriage today is still often initiated by sex and money," he pointed out, demonstrating the contemporary relevance of the issue. Discussion was lively. The women frequently disagreed with the rabbi and questioned the judgment of the sages as well as each other. After two hours, the issue had not been resolved, and we decided to continue the discussion the following week.

I attended these weekly classes for six months before I ever went to a service in the synagogue or interviewed any women at Beth Israel. My first visit was on Rosh HaShanah in September 1993. By this time, I had made friends with Sarah, one of the women I'd met in class, who had told me what to expect. Sabbath and holiday services begin with *Shacharit* (morning service) which is followed by a Torah reading and sermon, and *Mussaf* (additional service). Both Shacharit and Mussaf include the *Amidah* (silent individual prayers) and community prayers led by the *chazzan* (cantor) who stands on the *bimah* (center stage from which prayers are conducted). Rosh HaShanah differs from other services in that Mussaf includes blowing the *shofar* (rams horn) after the reading. Sarah has also warned me that "nobody ever comes to shul on time." Since services officially started at 7:45 A.M., I arrived around 8:30, which turned out to be still way too early. The men's section was about one-third filled, mostly with elderly men. There were two teenage girls whispering over their prayer books in the women's section. The balcony was empty. Through the mechitzah, a white lattice fence that separated the men's and women's sections, I watched the men, each wrapped in a blue and white *tallit* (prayer shawl), sway back and forth as they chanted Hebrew prayers. Over the next hour the men's section and much of the balcony gradually filled up with younger men, while most women did not arrive until about 10:30 when the Torah reading was about to begin.

The place was now packed. The men all wore yarmulkes (traditional Jewish head covering), dark suits, and ties. The women were decked out in their finest, silk and lace dresses, flowered hats, and fancy shoes and jewelry. I was struck by how much talking went on in the women's section during the prayer services. The women would greet each other, gossip a bit, pick up their prayer books and chant in Hebrew, quiet down the children, pray some more, say hello to a friend, and resume their prayers. I also noticed that not all of the congregants were fluent in Hebrew or familiar with the order of the service. The leadership seemed to be aware of this. Tucked in with the prayer books was a "Companion to the Rosh HaShanah Service" which explained and transliterated significant Hebrew prayers, as well as a booklet entitled *The Rosh HaShanah/Yom Kippur Survival Kit* which explained the structure and meaning of the holidays.

The day's Torah reading was about how Sarah gave birth to Isaac after Hagar had borne Ishmael. Rabbi Feldman's sermon related the passage to a contemporary image of repentance and renewal: Israeli prime minister Rabin shaking hands with PLO chairman Yassir Arafat the previous day. After the reading, two of the men opened the ark and removed several ornately decorated Torah scrolls. As they carried them down the aisles of the sanctuary, congregants reached out to touch the scrolls, many kissing their hands after doing so. Led by the chazzan, the congregants then began to recite a Psalm which was repeated seven times. Finally, one of the younger men stepped onto the bimah to blow the shofar, a long clear blast followed by several shorter ones. During the shofar service, many of the younger children climbed up onto the bimah; most were boys, but there were several girls as well. There were more prayers, followed by more shofar blasts, and additional prayers until the service ended around two in the afternoon.

The class and the service reflect many characteristics typical of Orthodox Jews as well as some that make this congregation unique. As in conservative Protestantism, there is considerable variation within Orthodox Judaism. The Hasidim and the ultra-Orthodox might be compared to Protestant fundamentalists in that their conservatism has led them to separate from society. Modern Orthodox communities are somewhat analogous to Evangelicals in that they seek to integrate their commitment to halacha with a higher level of involvement in mainstream culture. Beth Israel is a Modern Orthodox congregation; it is also young, intellectual, and, as one woman put it, very "ba'al teshuvah-ish", i.e., dominated by newly Orthodox Jews. The service, in which women play a minor role, is fairly typical for Orthodox synagogues. Even on regular Saturdays (as opposed to the High Holidays), the services are very long, people—especially women—arrive late, and men are more actively involved in the ritual than women. The women's Gemara class is more unusual. Yet allowing women to study Talmud, a new and controversial development in Orthodox Judaism, is part of what attracts so many ba'alot teshuvah to this synagogue. Most of the members of Beth Israel are young couples who came to Orthodoxy as adults and are now raising their children as religious Jews, often sending them to ultra-Orthodox Hebrew schools to "get a little extra." The community is close-knit. Due to the prohibition against driving on the Sabbath, most people live within easy walking distance of the synagogue. Many of the businesses in the area cater to Orthodox needs. There is a variety of kosher restaurants, including Thai, Chinese, and pizza, kosher food and wine markets, and stores selling Hebrew books, yarmulkes, and prayer shawls. Like Victory and St. Joseph's, Beth Israel provides its members with a sense of community that is otherwise lacking in Los Angeles.

Research Methods

Though the sense of community was a common theme in all three congregations, I was initially more impressed by the differences between them—differences that I only later learned were significant. At Victory, for example, my inability to distinguish who was the pastor and my discomfort with the militant tone of their songs and sermons point to characteristics that make conservative Protestants distinct from their Catholic and Jewish counterparts—the relatively egalitarian structure of Evangelical churches and their desire to shape the culture around them. At St. Joseph's, seeing a woman serve as cantor and noticing how her role is symbolically separate from the men at the altar reflects the hierarchical structure of that church and the dilemma Catholic leaders face in trying to accommodate both liberal and conservative members of the same parish. At Beth Israel, seeing the rabbi encourage women to actively participate in Talmud study, while maintaining their more passive involvement in religious services reflects the flexible nature of halacha and the fear—particularly poignant in a congregation of many newly Orthodox—that if women don't know the scripture, their children will fall away from tradition. I certainly make no claim that the congregations I studied are representative of all Evangelicals, Catholics, or Orthodox Jews in America. But the communities described do highlight patterns that can be found in those larger religious cultures as well. Moreover, I sought to avoid extremely atypical communities by selecting groups that resembled their respective demographic profiles drawn from city, state, and national survey data. Consistent with those data, the level of income and education are highest in the Jewish community and lowest in the Evangelical community I studied.[4] Also consistent with broader patterns is the fact that the Jewish community was mostly white, while both the Evangelical and the Catholic communities had a visible proportion of black and Hispanic members.[5]

At the same time, there are important similarities between the three communities that can provide a basis for comparative study. First, they were part of the same regional culture. All three communities I studied are located in greater Los Angeles, a sprawling metropolis where urban and suburban areas are becoming increasingly indistinguishable. Members of all these communities might be described as "worldly" or "integrationist" conservatives because they are involved in, and encourage involvement in, the secular society.[6] Their active maintenance of contact with people outside their traditionalist religious group—through employment, education, friendships, and/or political

activism—distinguishes members of these communities from certain fundamentalist Christians or Hasidic Jews who could be described as "isolationist conservatives."[7]

Second, the communities resembled each other demographically.
All were middle class and somewhat more educated than the national
average for the respective denominations they represented; and all were
relatively young, baby-boomer congregations with many children. The
women I interviewed were representative of these demographics.

At Victory Church, I talked to a total of twenty-seven women. They
ranged in age from twenty-eight to fifty, with an average age of thirty-
seven. Most had some college education, but many had not finished
college and only a few had advanced degrees. One-third of the respondents reported a family income between $40,000 and $69,999, another
third an income between $20,000 and $39,999, with the final third split
between those making less than $20,000 and those making more than
$70,000 a year.[8] Most (seventeen) were married; six were single, and
four were divorced. Only ten of the women were homemakers, while
the rest worked outside the home, most of them full-time.

Most of the women became Evangelicals as adults: eighteen were
raised Protestant, eight Catholic, and one Reform Jewish. Regardless
of denominational background, many had a strong religious upbring-
ing, though that was often downplayed. Several had been religious seekers who had experimented with a variety of spiritualities. Many tied their
move into Christianity to a need for stability and meaning. Some mentioned problems such as drug or alcohol abuse, promiscuity, or an abusive childhood. The criteria for measuring commitment to Evangelical
Christianity included the born-again experience, usually private, and
the public declaration of committing one's life to Christ, and the beliefs that Jesus Christ died for our sins and that the Bible is the inspired
word of God. Many of the women described their conversion as the
sudden realization, during a time of doubt and depression, that God was
the answer. Yet for many, conversion was followed by repeated periods
of "falling back" as they became increasingly committed to a Christian
lifestyle. For most, becoming Christian brought a shift in friendships.
As religion took up a bigger and bigger space in their lives, church became their social life—especially for single women since Victory Church

does not encourage dating. Following their born-again experience, many women had spent some time "church-shopping" to find a community that suited them. By the time I met them, the women had been members of Victory Church for an average of eight years.

At St. Joseph's, I talked to a total of twenty-seven women. They ranged in age from twenty-four to fifty, with an average age of thirty-nine. Most were college educated, but only a few had graduate degrees. About half of the respondents reported a family income between $40,000 and $69,999, a quarter between $20,000 and $39,999, and another quarter was split between those making less than $20,000 and those making more than $70,000 a year.[9] Most (seventeen) were married; six were single, three were divorced, and one was widowed. Only eight of the women were homemakers, while nineteen worked (most of them full-time).

The majority of women had been raised Catholic, though some had returned to active participation in the church after a period of "laziness" or adolescent rebellion when they experimented with a variety of spiritualities. Only three were raised Protestant and two Jewish. They all felt that their commitment had become stronger in their late twenties and early thirties, which was often the time that they began to have children. Their criteria for measuring commitment to Roman Catholicism always included partaking in church ritual, especially communion, and acting on one's beliefs. Yet there was considerable disagreement among self-identified liberals and conservatives over whether or not one must obey (or even try to obey) Catholic teachings. All of the women were very involved in church life. Protestant and Jewish converts to Catholicism reported strong tensions with their families. However, since most of the women had been raised Catholic, commitment to the church did not usually bring a move away from family or friendships. Still, due to their greater involvement, many women found that they spent much more time with other Catholics than with their non-Catholic friends. Almost all of the women had joined St. Joseph's because it was the parish they happened to live in. By the time I met them, the women had been members of this church for an average of twelve years.

At Beth Israel, finally, I talked to a total of twenty-seven Jewish women. They ranged in age from twenty-three to forty-four, with an average age of thirty-three. All were college educated; many had some graduate education (mostly two-year professional degrees). About half of respondents reported a family income between $40,000 and $69,999, a quarter an income between $70,000 and $99,999, and another quarter split between those making less than $20,000 and those making more than $100,000 a year.[10] Most (twenty-one) of the women were married; three were single and three were divorced. Only seven of the women were homemakers; of the twenty that worked, six worked part-time, and three were full-time students.

Most came to Orthodoxy as adults: sixteen were raised Reform or Conservative (eight each), nine were raised as Orthodox Jews, and two were raised Protestant. Regardless of denominational background, most were raised in religiously active homes or in families with a strong Jewish identity. Most tied their move into Orthodoxy to a need to explore and express their Jewish identity, often beginning with college courses in Judaic Studies and/or a trip to Israel. The criteria for measuring commitment to Orthodox Judaism are practice-based: does the individual observe the *mitzvot* (Jewish laws)? The minimal level of observance includes following the laws of kashrut (keeping kosher), being *shomer Shabbes* (keeping the Sabbath holy and refraining from prohibited activities, including driving and watching TV), and observing the family purity laws. Most of the women said their conversion was very gradual and often experimental, usually beginning with keeping kosher at home and gradually reducing activities on the Sabbath. For many, the decision not to drive was a turning point, indicating a full commitment to Orthodoxy. For most, becoming Orthodox brought a shift in friendships. As religion took up a bigger and bigger space in their lives, the Orthodox community became their social life, especially for homemakers. Many reported tensions with parents and childhood friends, sometimes due to the women's actions (e.g., refusal to eat in the parents' nonkosher home), sometimes due to the actions of parents and friends (belittling Orthodoxy). However, most had found ways to resolve the tensions and, in some cases, had brought their families closer to Orthodoxy. Like the Evangelicals, many of the Orthodox women had spent some time shopping around for a synagogue that met their needs, and several maintained membership in two synagogues because their husbands had different preferences. By the time I met with them, the women had been members of Beth Israel for an average of six years.

Finally, all three congregations were led by individuals who subscribed to traditional gender norms yet were concerned with not alienating their women members. Like the more famous religious conservatives described in the previous chapter, the leaders of the three communities I studied opposed the feminist movement but coopted some feminist ideas. At Victory, a moderate approach to gender roles seems to be part of the appeal to the baby-boom generation. Pastor Jordan considers himself theologically mainstream—as Evangelicals go. While he supports women working outside the home, he feels their primary responsibility is to care for home and children, and that their careers should be secondary to that. He supports equal rights for women in the workplace and in the larger society, though he is wary that such laws might lead to quotas. He does not think women should lead a congregation without a male "covering" (a senior pastor who supervises her), but he emphasizes that women in his church hold many important leadership roles, including functioning as elders, missionaries in Latin America and Africa, and pastors of "seed churches" in other California communities. He believes that women are naturally religious and should therefore step back in order to encourage men to take on religious leadership.

Rabbi Feldman considers himself progressive—as Orthodox Judaism goes. While he supports women working outside the home, he feels their primary responsibility is to care for home and children and a career should be secondary. He supports equal rights for women in the workplace and in the larger secular society (though he is wary of gender equality laws interfering with sex segregation in Orthodox schools). He does not think women should be counted in a minyan or take on the rabbi's role as leader of the congregation, but he does feel women who have achieved the requisite level of learning should be given an equivalent title and should have some role in developing halacha, particularly on women's issues (e.g., purity laws). He supports advanced religious education for women and is experimenting with allowing women to engage in rituals (separately from the men, of course) from which they are usually exempt but which are not halachically prohibited (e.g., dancing with the Torah scroll on Simchat Torah). Like Pastor Jordan, the rabbi wants to convince his female congregants that traditional religion already empowers women. By arguing that tradition meets many feminist demands, they seek to preserve that tradition largely unchanged.

Due to its size, St. Joseph's Church is led by a head pastor, Monsignor Edward Rivera, and several assistant pastors, one of whom, Father Thomas O'Reilly, was particularly esteemed by the women in this study. Monsignor Rivera considers himself a theologically conservative Catholic. He supports women working outside the home, as well as equal rights for women in the workplace and in the larger society. However, he is wary that equal rights legislation may facilitate abortion. He does not think women can be priests, but he is concerned about not alienating women. Thus he argues that the church is powerless to change a tradition instituted by Christ himself, and that the priest doesn't have much power anyway. Pointing to the many ministries that are headed by women, he insists that women are already the ones who are leading the church. Father Thomas O'Reilly, a big bearlike man with a thick beard and a warm smile, took many of the same positions on women's issues as the Monsignor. Father Thomas, however, had a much more personal relationship with many of the women because of his role as their confessional pastor. His influence, particularly on the issue of pro-life, was clearly reflected in many of the women I interviewed.

My goal in this study was to understand how women in different conservative religious communities respond to feminism. What makes these three communities good case studies is that they each reflect the typical characteristics of their particular tradition while at the same time they are similar enough demographically to make comparison meaningful. In the case of the Catholic Church, however, some of the very patterns that made my chosen community typical seemed to create a problem of comparability for my analysis. First, unlike Evangelicals and Orthodox Jews, most of whom had not been raised in their current conservative denominations, most Catholics *were* raised Catholic. Second, unlike many Evangelicals and Orthodox Jews, who expressed a strong sense of choice about the community they had joined, most Catholics did not. While many Evangelicals and Jews had attended and considered joining other churches and synagogues before joining Victory or

Beth Israel, most Catholic women went to St. Joseph's because they happened to live in that parish. The baby-boomer pattern of "church-shopping" appears to be more common for Evangelicals and Jews than for Catholics. Finally, unlike Victory and Beth Israel where the majority of members described themselves are religious conservatives, St. Joseph's was home to a large number of self-professed liberals.

These differences are precisely what makes a comparison interesting. To say that the women at Victory and Beth Israel chose to become religious conservatives, while the women at St. Joseph's did not would be incorrect. It's just that for Protestants and Jews becoming conservative means switching denominations while for Catholics it does not. While conservative Protestants and Orthodox Jews have separated themselves from their more liberal counterparts, conservative Catholics do not feel they have that option. Indeed, their very traditionalism compels them to remain committed to the larger body. A vocal minority in an increasingly liberal church, they are fighting to retain influence over its direction, while at the same time adapting to the realities of our times. If conservative Protestants are struggling to regain cultural dominance and Orthodox Jews are struggling to survive, the Catholic Church is a deeply divided community that is struggling for a coherent identity.[11]

The case study approach, then, can help us see patterns that might be overlooked in a broader survey. Finding out how women construct the meaning of gender requires listening to how they talk about themselves, their beliefs, feelings, and actions. Understanding the similarities and differences between Protestant, Catholic, and Jewish conservatives requires spending time in these communities and observing both formal and operational norms. A survey might tell us that women in all three traditions oppose abortion and homosexuality, but unless we talk to them and spend time with them, we will not realize that they oppose it for very different reasons and to different degrees. Both the formulation of questions to guide the interview and the interpretation of responses are enhanced if the researcher is able to engage in the religious community she is studying.

The comparative case study poses particular challenges. Besides making sure that cases meet some standard of representativeness and comparability, there needs to be consistency in the method of gathering and analyzing information. I gathered data from the same combination of sources in each community studied: participant observation, personal interviews, demographic surveys, and documents distributed by each group. I analyzed the data using linguistic, psychological, and statistical models.

PARTICIPANT OBSERVATION

At Victory Church I attended many Sunday services, including Easter and a wedding, as well as midweek evening Praise Meetings. I also went to Women's Fellowship dinners, a Valentine retreat, and political organizing meetings. At St. Joseph's I attended Sunday Masses, festivals, and retreats. Several of the women in both churches invited me to share a meal with them and their families. At Beth Israel I attended the Gemara classes for more than a year. I also attended religious services at the synagogue, both on the Sabbath and on all of the major holidays: Rosh HaShanah and Yom Kippur, Sukkot and Simchat Torah, Hanukkah, Purim, and Pesach. Following many of the services, I was invited to lunch or dinner at somebody's home, which gave me a more intimate look at family life.

Like most researchers who engage in participant observation, I was faced with the problem of how to represent myself. Although I was an outsider to all of the groups (I was not raised Protestant, Catholic, or Jewish), many of the women (most of the Evangelicals and, surprisingly, some of the Orthodox Jews) saw me as a potential convert. I had expected this to happen with the Evangelicals, since proselytization is one of their religious duties. In the Orthodox congregation, this impression may have come about because the women saw me attending so many events and knew that I drove all the way from Santa Barbara to do so, which made me seem more committed than some of the women themselves. I told the women that my interest was academic; when pressed about my own spiritual leanings, I told them honestly that I have not yet found anything I feel comfortable committing to.

Another challenge that I encountered was how to deal with friendships that developed during research. Though I initially intended to maintain complete "critical distance," my friendships with women in two of the congregations seemed too natural to resist. Both women were my age and single, and both helped me find my way in communities to which I was a stranger. We seemed to have similar interests, would call each other weekly, and, on occasion, would go out to dinner or see a movie. Once my research was over, and I started spending less time in their respective congregations, one of the relationships faded but the other has continued to this day. In retrospect, it is clear that I made the right decision. The myth of objectivity has been thoroughly covered elsewhere (e.g., Davidman 1991; Griffith 1997). Rather than repeat that discussion here, I would like to acknowledge that my friendships with these women provided me with an insight into both communities I would otherwise have missed.

INTERVIEWS

I tried to interview a cross-section of women in each community, that is, I made sure that each sample included married, single, and divorced women, as well as homemakers and women employed outside the home. At Victory Church, I began with a list that Pastor Jordan had given me. With the help of some of the women I met, I then identified additional interviewees, some of whom the pastor might not have recommended. At St. Joseph's, I started out with the parish directory and a short list of parishioners given to me by Father Tom which was gradually expanded through contacts I made in the church. Because much of the literature has pointed to the liberalization and lack of active participation of American Catholics, I had asked to be referred to religiously active women who defined themselves as traditionalists, but as it turned out, not all of them were conservative. At Beth Israel, I began by interviewing women I'd met in the Gemara class. Other interviewees were people they recommended, as well as women I met at various events I attended. Most of the interviews lasted about ninety minutes and were held at women's homes, some at restaurants or offices, and some in an empty room at the church or synagogue.

I used the same interview guide for all three groups (see appendix A), modified in accordance with the obvious differences between Protestants, Catholics, and Orthodox Jews (for example, I asked only Jewish women about covering their hair and the family purity laws). The interview covered three main areas: (1) background (how and why they committed themselves to Evangelicalism, Catholicism, or Orthodox Judaism); (2) women's roles in church or synagogue, in society, and in the home; (3) social issues, including feminism, abortion, and homo-sexuality. I concluded each interview by asking the women to tell me what they felt was most challenging and what was most rewarding about being an Evangelical, Catholic, or Orthodox Jew in today's society.

DEMOGRAPHIC SURVEY

After each interview, I asked the women to complete a brief demo-graphic survey (see appendix A). The survey was the same for each group, requesting information about age, marital status, number of chil-dren, education, income, religion they were raised in, time of conver-sion or active commitment to Christianity or Judaism, and number of years they had belonged to their respective congregations.

DOCUMENTS

I collected a wide variety of printed material in each community. At Victory Church, documents included worship schedules, flyers for vari-ous church-sponsored events (fund-raisers, retreats, etc.), anti-abortion literature, homeschooling information sheets, and Christian magazines, such as James Dobson's *Focus on the Family*. The documents I collected at St. Joseph's were similar, except for the absence of homeschooling literature. Instead, there was a great deal of information on Hispanic outreach and efforts to feed the homeless in Los Angeles. I also reviewed two conservative Catholic magazines, *Voices*, published by Women for Faith and Family, and *Hearth: Journal of the Authentic Catholic Woman*. At Beth Israel, documents included the service schedules, flyers for up-coming events (a *shabbaton*, Talmud-study groups, etc.), the synagogue newsletter, instructional items for newcomers (e.g., *The Rosh HaShanah/ Yom Kippur Survival Kit*), and Orthodox newspapers, such as *The Jewish Women's Journal*.

ANALYSIS

It took me about a year and a half to complete the field research. In many ways, leaving the field was sad, particularly because of the friend-ships I had made in each of the communities I studied. In other ways, finishing was a relief. The commute to Los Angeles (two hours each way), which I made several times each week, was exhausting, especially because I often returned home late at night and spent another couple of hours at my computer, typing up fieldnotes. By the time I had finished my fieldwork, I had over two thousand pages (single-spaced, typed) of interview transcripts and fieldnotes, seventy-five demographic surveys, and three folders full of documents. The present analysis draws on these sources, as well as memories and images that were never written down.

I analyzed interview transcripts and fieldnotes by looking for common themes, use of language, emotional expression (e.g., humor, anger, evasiveness), inconsistencies, repetition, and connections between events. I entered data from the demographic surveys into the computer and ran it through a statistical software package to produce the quantitative findings summarized above. I separated documents into publicity and outreach materials and reading materials, including magazines that some of the women subscribed to. Both served to supplement my impressions of each community and the women within it.

Long before I finished the analysis, I realized that the women at Victory, St. Joseph's, and Beth Israel were far more different from each other and far more similar to feminists like me than either conservative or feminist leaders would acknowledge. The question I kept returning to was how do the differences between Evangelicals, conservative Catholics, and Orthodox Jews shape the ways in which their women members come to term with feminism? The rest of this book presents my answers to that question. In order to provide a meaningful answer, I have distinguished between two types of feminism: feminist values (personal norms of behavior) and the feminist movement (a political entity). How Evangelical, Catholic, and Orthodox Jewish women have been influenced by feminist values is explored in part 2, while the women's responses to the feminist movement are the subject of part 3.

Part II

Yes to Feminist Values

Chapter 4

Feminists in Society

*I realized that I had all these intellectual talents which
God has given me, and that I was much better off giving
love using my own talents than accepting the burdens of
the housewife role.*

————CONSERVATIVE CATHOLIC WOMAN

*I think it's OK for a woman to be the boss. I mean, if
God's given her the ability.*

————EVANGELICAL PROTESTANT WOMAN

*I would like to see more women elected to political office.
It would benefit our country, because women are equally
qualified.*

————ORTHODOX JEWISH WOMAN

THE OFFICIAL PUBLICATIONS of conservative religious communities as well
as the pronouncements of their leaders suggest that women's place is
the private sphere of home and family and that women should submit
to men. Yet most of the women I spoke to were employed outside the
home, some of them in traditionally male occupations and some in positions of authority over men. How do they reconcile such positions with
the norms of their communities? The answer has to do with the social
context they find themselves in.

Context matters. In chapter 1, I suggested that Katrina, Miriam,
and Barbara are adapting themselves to different social contexts: in the
secular context of work and politics, they take on a "feminist" identity;
in the religious context of church or synagogue, they maintain a "traditionalist" identity. By "traditionalist" identity I mean a self-conception
based on the assumption that because men and women are by nature
different, they have different roles to play and, as a result, should
be treated differently. "Feminist" identity is more difficult to define, since

the liberal feminists who dominated the movement in the seventies downplayed gender differences in order to justify equal treatment, while the "new" feminists of the eighties and nineties emphasize gender differences in order to justify meeting a diversity of needs. In contrast to traditionalism, however, both types of feminism elevate individual choices and rights over community mandates and responsibilities, promoting what Robert Bellah has called "expressive individualism." I will therefore define "feminist" identity as a self-conception based on the assumption that natural gender differences do not in themselves mandate differential roles. Rather, society must allow both men and women an equal right to choose what role they want to play. It is in this sense that the attitudes and behaviors of Katrina, Miriam and Barbara can be defined as feminist—even though they do not think of themselves as such.

But context isn't everything. There are certain aspects of a religion that are accepted as given by members of that community. A "given" is something that is accepted as true and right, that isn't questioned no matter how many doubts one may have about other aspects of the religion. A "given" provides the community with an anchor, a basis from which potential conflicts can be resolved. Evangelicals, for example, believe that the Bible is God's word and therefore literally true. This is reflected in how they talk about the Bible, which they refer to as "the Word," a term not used by conservative Catholic and Orthodox Jewish women. The literal truth of the Bible is accepted as a given and is not questioned. When women at Victory Church sought to legitimate an opinion, they would cite the Bible, saying things such as: "the Word says," or "according to God's word," or "God's word requires." Conservative Catholics, by contrast, accept the hierarchy of their church as given. Unless I specifically asked them about the Bible, women at St. Joseph's almost never cited it to back up an opinion but instead said things such as: "the church teaches," or "the magisterium teaches," or "the bishop has said." For Orthodox Jews, finally, it is halacha that is given. Halacha is the process by which Talmudic law is applied to real-life situations. Because the rabbis disagree on how it applies, this process has generated a huge body of legal opinion, which continues to grow. The women at Beth Israel consistently justified their choices by referring to the halachic process, saying things such as: "it's not halachic," or "I try to live a halachic lifestyle," or "my rabbi says." Though there is diversity in interpretation, it is a given that every decision must be subjected to halachic scrutiny. Indeed, one of the hallmarks of a conservative religious community is its emphasis on such "givens" (and many conservatives see this as what distinguishes them from liberals where "nothing is given").

A "given" provides clarity and security, but it can also create a painful choice for an individual seeking to express and develop her unique identity. Identity can be adapted to context, but some things are given in all contexts. As members of Evangelical, Catholic, and Orthodox Jewish communities, Katrina, Barbara, and Miriam respectively accept the literal truth of the Bible, the authority of the magisterium, and halacha as given—an acceptance that sets them apart from secular (or even liberal religious) Americans and would seem to exclude them from the renegotiation of gender roles that is occurring in the larger society. In the secular context of work and politics, however, these three women are more similar to than different from other Americans and appear to be active participants in society's reconstruction of gender roles. Although they are critical of the feminist movement, they embrace feminist values in the sense that they think men and women should be treated equally despite the differences between them. More importantly, they seem to be able to reconcile those values with what is given in their traditions. In assessing how a woman defines her role in secular society, I used the same indicators of "feminist values" in all three communities: support for women's employment as career rather than as temporary supplement to family income, support for laws that prohibit gender discrimination, support for women taking on leadership positions in which they have authority over men, and support for women working in traditionally male occupations such as the military. While these indicators are clearly present in the responses of Katrina, Miriam, and Barbara, we must ask how representative they are of others in their respective religious communities and how those communities are similar to or different from each other. Let us take a closer look, then, at how women at Victory Church, St. Joseph's Church, and Congregation Beth Israel understand their roles in secular contexts.

A Tradition of Working

When I began my research at Beth Israel, it was surprisingly difficult to schedule the women for interviews. Only a few were stay-at-home moms, while nearly three-quarters were employed outside the home. While that figure includes single and divorced women, all of whom worked, almost two-thirds of the married women were employed as well. Due to their relatively high educational attainment (all had obtained college degrees and several had or were working on getting an advanced degree), most of the women were employed full-time in professional or managerial occupations, including a college professor, a chemical researcher, an engineer, a marketing executive, a therapist, lawyers, nurses, and teachers. Only six women had nonprofessional jobs (work that does not require an advanced degree) such as receptionist; these women worked part-time only.

The women at Beth Israel strongly believe in gender equality in the workplace. When I asked if they supported laws that mandated equal rights for men and women, all of the women interviewed said "yes." While acknowledging gender differences, they feel these differences are not important enough to mandate that women play different roles in society from men's. Judith, for example, is a single mother of two who works full-time as a registered nurse in a nearby hospital. We talked at her home; it was her day off. A short, plump woman with dark curly hair, she wore loose-fitting pants under a plaid shirt as she sat on a well-worn sofa sipping a cup of tea. She describes herself as "more orthodox than many other women in this congregation." Yet she divorced her husband because he was too traditionalist: "He didn't want me to work. Very annoying . . . he didn't let me see how much money we had in the bank. I had a certain allowance but I didn't have access to the account . . . and then when I was going back to get my Masters, that's when the whole marriage ended." Judith's conception of "more orthodox" apparently includes her right to work outside the home. Marcia, a college professor, would agree. She was sitting at her office desk grading a stack of blue-books when I entered her office. As fellow academics we were soon engaged in a conversation about the joys and pains of teaching and research. Marcia is deeply committed to her career and sees that commitment as consistent with Jewish tradition: "A lot of the things on a day-to-day basis that the women's movement addressed and has gotten changed, don't exist in Orthodoxy. It was never an issue. In many Orthodox homes, very *frum* [pious, observant] homes, you see the woman working alongside the man . . . the woman contributes to the family income." Both men and women should choose what they want to do with their lives. As Judith put it, "We're equal mentally and we're equal intellectually, the only thing we're not equal in is that we happen to have children. So we have that extra role . . . it's a very important role, but it's not the only one if a woman is not satisfied doing that." Seeing herself as equal to men in all respects save childbearing, she feels that women's biological differences from men should provide them with more rather than fewer options.

While we might expect such opinions from working women, I was surprised to learn that full-time homemakers share this view. Chana, for example, stays home to care for her three children, but feels strongly that "women should be able to do whatever they want to do—and be rewarded for it just like the men." I interviewed Chana at her home where she was keeping an eye on her toddler while the other two children were in school. A tall, thin woman with straight red hair and wire-rimmed glasses, she seemed very much at ease with her two-year old son, who, singing and banging his toys on the floor, was driving *me* crazy. Chana believes that gender discrimination continues to be a problem in various secular institutions and supports legislation to alleviate it: "I know in schools, for example . . . teachers unwittingly favor the boys over the girls, you know, giving more praise to boys and that kind of stuff. My daughter tends to be outspoken and she tends to get her needs met, but I know when she has played sports . . . even in this day and age, head coaches don't want to coach her because she's a girl . . . I mean, I'd rather we not need the laws but I think that we do need them, and yeah, I support them." Chana told me that before she began to have children, she had been working full-time as a sales manager for an appliance firm. She chose to stay home because she felt that "somebody should, and my husband (a lawyer) makes a lot more money." Yet she insisted that it was her choice, not her responsibility to stay home. Like Judith and Marcia, she believes the fact that women are different from men should give women more, not fewer choices.

The women at Beth Israel also believe that it is a good thing for women to take jobs traditionally held by men. When I asked about women in the military, a typical answer was: "I think women can do anything they want. Whoever is qualified, man or woman, should be hired for the job." Most Orthodox Jewish women say that they personally would not want to be in the military, but they insist that the opportunity should be there for women who do. This is not a merely theoretical position. Many women in this community have had personal experience with working in male-dominated fields. Tamar, for example, is in music school, studying to be a composer. Because of her many engagements, she is rarely home. I was lucky to catch her in the afternoon before she left for a concert that evening. A tall, slim woman, elegantly dressed in a black silk suit, she sat on a white leather couch in the small, but exquisitely appointed apartment that she shares with her physician-husband. They do not yet have any children. "There aren't many women composers," she told me. "I'm the only woman in my class, the only Jewish woman, and the only Orthodox woman that they have ever had. So in the field that I am involved in it is purely a man's world still. . . . I was at a conference this past summer, and I was definitely treated much differently than the male composers who were there. I don't think [the conductor] did a very good job with my piece . . . because I wasn't taken as seriously." If Tamar stuck to traditionalist values, her experience with discrimination might lead her to conclude that she is intruding where she doesn't belong. Yet when it comes to her job, Tamar adopts feminist values: she feels she has a right to be in this field and is being treated unfairly. Debra, an engineer at a large aerospace company, is another example. We talked in her office, a bright neon-lit room, sparsely furnished with a desk, a file cabinet and two computers. In contrast to her stark surroundings, Debra, dressed casually in slacks and a red turtleneck, appeared lively and colorful. One of a handful of women in her firm, she is unabashedly feminist. She admits that she has benefitted from affirmative action programs: "When I graduated from UCLA with a masters in engineering, I was hired by another aerospace company . . . and my boss would say, oh, the government was giving a subsidy to all companies for hiring women . . . so they picked me probably because I'm a woman." Yet she feels she is just as qualified as any man. "I had excellent credentials . . . and I would like to see more women in my field. There are more and more women engineers, in my view equally qualified, intelligent, and of equal experi-

ence . . . but it's not yet enough." Not surprisingly, Debra strongly supports women in the military. If they meet the standards, she argues,
women should participate equally in all aspects of the military, including combat. A man may be physically stronger, but "anything that requires intellect, a woman is equally qualified to do . . . like flying combat
planes takes reaction time, it's not necessarily strength, so I think a
woman can do that equally well." Like Judith, Marcia, and Chana,
Tamar and Debra acknowledge differences between men and women
but reject the conclusion that such differences justify categorically different roles or separate spheres. Instead, difference should be the basis
for expanding rather than narrowing women's roles.

One area in which Beth Israel's women feel their presence should
be expanded is political leadership. They clearly reject the traditionalist argument that a woman's nature is to follow rather than to lead.
Some women argue that there are too many variations among women
to categorize all of them as different from men. As Debra put it, "I would
like to see more women elected to political office. It would benefit our
country, because women are equally qualified. I think it would change
the view of women. Maybe some women like the idea of being in the
traditional role of being a homemaker, but for those women who don't
like to be that way, and would like to be accepted equally in the work
force, having women in political power could help the image of women."
The image she is talking about is the traditional depiction of women
being different and therefore less competent leaders than men. Other
women emphasize those very differences. Interestingly, they used the
notion of male-female differences—traditionally used to justify the exclusion of women from positions of power and leadership—to empower
women. A good example is Michelle, a homemaker with three young
children who runs a greeting-card business out of her home. A pretty,
vivacious blonde, dressed in pink tights and a long turquoise sweatshirt,
she looked like a typical "Valley girl"—once again diversifying my image of Orthodox Jewish women. Judaism, according to Michelle, not
only allows but encourages women's leadership in the secular world. "I'm
not a feminist," she told me, "but . . . from a Jewish standpoint, and from
a practical standpoint, I think women are much better suited to be leaders than men. They have innate qualities of empathy and compassion
and sensitivity that, for better or for worse, men just don't have, and I

think when you're making decisions that affect millions of lives, you have to have those qualities." Another woman put it even more bluntly. "I think we should definitely be in charge of the world. I think it would be much better, I really do." These women emphasize their differences from men. Yet it is precisely these differences, they feel, that uniquely qualify women to hold many of the jobs from which they are often excluded. The women at Beth Israel, then, sound more like the new difference feminists than like the antifeminist religious right.

Although the women's support for working outside the home reflects a uniquely Jewish outlook, their understanding of what work means goes far beyond their religious tradition. Orthodox Jewish gender roles emerged in a pre-industrial culture that did not separate work from home. To assign the home as woman's place therefore does not necessarily suggest that she shouldn't work. Indeed, Judaism has a long tradition of women providing for family income, partly because it would allow their husbands to dedicate themselves to the study of Talmud, and partly because Jewish men faced intense employment discrimination. That tradition, however, does not negate a basic commitment to separate spheres for men and women. A woman's primary role is motherhood, whereas working outside the home is an exceptional, temporary responsibility she adopts as a means of supplementing family income. To the women at Beth Israel, by contrast, work can also be a permanent right to express individual talents. In the words of a mother and advertising executive: "If you're going to live in LA it's very expensive and you can't really make it on one salary, but anyway, I probably would want to be doing something just to get out." What determines a woman's role in the secular context of work and politics is choice, and, according to these religious conservatives, women must be ensured the same right as men to make that choice.

God's Calling to Work

Compared to the women at Beth Israel, those at Victory Church appear less feminist in their understanding of women's role in secular society. Nonetheless, they too have integrated feminist values into parts of their lives. The proportion of Evangelical women who were employed (about two-thirds) is slightly lower than for Orthodox Jewish women, and almost three-fifths of married Evangelicals stayed home with their children. Due to their slightly lower educational attainment (most had several years of college, but only a few had advanced degrees) fewer of the Evangelical women worked in professional or managerial occupations. These included a school principal, a lawyer, a sales manager, and several nurses and teachers. As at Beth Israel, there were six women in nonprofessional (clerical, sales) positions. Perhaps because family income tended to be lower for Evangelicals than for Jews, most of the women who worked did so full-time.

Regardless of their own employment status, most of the women at Victory Church support equal gender roles in the workplace. Employed women in particular think of themselves as equal to the men in their workplaces and adamantly support equal opportunity and equal pay legislation. Lisa, for example, is a doctor's assistant who attends night school for a master's degree in psychology. Although Lisa, who is currently single, hoped to someday find a good Christian husband whom she "would *want* to submit to", she does not extend that traditionalist view to the workplace. She does not object to women in power and thinks that "a woman who has the same level job as a man, does the same amount of work, has the same responsibility, should be paid the same, have the same opportunities for raises or promotions." Like the women at Beth Israel, Lisa emphasizes the qualities of the individual. She acknowledges that men may differ from women as a group, but insists that those differences are superseded by each individual's qualifications for a particular position, including positions of authority. Not surprisingly, Lisa considers herself eminently qualified for such a position.

Working women like Lisa have a certain amount of self-interest in supporting gender equality on the job. Homemakers like Jennifer do not, but she too supports feminist values in the secular context. A couple of months before I spoke to her, Jennifer had left her job in order to spend more time with her two children. Red-haired and freckle-faced, she wore a blue, flowery dress, covered by a long, white apron and was stirring a big pot of spaghetti sauce during much of the interview. She believes that many women with children would prefer not to work outside the home, yet insists that those who choose to do so be treated equally. In her view, this does not contradict Christian teaching. "Based

on my experience," she told me, "I think it's OK for a woman to be the
boss. I mean, if God's given her the ability... like when I worked at
UCLA in the registrar's office, we had a woman, she was the boss, and
there was a guy that was directly under her. I don't think there's anything wrong with that. She's not going to tell him how to run his life.
She's just going to tell him what to do on the job. I think there's a big
difference in that." Jennifer here makes a clear distinction between
women holding authority over men in the workplace and other spheres
of life. Although she and other Evangelical women emphasize the natural differences between the sexes (e.g., men's physical strength and ag-
gression versus women's weakness and nurturing capacity), they insist
that the roles they can play at work and elsewhere in secular society
should be no different from those held by men.

Still, the women at Victory Church are more ambivalent than those
at Beth Israel about women working in traditionally male occupations.
Many Evangelicals, for example, are opposed to women in politics. The
reason, however, is not that they consider women less able to lead but
that most of the women politicians they know of are pro-choice. It is
not the fact that they are female, but the fact that they hold the wrong
political views that disqualifies most women politicians from holding
public office. An excellent example of this perspective is Valerie, the
wife of a local politician. A regional sales-manager for a computer company, Valerie travels a great deal and is often away from home for days
at a time. Due to her hectic schedule, we decided to "do lunch" at a
restaurant near the office of one of her clients. A slim, attractive woman
dressed in a gray business suit whose direct manner and firm handshake
conveyed an impression of professional confidence, Valerie defied the
stereotype of the meek Christian woman. "I don't think there's anything the matter with women running for political office," she told me.
"It's not the same thing as being actively involved in speaking in a
church [which she opposes]. It's not the same thing at all. But we see a
lot of people just go down the ballot and check off only women because they were women... I would not do that. More than gender, it
matters to me what their values and ideals are. Most of those women
candidates don't have the right values. If they were pro-life I would vote
for them. But you don't get a lot of that, because it's tough [to be a
Christian in this area]." Based on her husband's experience, she feels

that openly opposing abortion is a political liability in California. "I don't actually go and sit down at abortion clinics . . . you have to be careful when you're a politician's wife, 'cause it can come back to haunt you later." But being pro-life is central to her identity as a Christian. "I used to be like everybody else. I said, I'm a Christian but I believe it's a woman's right [to have an abortion], it's not the government's business. Now I realize that I was wrong." In this respect, Valerie is representative of many of the Evangelicals in this study. If women politicians were pro-life, the women at Victory Church would support them.

Evangelical women also express ambivalence about women in the military. Sandra, for example, is a plump, good-natured woman who stays at home with her four children, but has worked intermittently as a substitute teacher to help bring in additional income. Her husband is a cabinetmaker who works in the film industry. During our interview, she proudly pointed out that he had made most of the furniture in their house. I had a hard time pinning down exactly whether Sandra's understanding of women's role in secular society is "feminist" or "traditionalist." When we discussed women working in general, she expressed feminist values, downplaying gender differences and emphasizing personal choice: "I think there's a lot of capable women in the work force . . . and I know I could be too. I could be out there and able to run a crew of people or manage an office . . . this is just what I have chosen to do. I good friend of mine, a woman, is a doctor, and I don't think our minds run any differently that way. Sometimes you see men that do have a problem working for a woman, but that's *their* ego-trip, it's *their* problem." She laughed. "If women are doing a good job, what can you argue with?" But when we discussed women working in historically male occupations, she shifted to more traditionalist rhetoric, emphasizing gender difference as a reason to exclude women: "Now being in the military, though, that's different. The woman is simply not capable of the same job as a man, period. We just don't have the same anatomy as a man, we are weaker, and weaker is better because it really is what God created us to be: helpmates." Minutes later she shifted again, arguing that women should be free to fill any role they choose:

> I had a really good friend who worked for the phone company,
> and she was the one who climbed the power lines, with the

safety belt and hard hat, and she loved her job, but she's no less feminine because of it. She would look kind of tough when you'd see her up there in her outfit, but at home she wears dresses and make-up. She has two children and is a good wife, has a good home. But many women who work on road crews or in the military just have an attitude: I'm tough and don't mess with me . . . and they miss out on what God created them to be, the pleasures of being a woman. So actually I have no problem with women taking those jobs, so long as they don't try to be men.

Sandra has come full circle, returning to her original position that gender differences should not limit a woman's options.

Sandra's comments are inconsistent but reveal much about how women in Evangelical communities think and act. At one level, her inconsistency reflects an ambivalence about feminism that is shared by many women who are not religious conservatives. What she is rejecting is not feminist values per se, but the liberal feminist movement which has downplayed male-female differences in order to gain equality. Like the women described by Elizabeth Fox-Genovese (1996), women like Sandra want to be acknowledged as different *and* treated equally. At another level, her inconsistency reflects a struggle particular to women in conservative religious communities: the difficulty of applying gender norms that emerged in cultures very different from today's. Her apparent flip-flopping suggests that one way in which these women resolve those difficulties is by thinking and acting situation-specific. Rather than apply a single preconceived notion of what it means to be a woman (such as wife and mother) or what is appropriate behavior for women (such as serving and submitting to men), most women in this study constructed and reconstructed their identities and the roles they felt women should play as they deemed appropriate for different contexts.

Finally, Sandra's ambivalence reveals a challenge unique to Evangelical women: the fact that—compared to Catholic and Jewish conservatives—conservative Protestant leaders are the most adamant about the homemaker ideal. Male Evangelicals have argued that because women are different from men—weaker, more emotional, less aggressive—society would be better served if women did not enter traditionally male jobs such as the military or the police force. According to this view, women's competition with men in the job market is detrimental to the economy (lowering wages and raising unemployment) as well as to men's self-esteem (undermining their primary role as breadwinner). Women therefore should work only if it is absolutely necessary to supplement the family income (LaHaye 1976; Lienesh 1993). To ordinary Evangelical women, however, work is much more than a supplement to income. For many women, especially those who themselves hold positions of authority at work, or who have (or are in training for) jobs that provide at least some upward mobility, work is a choice. A good example is Patty, a married woman with three children, who is the principal at a nearby Christian school. A short, big-boned woman, dressed in a conservative navy-blue suit, she talks in a soft voice that belies her inner strength. I interviewed Patty in her office, a cramped space filled to capacity with a large desk, several bookshelves, a computer, and a phone that wouldn't stop ringing. She told me about her dream to start a school of her own. "When I first came to Los Angeles, I was getting my teaching credential at Northridge, I got a scholarship there, and I was also working . . . I taught down near the inner city, down in Watts . . . and I just started seeing the way the system was, and that there wasn't much I could do to change it . . . so I just felt like I wanted to start a school . . . I told my husband before we got married that I would always be in education, probably my whole life . . . so that he would know I wouldn't—not that I object to staying home, but that wasn't what I felt I was going to be called to do." The school she now directs is the product of that dream. Patty makes it very clear what her primary identity is—not a wife, not a mother, but a teacher—and draws on the classic Protestant notion of a calling to legitimate that role.[1]

Like their Jewish sisters, the women at Victory Church see their roles in society through the interpretive lens of their tradition but are focusing that lens in new ways. Because conservative Christian gender roles were developed before the Industrial Revolution had separated home and work, the designation of home as woman's place need not imply that she shouldn't work. The Protestant understanding of work as a religious calling further legitimates a woman's choice of employment. Protestant reformers rejected the Catholic monastic tradition by arguing that God calls individuals to serve in many different ways, including working in secular society. This argument not only elevated work to sacred status but transformed it into an expression of individual choice. Patty's assertion that God calls her to work outside the home is thus not essentially different from Sandra's or Jennifer's assertions that they have chosen to stay home in order to be full-time homemakers or to homeschool their children. For Evangelical women, the choice is not whether or not to work, but whether to work inside or outside the home. In making this choice they are challenging not only the traditional assumption that women should be homemakers, but society's assumption that homemaking isn't work.

Bringing in Feminine Gifts

The Catholic picture is more difficult to sort out because so many church members do not consider themselves conservatives. Overall, just over 70 percent of the women at St. Joseph's were employed, including over half of married women. Among self-proclaimed conservatives, however, only single women and married women with grown children worked outside the home. Conservative Catholic educational attainment was higher than for the Evangelical women but lower than for the Jewish women (most Catholics had completed college but few had obtained advanced degrees). Many women worked, or—if they were homemakers—had previously worked in professional occupations, including a professor, an editor, an accountant, and several nurses and teachers. Four women jointly managed businesses with their husbands, and one, Barbara, ran a childcare center.

Regardless of their employment status, conservative Catholic women support gender equality in the workplace. Jill, for example, is a single woman who works as an accountant by day and a jazz musician by night. I interviewed her at home, a two-bedroom apartment she shares with another young woman. We sat in the kitchen, a small space crowded by a long table cluttered with papers, empty coffee mugs, and a half-eaten TV dinner. Thin and pale and dressed in black, Jill looked as if she hadn't had enough sleep. She confided that before coming to St. Joseph's, she had spent about five years with the Tridentines, a group of ultra-conservative Catholics led by Archbishop Lefevre who has rejected the Vatican II reforms. Jill had left the Tridentines because of personal problems she had with members of the group and because, as she put it, "my religious needs changed." Jill continues to identify herself as a conservative. She plans to quit her job when she gets married, feels that "it works best when the husband is the head of the family," and opposes women priests. "But aside from that, no! We are all equal. It says so even in scripture. I know a lot of men who would love to make that case [that traditional roles apply in all situations]. In fact, when I was with the Tridentines, they tended to believe that, that the women in general should submit to men. Many times I would say something and be passed over, and my friend Peter, who was studying to be a seminarian, which gave him extra clout, he would say the same thing, and they would listen to him. " Jill draws a clear line between gender roles in the church or family and gender roles in the workplace. Though she believes that men and women are essentially different, she does not think that this justifies differential treatment, and she insists that legislation is necessary to prevent it: "I don't believe that women should be treated disrespectfully . . . I've had my own share of sexual discrimination and harassment, and it's just not right." Conservative Catholic homemakers would agree with Jill. Bridget, for example, quit her job as a manager of her husband's bookstore in order to stay home with her two children. She was a soft motherly type whose kitchen smelled of fresh baked cookies. The children, a boy and a girl, aged two and four, were splashing in a wading pool as we talked. Though Bridget sees mothering as women's primary role, she also insists that "I support equal pay for equal jobs, all that stuff" as necessary to protect women who choose to work.

These women's support for feminist values often derives from personal experience with gender discrimination. As we have seen in chapter 1, Barbara's realization that she was paid less than a less-senior male employee radicalized her and encouraged her to think of herself and other women in more feminist terms. This feminist outlook carries over into how conservative Catholic women think about women entering historically male fields. Although most say that they personally do not want to be in the military, they believe the opportunity should be there for women who do. And although conservative Catholic women are sometimes reluctant to support female politicians, the reason is not that they think women unqualified but that so many women candidates are "pro-abortion." Bridget, for example, does not oppose women politicians per se. "I'm not antiwoman, OK? In most instances, we can do anything a man can do . . . though I believe that God gives us very definite gifts." She acknowledges that those gifts may include political leadership. Hillary Clinton, for example, "is the co-president in my opinion." Though she admits that Hillary is competent, Bridget opposes her because "on abortion she's radical. She wants it on demand, and we pay for everything, and all protest should be squelched." She opposes both of California's female senators for the same reason. "I don't think you could believe in abortion and consider yourself a Catholic," she said. "It's just so utterly against everything that the church teaches, and everything that we stand for as Christians and as a Catholic community." For Bridget and other conservative Catholic women, a pro-life position is *the* criterion for authentic Christianity, and they would vote for any candidate—male or female—who supports this position.

Bridget's argument that anyone who supports reproductive choice cannot legitimately call themselves a Catholic and her feeling that a woman should put family before career reflects the official teaching of Catholic leaders which encourages motherhood as women's primary role. Catholic bishops are among the most vocal opponents of cutting government support for poor families, arguing that women should not be forced to work (NCCB 1980; O'Connor 1986). In addition, they have firmly opposed contraception and abortion, a rule which, if followed, has the effect of encouraging women to devote their lives primarily to motherhood. Unlike most American Catholics, conservatives actually follow this rule and accept the natural law theology in which it is grounded. If human reason can discern God's will in the laws of nature, they argue, then women's capacity to bear children suggests that God wants women to be mothers. As Bridget puts it, "I think there are things that we are suited for, that God gives us very definite gifts that can vary from person to person, but he also made men and women differently. We're different physically and psychologically, and I think God has it that way for a reason. Man and woman are different so that they can become one in marriage. It's like there's a completion when the two are one. I've always thought that. I can't see why some women are so intent on being just like men . . . Women have a more nurturing role."

Bridget's understanding of mothering as a divine gift is representative of the views of many women at St. Joseph's. Yet their interpretation of what mothering means goes beyond traditional gender roles. Raising children, according to these women, is not the only way to express the unique gifts God has granted to women. Working is another. Liz, for example, is a professor of theology at a local college. We met over lunch at a small, home-style restaurant near her office. Liz is a tall, olive-skinned woman in her mid-forties, with long dark hair tied into a thick braid. She was dressed informally in a flowing, Indian-cotton dress and Birkenstocks and impressed me as cheerful, direct, and very energetic. Liz told me that before she had committed herself to the Catholic faith, "I was in despair. I had no moral standards . . . no commitments in my life to anyone or anything." Having been "brought up to be selfish," it was difficult for her to "try to become more humble and accept my limitations." But notice how she interprets humility and selfless love: "I realized that I wasn't really cut out to be a good person in the particular mold that I had in my mind, which was the sacrificial mother image for a married woman. [I realized] that I had all these intellectual talents which God has given me, and that I was much better off giving love using my own talents, than . . . accepting the burdens of the housewife role." Liz clearly rejects the notion that women are naturally inclined to be homemakers. Expressing more feminist values, Liz insists that women can do anything men can do. "I'm in a very masculine field . . . there are many, many more male theology professors than women professors, and I am good at what I do." She also notes the difficulties faced by women who work in male-dominated professions. "Unfortunately, the masculine personality is still the paradigm . . . my way of teaching is not as highly valued as theirs." While insisting that women are different from men, she sees those differences as a reason for women to share the same sphere as men: "I think it's good if [women] come bringing their feminine gifts, like if they warm up the place . . . because most women are just so made by God, by their nature, to be nurturing . . . to do those same tasks with less ambition and competitiveness, to be affirming to your colleagues."

Conservative Catholic women agree with their leaders that mothering is women's unique gift but they insist that this gift be applied not only to children but to society at large. Such an interpretation challenges not only conservative notions of motherhood as women's primary role, but the assumptions of secular society which has defined the nurturing qualities required for motherhood in opposition to the competitive character of work and politics. Like their Evangelical and Jewish counterparts, conservative Catholic women build on women's difference to broaden their choices, integrating traditionalist norms with feminist values.

Pushing Boundaries

As conservative Christian and Orthodox Jewish women define their role in secular society, they are pushing the boundaries of their tradition. Rather than ignore or reject traditional norms, they reinterpret them by drawing on the unique resources of their respective religious communities. The notion that women working outside the home is part of Jewish tradition makes it easier for women at Beth Israel to justify having a career. Women at Victory Church draw on the Protestant concept of calling to legitimate their choice to work, while women at St. Joseph's reinterpret their church's emphasis on motherhood to apply to the workplace. In the secular context of work and politics, these women find ways to reconcile conservative Christianity and Orthodox Judaism with the expressive individualist feminism these communities explicitly reject.

But conservative religious women are also pushing the boundaries of secular society. By arguing that difference is an asset that makes women better political leaders, that homemaking is work, or that mothering should be applied to all spheres of life including work and politics, they are challenging modern industrial society's separation between home and work and its organization of economic and political institutions according to male needs. Such arguments are strikingly similar to the demands made by feminists, particularly the new difference feminists. Women who have returned to conservative religious communities, then, have not simply withdrawn from secular society in rejection of feminism, but are actively participating in the larger cultural debate over gender roles.

Their desire to participate raises at least two questions. First, why are these women (adults who have chosen to join conservative communities) so supportive of feminist values? One reason is education which has long been found to have a positive correlation with more feminist attitudes (Alwin 1993). This would explain why the women at Beth Israel (the most educated in this study) sounded more consistently feminist than the women at Victory Church (the least educated in this study). Another reason these women embrace feminist values could be workplace participation. Schmalzbauer (1993) demonstrated that working in professional or managerial occupations had a liberalizing effect on Evangelicals' perceptions of gender roles. Wilcox and Jelen (1991) found that labor force participation was strongly and positively related to feminist attitudes among both Catholics and Evangelicals. Cohen-Nusbacher's (1987) study of Orthodox Jewish women found that those who worked developed more feminist attitudes. The fact that all of the women in this study—even those who are currently homemakers— have experienced working outside the home may make them more supportive of gender equality.

A second question is whether the support for feminist values that these women express in secular contexts carries over into the all other aspects of their lives. If women support gender equality at work, one would think they would support it at home and in church or synagogue as well. If Victory Church, St. Joseph's, and Beth Israel are filled with women who want the option to be a president or general, we may soon find them wanting to be priest and rabbis as well. As we shall see in the following chapter, however, church or synagogue is an entirely different context and induces very different responses.

Chapter 5

Traditionalists in Church and Synagogue

I would feel uncomfortable having a woman rabbi . . . I just feel it's against Judaism for a woman to be in front of a pulpit running a whole congregation. Men have that role in Orthodox Judaism, and women have other roles like raising children and maintaining the household.

—ORTHODOX JEWISH WOMAN

We believe that a woman cannot have spiritual authority over a man because God has given that role to the man . . . a woman needs to be accountable to someone.

—EVANGELICAL PROTESTANT WOMAN

I don't think women should be priests any more than I think women should be fathers.

—CONSERVATIVE CATHOLIC WOMAN

IT IS HARD TO BELIEVE that these statements were made by some of the same women presented in the last chapter. These are women who, in secular contexts, insist that they have a right to choose any role they please regardless of gender differences. These are women who, despite their stated opposition to the feminist movement, have clearly integrated feminist values into their lives—women who are successful in their careers, who oppose gender discrimination and support the expansion of women's leadership. If one met a woman like this while she was on the job, one would never know she's a religious conservative.

A totally different picture may emerge if one followed this woman to church or synagogue. In this religious context, she appears to accept the traditionalist argument that gender differences mandate different social roles. In assessing how a woman defines her role in church or synagogue, I used opposition to women's ordination as the primary indicator of "traditionalist values." By "ordination," I mean an official policy that allows a person to be a pastor, priest, or rabbi of a congregation (even Evangelical churches that reject the term "ordination" have such policies). While this indicator is imperfect (liberal denominations that permit women's ordination may discriminate against women pastors and surveys of members of such denominations show ambivalence about women's ordination), it is useful for two reasons. First, many conservative religious denominations, including those studied here, see women's ordination as a symbol of the liberal world they are trying to define themselves against. Thus the women themselves see their opposition to female religious leadership as an indicator of their commitment to tradition. Secondly, the reasons women cited for opposing ordination clearly reflect the traditionalist assumption that natural gender differences should mandate different social roles.[1] We saw in chapter 1 that Katrina, Miriam, and Barbara adopted such traditionalist values when they were in church or synagogue. Let us now look more closely at how other women at Victory, St. Joseph's and Beth Israel understand their role in a religious context.

Women are Exempt

Every time I attended religious services at Beth Israel, I was struck by how peripheral women's participation seemed. The men always arrived first, sometimes several hours before the women. The men wore special ritual garments (prayer shawls and yarmulkes) while the women did not. The men sat in the center of the sanctuary, surrounding the bimah, and participated continually in prayers and readings, most of them apparently quite fluent in Hebrew. The women sat in the back and on the sides of the sanctuary, separated by a mechitzah. Many of them appeared to have difficulty following the Hebrew, and they frequently interrupted their prayers to whisper to each other or to the children. From an outside observer's perspective, the synagogue of Congregation Beth Israel was clearly a man's place.

A look at Orthodox Jewish teaching confirms that observation. The Orthodox explanation for why women cannot be rabbis is rooted in a larger system of ritual segregation. Because of their responsibility for the home, women are exempt from most positive time-bound mitzvot (religious commandments that must be performed at certain times, such as communal prayer).[2] While men attend services on Friday afternoons, women are preparing the home for the Sabbath. Women's exemption in turn is used to justify excluding women from a minyan (quorum of ten necessary for public prayer), from having *aliyah* (being called up to the Torah), from studying Talmud, or from leading religious services.[3] The segregation of men's and women's seating areas follows logically from this argument. Since women need not fully participate in the ritual, they will only distract the men from their religious duty.

The women at Beth Israel support these norms. Not only do they oppose women rabbis and support the mechitza, but their reason for doing so reflects their acceptance of the traditionalist view that natural differences between men and women mandate different social roles. Despite their insistence that women can and should hold the same leadership positions as men in the secular society, most women in this congregation feel that they should not be rabbis. Take Judith, for example. You'll recall from the last chapter that she left her husband because he forbade her to work and sought to limit her to the traditionalist role of wife and mother. Yet she also told me, "I would feel uncomfortable having a woman rabbi . . . I just feel like it is against Judaism for a woman to be in front of a pulpit running a whole congregation . . . Men just have that role in Orthodox Judaism, and women have other roles like raising children and maintaining the household and going to the *mikveh* [ritual bath] and making challah, and all these other things that are also very important . . . Women have enough to do without being rabbis." Judith is angry at feminist efforts to push for ordination. "It's just not necessary and I don't think the rabbis will permit it." Rivka expresses similar resentment. A big strong woman who runs a contracting business with her husband, she was clearly the dominant partner in her marriage. Having previously worked as an engineer, she was strongly supportive of gender equality on the job. When it came to the synagogue, however, she is very critical of any effort to train women as rabbis. "A lot of times it just creates friction when you're trying to pull from what the man's job is. I don't know, I just don't see a real need for that. . . . It makes you feel like you're a second-class citizen that you're always having to push, push, push for these equal rights. If you would just step back a little bit and say, 'this is what I have to work with,' then . . . I think there's many other areas besides the Talmud that women can learn and really excel in, I mean, I believe there is a reason why men were chosen, why it was designated for men to learn this and women not." When talking about secular society, Judith and Rivka feel that differences between the sexes do not warrant different roles and that child rearing is an option that broadens women's choices vis-à-vis men. By contrast, when they talk about the synagogue, they argue that there are some roles like being a rabbi that a woman cannot play because her main responsibility is home and children.

I noticed a similar contrast in how the women viewed the mechitza. While they support gender integration in the military, they believe male-female segregation in the synagogue reflects natural patterns. Dana, for example, is a public relations manager at a large Jewish organization. A political liberal, she actively opposes the exclusion of women from the military. Yet she feels that the mechitza merely institutionalizes natural patterns of male-female separation. "I find it so funny when we're out in a social situation, and all the men are together and all the women are together, because that's how people *are*." By affirming the differences, the mechitza actually benefits women. As Michelle explains: "I grew up without [a mechitzah]. We were Jews on Friday nights, and it was a family thing, and we all sat together . . . that was [our] Jewish experience." Now that she is Orthodox, she values gender separation: "I have no problem with [the mechitzah]. Sometimes I wish I had a mechitzah completely around me, so I wouldn't be distracted while the other side is talking. I get distracted very easily. . . . we all do. And the truth is, look, it's not such a barrier that I can't look over and motion to my husband to go outside and check on the baby." The synagogue, according to these women, is indeed "a man's place," but that does not make them feel excluded.

Given their condemnation of women's exclusion from historically male occupations in secular society, one wonders how they can accept it in their religious community. They accept it because women's exclusion from the rabbinate is part of halacha. As we saw in the last chapter, commitment to halacha is a given in this community, a basic tenet that is not questioned because it lies at the heart of Orthodox identity. The most frequently cited reason for their opposition to women's ordination was that "it's just not halachic." As Judith puts it, "It's just not allowed, and that's the bottom line. There are too many halachic

problems with it . . . rabbis do a lot of counseling, and a woman cannot be a counselor for a man. Occasionally a rabbi has to act as a witness, and she cannot be a witness. She can be a teacher but she cannot
run a whole congregation." Judith believes that even if a woman could
be given the rabbinical title for achieving the requisite level of Jewish
learning (as some Jewish feminists have suggested), she could not fulfill most of the functions of a rabbi. It does not seem to occur to Judith
to question why a woman is excluded from those functions the way she
questions traditionalist gender roles outside the synagogue. Being an
Orthodox—rather than a Reform or Conservative—Jew, means observing Jewish law, and according to Jewish law "our role is important but
it's quieter than that of the man, less demonstrative. Women should
not be running an entire community." Enforcing halachic rules about
ritual segregation, including the prohibition against women's ordination, is what makes Beth Israel distinct from other, more liberal synagogues as well as from the secular society.

It is therefore rather ironic that Orthodox Jewish women would find
affirmation of halacha in the secular field of popular psychology. Pay a
visit to a commercial bookstore anywhere in this country and you will
find scores of books such as the bestselling *Men Are from Mars, Women
Are from Venus* that reaffirm old stereotypes of natural and unchangeable psychological differences between the sexes. Men are more aggressive, independent, rational, while women are more nurturing, relational,
emotional. Traditionalists usually argue that these differences disqualify
women from leadership positions. The women at Beth Israel, however,
give this argument a different twist. They claim that their role in
the synagogue is limited because they are naturally spiritual and therefore don't need the practice. Men have more religious obligations,
including leadership, because they need that structure to maintain their
spirituality.

This is the position taken by Naomi, a single mother of two who
works as a therapist in a private clinic. Due to her hectic schedule, we
had agreed to meet for breakfast at 8:00 A.M., right after she dropped
the boys off at school and before she had her first appointment at ten
o'clock. Naomi is tall and blonde and was dressed for work in a dark
skirt and pink sweater. In her mid-thirties, she looks pale and harried,

the lines of stress beginning to show in her face. The previous year she had gone through a rather ugly divorce in which her husband refused to give her a *get* (the Jewish divorce document) unless she accepted the financial settlement he requested. Needless to say, her impression of men is less than glowing. Yet she feels it is only men, not women, who should lead a synagogue. "Men need more structure and they need more obligations. . . . I hate to say this, but I think they're not as inherently spiritual and giving and responsible as women unless they have some kind of structure atmosphere." Naomi's perspective may reflect the negative experiences she had with men. Yet several seemingly happily married women make similar arguments. Thus Vicky, a part-time lawyer and new mother, was basking in the joy of having just given birth when she told me that "I wouldn't want to be a rabbi . . . we don't need to. Women are just naturally more spiritual and they are closer to God, so they don't need to go through some of the rituals and do some of the things that men do." Ironically, this reasoning implies that women are actually more capable of religious leadership than men. Ellen, who had worked as a family therapist before deciding to stay home with her four children, suggests that it means exactly that:

> Women in many ways are more spiritual and better at these things than men. If women are allowed to do it, I think a lot of men will shy away from it . . . in social situations I notice that women are more comfortable and more involved and more connected. . . . If you go to a party, you'll see how women are talking and how many of the men are sitting in a corner, not knowing what to do with each other. . . . I find in the synagogue it's the reverse. It's the men who are more comfortable. They really feel like it's their place. . . . So I don't think anyone would actually admit this, but I wonder if that's part of it, that if you let the women do it, and they do such a great job at it, will the men stop doing it?

Ellen assumes that gender differences matter—indeed, it is their very difference from men that makes women more qualified to lead than men. Such assumptions suggest that despite their acceptance of halacha as a given, these women do feel some ambivalence about the role it assigns to them.

A Woman Needs a Covering

A similar dynamic can be observed at Victory Church. The women here initially appear more integrated into religious services than their Orthodox Jewish counterparts. They announce upcoming church activities, witness to their experience with the Lord, and may even lead the congregation in song. Yet if you stick around long enough, it quickly becomes clear who is really in charge. It is always a male pastor who gives the sermon—the core of the Evangelical service. Pastor Bill and his male assistants teach Bible-study groups and provide counseling to both men and women, while women can only teach and counsel children or other women. And at the time of my research, the pastor was in the process of replacing Victory School's female principal with a man—not because church members were unhappy with her performance but because the pastor believed the position should be held by a man.

The pastor's actions reflect common Evangelical teachings. Like Orthodox Jews, most Evangelical churches prohibit women from leading an entire congregation. But unlike Jews who exempt women from much of obligatory synagogue participation, Evangelicals expect women to attend services as much as men. Instead of exemption from duty, Evangelicals emphasize male headship, arguing that it is inappropriate for women to have authority over men (Lienesh 1993; Clouse and Clouse 1989). Interpreting the Bible literally, they rely on Paul's exhortations that women should be silent in the church and that the husband is the head of the wife as Christ is the head of the church. Thus many Evangelical churches allow women to teach women, but not men or mixed groups (the stricter view, that women have no public role in the church is less common). Some churches, particularly charismatics such as Victory, make exceptions to this rule so long as the woman has a male "covering," i.e., her actions are under the authority of her husband or a male pastor. The exceptions confirm the rule that church headship is male.

The women at Victory support these norms. Not only do they oppose women pastors, but their opposition reflects acceptance of the traditionalist view that natural differences between men and women mandate different social roles. Gender differences that are downplayed in discussions of the workplace are, in the context of the church, emphasized as significant. Patty, who as we saw in chapter 4, is herself in charge of an entire school, feels that "a woman should not be in running a congregation." Similarly, Lisa who, when discussing secular roles for women, insists on gender equality, makes a complete turnabout when I ask her about women's role in the church: "I never, never have believed that women and men are equal. I believe they can do equal types of work, in certain areas, but I believe they are created differently because they have different roles to fill. And I don't see that as a role for a woman to fill, being the leader of a whole congregation of men and women together." Both Patty and Lisa make a clear distinction between who they are at work and who they are at church. In the former context, they are equal to men in every respect; while they acknowledge that differences between the sexes exist, they do not see them as sufficient to justify separate spheres. In the latter context, however, these differences matter and mandate that men and women play different roles. The inconsistency between these two identities does not seem to be an issue.

The arguments Evangelical women make to justify their support for traditionalist norms are very similar to those made by Orthodox Jewish women. Just as the women at Beth Israel refuse to question religious law that excludes them from synagogue leadership, the women at Victory Church accept scripture without questioning it the way they do secular laws. Many Evangelicals are able to cite, often including full biblical references, the arguments about headship and "male covering" found in conservative Christian writings. Ronda, a single woman who teaches history at a local high school, explained to me that while women can teach other women or children, and lead various church ministries, they cannot be head-pastors of a congregation. Citing Paul's first letters to the Corinthians and Timothy, she told me:

> We believe that a woman cannot have spiritual authority over
> a man . . . because God has given that role to the man. . . . And
> I really believe that a woman needs to be covered. God just
> created us that we're more emotional . . . and when you look in
> the Bible, God did use women, but the majority of the time he
> used men, and a majority of the time when women were used,
> there were men very close by for accountability purposes. A
> woman needs to be accountable to someone. It's like a cover-
> ing . . . the covering is submission to a pastor she can turn to

and say, "This is the way my ministry is going, I feel like God is
leading me in this direction. What do you think about it?" She
needs someone to bounce things off of.

Ronda emphasizes that *her* views ("I really believe") are fully in line
with those of her community ("we believe"), and that the gender norms
prescribed by conservative Christian leaders not only apply to her life
but make sense—at least in the context of the church. Implicit in her
scriptural argument is the assumption that women are fundamentally
different from men: more emotional and therefore in need of direction
and supervision. While she does not believe that these characteristics
should prevent women from holding any leadership positions in the
secular world, her insistence on biblical inerrancy forces her to conclude that gender differences are sufficient to deny women authority
over men in the church.

Evangelical women see their acceptance of scripture as a given as
what distinguishes them from liberal Protestants and secular Americans.
Yet they seek affirmation of scripture in secular psychology, and they
interpret that psychology in ways that seem to undermine traditionalist assumptions that women are less qualified to lead. Like Vicky and
Naomi at Beth Israel, many women at Victory believe that because they
are naturally more spiritual than men, they should step back in order
to encourage men's spirituality. As Patty explains:

> There's a couple of [women pastors] in the valley . . . if they're
> submitted, OK—apparently most of them have a pastor to
> relate to—but I just don't think it's a good role model for the
> men. And the men are the problem! There's just a weakness in
> men. I don't see a problem with women being weak. . . . When
> you go to churches and you look around, you'll see . . . that
> numberwise it's the women who predominate, and it's the
> women that are a lot of times leading the families. . . . Women
> just have that fortitude to keep going. I'm not saying that men
> don't, but if you saw all the single parent families, headed by
> women, that I see . . . so we need to encourage men.

Because men are spiritually weak, they need male role models to emulate and leadership opportunities that challenge them to become stronger. While explicitly traditionalist in its assumption that it is men's role

to lead and women's to follow, the argument implicitly inverts itself by assuming that women are actually stronger and more capable than men—so capable, in fact, that they are already running the show. Thus Marisa, a single woman who teaches at Victory elementary school, said "women in this church lead the church. . . . I'm praying for men to do more. Shoot, we do everything!" Charleen, a big woman with a loud voice who is active in church fund-raising, echoes this sentiment. When asked what she thought about women's leadership in the church, Charleen is emphatic: "You can't have a church without it! The women do all the work. . . . I think that the man is the overseer, according to God's word, but none of these men would be anywhere without the support of their wives. . . . We're doing this tea for the school [a fund-raiser], and it's the fourth year in a row, and there's not one man on the committee. Now the men are out there being evangelists and all of these so-called important things, but the women, in my opinion, keep the church going." Neither woman challenges the assumptions of gender difference that prohibit women's official leadership. Charleen does not question the notion that "the man is the overseer," and when Pastor Jordan told Marisa that she was becoming too visible in the church, she agreed. Instead these women complain that men are not living up to their God-given responsibilities. Because men are weak, Marisa feels women must pick up the slack. And Charleen's jibe at evangelists implies that women's work, although not officially acknowledged, is actually more important than that of men. The women at Victory Church accept the traditional role assigned to them but their acceptance is not without misgivings.

A Woman Can't Represent Christ

The picture is even more complex for Catholic women. While conservative Protestant and Orthodox Jewish opposition to women's ordination is fairly unified, the Roman Catholic Church is deeply divided over this issue. Both feminists, who seek to expand women's leadership in the church, and the Catholic hierarchy, which opposes that, have received extensive media coverage. The exclusion of women from the Roman Catholic priesthood and feminists' inability to change that is old news even to people who have never set foot in a church. When I attended services at St. Joseph's, I was therefore surprised to see women in visible leadership positions (cantor and reader). As I got to know the community, however, I realized that the inclusion of women is clearly limited. Women are allowed to actively participate in leading services but are clearly excluded from any sacramental function: they do not wear any special garments like the men's and altarboys' and never set foot on the altar. Women are encouraged to lead committees and small groups, but all of these are ultimately accountable to the male priests. The selective inclusion of women seems to be a very deliberate strategy to keep both liberal and conservative parishioners happy.

Conservative Catholic opposition to female priests is consistent with church teaching. That teaching is quite different from Jewish and Evangelical arguments against women's ordination. While the former exempt a woman from synagogue duty and the latter prohibit her from having teaching authority over men, Catholics specifically exclude women from performing the sacramental function of a priest. Because the priest, especially when he is celebrating Mass, is acting *in personae Christi* and Jesus was a man, only males can serve as priests. Furthermore, the doctrine of apostolic succession states that the first bishops were the direct successors of the apostles whom Christ chose himself and that there is an unbroken line from them to present day bishops and priests in the Roman Catholic church. If Jesus didn't admit women to his founding circle of twelve, conservatives argue, the church cannot do so either. In contrast to Evangelical teaching, this sacramental argument allows women to teach mixed audiences of men and women (in Bible-study groups, for example), but it excludes women from any functions that would put them on the altar (for example by serving as altar girls). And in contrast to Orthodox Jewish teaching, Catholic doctrine does not exempt women from their duty to attend mass—only from leading it.

Conservative women at St. Joseph's support these norms. Not only are they adamantly opposed to ordaining women, but their opposition to change reflects their acceptance of the traditionalist view that natural differences between men and women mandate different social roles. Take Liz, the theology professor, for example. When we talked about her job she complained that theology is a male-dominated field that has yet to learn to value a woman's input. But when we talked about the church, she accepted women's exclusion: "The male priesthood is a special role for the men which women can't have in the Catholic Church." She explained that "there are several reasons for this. . . . One of them would be the whole symbolic thing that Jesus was a man. The priest is supposed to represent Jesus. The priest is saying, 'This is my body.' Jesus had a male body, so the priest should have a male body. Then there's the whole aptness argument, it's called apt symbols . . . so if you were doing a nativity play, you wouldn't want Nick Nolte for Mary. So there's that whole Catholic thing about drama and symbols that comes in there." In contrast to her statements about her job, Liz now says male leadership is natural and should not be challenged: "I notice that women—unless the boss is an ogre or something— many women prefer having males in leadership over women rather than other women. . . . I prefer working with women on a project together because there's that very immediate understanding, but I prefer having males in leadership." Even her perspective on work—previously feminist— is now colored by her effort to justify the traditionalist position.

How do conservative Catholic women, so supportive of women's leadership in secular contexts, explain their rejection of the female priesthood? Some of their arguments are similar to those I heard at Victory Church and Beth Israel. Just as Jews and Protestants accepted halacha and the Bible as a given, so conservative Catholics accept the doctrine of their church without questioning it the way they do secular laws. Liz, as we have seen, cites the argument about men representing Christ. Other women I interviewed cited a variation of the doctrine of apostolic succession to justify excluding women from the priesthood. Donna, a homemaker who has been very active in the pro-life movement, put it this way: "The church bases its belief on the fact that Christ only picked men for his apostles, and there are people who would say that Christ was just conforming to the cultural patterns of his time. But if you look at other things our Lord did, he did not conform to the patterns of his time. There were many times when . . . that's why he got crucified, 'cause he differed from everybody. When it was right from wrong, he just did it. So if you believe he was God, you would say to yourself, he would not conform, he's beyond the patterns of time. If it was wrong to exclude women, he would have included them." Donna is clearly aware of feminist arguments that interpretation of the Bible must take into account that its authors lived in a patriarchal society. But she rejects those arguments by asserting that placing Jesus' actions in historical context would challenge his divinity. Interestingly, she has no problem with a contextual reading of other passages of the Bible. Fundamentalists who take literally Paul's exhortation for women to be silent in the church are, in her opinion, irrational because they fail to see that "those were different times." A good Catholic, Donna accepts only those interpretations—either literal or contextual—that are officially sanctioned by her church.

Like Evangelicals and Orthodox Jews, conservative Catholic women find the laws of their church affirmed by popular psychology, but unlike the former, they interpret that psychology in more traditional ways, suggesting that women are not capable of religious leadership. Beatrice, a tall, elegant woman who left a university teaching career in order to stay home with her seven children, resists women's ordination because "women aren't suited to that role. They tend to be somewhat more strident or something . . . we don't have the natural qualities [for leadership]." Conservative Catholic women accept popular theories that dichotomize male and female psychological characteristics. While they acknowledge that "female" traits (e.g., being relationship oriented) can be useful to business leaders, they see these same traits as inappropriate for religious leaders. I talked to one woman who, widowed at twenty-five, spent the next twenty years working full-time as a manager of a bookstore while raising five children. Yet when it comes to the priesthood, she didn't think women could handle it: "I seriously wonder, even with the strongest women, like when they're really good in business, I seriously wonder if [given] the emotions and the strengths in a woman [it] would not be difficult for her to carry out the business of being a priest. . . . Women have maternal instincts, their mood is more emotional for the most part. Although we're strong and we can handle emergencies, we don't have the qualities of a man . . . there is a certain ability that men have to deal with another's emotions without getting emotional themselves." Female psychology disqualifies women from being religious leaders because their primary role is to be mothers. As Bridget explained: "I think there are things we are suited for . . . that God made men and women differently. And I think women have a more nurturing role. And you can say, 'Well, priests need to nurture, too.' But I think, by and large, if a woman can she should be a mother. And I think the job, the role of the priest is to be out there for everyone, to be there for your needs, my needs, anytime, day or night. And I don't think that's a good role for a woman. I don't see how you can do that and be there for your family all the time when they need you. Because it's most of the time that they need you." Because mothering their own family is women's first responsibility, we cannot expect them to take care of an entire community. Hence that role is assigned to men. None of these women would accept the argument that women's mothering duties preclude them from leading a corporation or running for public office—especially if their children are no longer infants. Yet they fully embrace the assertions made by conservative Catholic leaders that the psychological characteristics that make women good mothers also render them ineffective priests.

Using popular psychology and religious law to justify separate gender roles in church is common in all three communities I studied. Yet women at St. Joseph's added a third argument that I did not hear at either Victory Church or Beth Israel. That reason is biology. Rita, for example, is a conservative Catholic who gave up her medical career to stay home with her children. A slim, gray-haired woman, she now heads up St. Joseph's pro-life committee. Like Barbara, she thinks that the feminist push for women's ordination is bad for the church. "I don't think women should be priests any more than I think women should be fathers. To me it's another example of misconstrued feminism, to think that for women to be priests is absolutely no different than women wanting to be corporate executives. It *is* different!" It is different because in order to be a priest you need a male body. Donna, for example, rejects what she calls a fundamentalist notion that women should not have authority over men. She approves of women leading co-ed Bible-study classes and thinks that "women can be school principals, heads of corporations, even president of the United States." But they cannot be priests because "there's certain things, like physical things, that men can't do, that women can do, like having a baby, nursing a baby, that's one example. And so it doesn't hurt my pride that there could be, on a spiritual plane, something that would be only open to men. So if the church tells me [the priesthood] is only open to men, that's fine by me, it doesn't bother me, it doesn't make me a lesser person." While Donna rejects any hint of biological determinism with respect to women's role in the workplace, and repeatedly emphasizes that "I chose to stay home," she fully accepts such determinism in the context of the church.

Of course, the Protestant and Jewish arguments against female ordination also rely on biological differences between the sexes, but they do so more indirectly. In their view, the biological fact that women have babies results in certain psychological tendencies or social responsibilities that make it impractical for them to hold the highest religious leadership positions. But Evangelicals and Jews rarely go so far as to argue that it is her female body that makes it impossible for a woman to lead a congregation. This kind of overt biological determinism is unique to conservative Catholics because of the sacramental emphasis of the Roman Catholic tradition. The doctrine that the priest personifies Christ is an idea that magnifies the importance of gender differences because it bases the separation of male and female roles on biological, and hence unchangeable, fact. It provides perhaps the strongest case for maintaining separate gender roles in the church.

Conservative Catholic women accept this case completely, expressing much less ambivalence about traditional religious roles than Evangelicals or Orthodox Jews. This difference is significant. In contrast to Victory and Beth Israel, conservative women at St. Joseph's must share the pews with liberal church members. Their acceptance of Catholic doctrine is thus the only way they have of asserting their conservative identity.

Maintaining Boundaries

Maintaining a distinct conservative identity is key to understanding why the women in this study accept inequality in the religious context of church or synagogue even though they reject it in the secular context of work and politics. Calling oneself a conservative Protestant or Catholic, or an Orthodox Jew presumes that one accepts scripture, magisterial teaching, or halacha as a given. While women's equality in secular society is perceived as compatible with those "givens," women's ordination as religious leaders is not. Their acceptance of traditional roles in church or synagogue, then, is a symbol of conservative identity.

The symbolic meaning of rejecting women's ordination also explains why these women support female religious leadership in positions other than pastor, priest, or rabbi. Secondary levels of authority (even when they wield considerable influence) are compatible with what is given. Thus several conservative Catholics with whom I spoke would gladly expand women's role as far as church law will allow. Donna, for example, has noticed that the church is "opening up all kinds of other things for women, and I think that's basically good. On commissions, on encyclicals, women are part of all this now, and there's nothing wrong with that." Despite her insistence that the priesthood would interfere with a woman's maternal obligations, Bridget asserts that "I don't see any reason why women can't function within the parish and have various leadership positions without sacrificing their families. That's all just fine, I mean, I don't have a problem with that. I think it's great. I don't see why they can't lector, why they can't cantor, can't be teachers, or can't head committees"—all positions that women actually do hold at St. Joseph's. Liz noted, "I myself am a lector, and I used to do Eucharistic ministry, and I loved it, and I love being a lector." And the spunky young Mexican American woman who heads St. Joseph's youth ministry, observed, "I see women everywhere—leading. Most of the religious education teachers at parochial schools are women. A lot of the leaders in administration are women, and they aren't necessarily women religious. They are laity. Also you have what's called Sacristal Ministers, they take care of the sacristy and stuff, not just administration, and a lot of them are women. . . . I mean it's really increasing. I'm not sure how many women are involved in the training for the deaconate, but I think that's going to be the next step, you know, to have that kind of leadership by women."[4]

Similarly, Evangelical women support women's leadership in areas such as foreign missions, healing ministries, and even founding local "seed" churches, which, once established, would be taken over by men. Stephanie, a homemaker with five children, feels that all positions other than the head pastor should be open to women. "That's the only office I think that women should not lead in . . . anything under that is OK. And there's a multitude of things you can do—you don't even need the pastor. There's elders, deacons, there's a ton of women's ministries, like I'm a homeschool leader for the church." Tanya, a woman in her early forties who was a long-time follower of an Indian guru before being born again as a Christian, put it this way: "The Bible says men should lead, but God uses whoever he can. . . . If there's not enough men who are willing and ready, he'll use a woman. . . . I know this woman missionary, she's a powerful preacher . . . and she goes out to all different countries and does great work for God. . . . So women should not be head over men, as in pastoring a church, but as far as being in leadership in healing and ministering—definitely!" Such comments are not just wishful thinking but are based on the women's own experience at Victory Church.

The same is true of Orthodox Jewish women. The synagogue is defined as a house of prayer and study, and several women at Beth Israel want to participate more fully in both areas. As Rachel put it: "We need to make sure that women are represented in the shul and in Jewish life to the fullest extent that we can be—not as much as men are, but the fullest extent that women can be. . . . That's why I'm involved in the women's *Gemara* class and the *Shabbes shiur* [a scripture-study group] . . to really push the front on Orthodox Judaism." Rachel is a student finishing her master's degree in early childhood education. She is also the mother of a three-year-old girl. As such, she is representative of a broader pattern at Beth Israel: the desire to push the boundaries of tradition is most common among women who have daughters.

Even those women who are quite comfortable with traditional roles that limit their own participation in synagogue ritual want their daughters to have greater involvement in "the house of prayer." The bar mitzvah ceremony, for example, is generally reserved for boys in Orthodox communities. Even though none of the women had themselves received bat mitzvah, and some felt uncomfortable with the thought of doing so, many women insisted there should be a parallel celebration for the girls. Leonora, a chemical researcher in pharmaceutical company, told me that her daughter had partaken in a such a ceremony. "My daughter was bat-mitzvah'ed this summer . . . and my husband had wanted very much for her to do it—the regular way [i.e., like the boys], and I thought I'd be very uncomfortable with that [since] I've never had a bat mitzvah. So I just thought it would feel funny. But at Beth Israel, the way they handled it was . . . on one day she read Torah at the shul, during the board member's breakfast there, and the faculty [of her school] were there too, and then on Shabbes she talked about some

Mishnah that she had learned . . . and it was just great!" Unfortunately, in Leonora's view, not all rabbi's are as open to change as Rabbi Feldman. "They had started doing bat mitzvahs at another synagogue, where my husband and I used to go, and the way they did it is the girls came up after the shul was over and gave *devar Torah* [an explanation of a passage of scripture]—and they covered the ark with a tarp, to sort of desanctify the room, like 'now it's a hall, not a shul.' To me that was so incredibly offensive! I couldn't look at it. I thought it would be better if they wouldn't do it at all, if they just had no bat mitzvah at all. But to have a young girl go up there and cover it up. . . . I just couldn't stand it." Leonora accepts the separation of the sexes in the synagogue and the restrictions of women's public ritual participation: she has no problem with the fact that her daughter's bat mitzvah was held separately, structured differently, and did not last as long as that of the boys. But she is deeply insulted by the notion that those restrictions mean women are somehow less worthy, more profane than men, so that their very presence would desanctify an otherwise sacred space. Leonora does not question complementarity; rather she believes it means separate but equal.

The women also want their daughters to participate equally in "the house of study." They see "Jewish learning" as essential to Orthodox identity and complain bitterly when local Hebrew schools do not provide that opportunity. Dana, for example, told me that, beginning in fifth grade, "the boys go to school half an hour earlier than the girls because the curriculum is different. Well, I think that's terrible, if for no other reason than that the school is far away and I can't get to work on time. But that's not the real issue—that's just when I noticed that [they were treated differently]. Not that it needs to be the same—what men do and what boys do is going to be different—but everyone needs to feel that they have a role, that they have a place, and they can be different, but still equal. . . . I think the girls need to be treated with respect!" She related a story about another Orthodox woman in her office who has two boys at another Hebrew day school. "So I asked her about the time difference, and she said at her school the boys stay later." Dana told the woman that she thought girls and boys should spend the same amount of time in school. "And she said, 'Yeah, give 'em home-ec.' And I looked at her—she's working because she needs to work, not a career woman, she's a secretary—and I said, 'Well, I would say that is not acceptable! To me it's not treating the girls with any kind of respect . . . and that's not what I want for my girls.'" Dana's earlier assertion that Judaism merely institutionalizes natural differences between the sexes apparently does not extend to her daughter. She herself does not have the Jewish education her husband has and makes no effort to acquire it—even though Beth Israel offers several relevant classes—because she believes her ritual role in the synagogue does not require it. Yet what she wants for her girls, if not for herself, is equality—especially in religious education because learning, she believes, lies at the heart of Judaism.

Conservative religious women, then, support changes in women's role only if they are consistent with what is given by their respective tradition. Although conservative Catholic women enjoy having female lectors, cantors, and Bible teachers, they accept magisterial teaching that only these nonsacramental positions are appropriate for women.[5] Although some Evangelicals feel that the church positions held by women are actually more important than those held by men, they do not question the biblical assumption that those positions should be different. And although Orthodox Jewish women push the boundaries of halachic restrictions on women, especially for their daughters, they do not reject the restrictions themselves. Thus a woman reading the Bible during Sunday services at St. Joseph's Church does not contradict the doctrine that a female body cannot represent Christ. A woman preaching the gospel to teenagers at the shopping mall does not contradict Victory Church's teaching that women can't have authority over men. And attending women's Talmud-study classes at Beth Israel is justified so long as classes are held separately from men's. Although these women set limits on traditional restrictions, they generally do accept traditional roles in the context of church or synagogue.

The ways in which women adapt themselves to traditional roles reflect important differences between their respective religious communities. Because Orthodox Jewish women are perhaps most visibly excluded from leadership or even participation in synagogue ritual, it makes sense that they would push harder for change than say Evangelicals who participate equally in most aspects of church services except for the pastorship. The relatively democratic leadership style of many Evangelical churches may make it easier for the women to accept male authority. Many Evangelicals, including Pastor Jordan, believe that religious leadership should be determined by a call from God—seminary training or ordination rituals are unnecessary. The fact that any man or woman at Victory Church could get up and "give the Word" to the rest of the congregation blurred the distinction between leaders and regular members. In some ways, all members are leaders, and all leaders are laity. An Evangelical woman can embrace a traditionalist role in church because, in practice, it hardly limits her role at all.

While Evangelical and Orthodox Jewish women adapt to traditionalist roles shared by the majority of their congregation, conservative Catholic women must defend these roles against the dissenting views of many church members. Knowing that two-thirds of American Catholics support women's ordination, conservative women see it as their mission to stem the tide and reject female priesthood. Fully accepting their exclusion from authority has become a symbol of their identity as conservative Catholics. To embrace a traditionalist role in the church gives them a sense that they are "real Catholics"—as opposed to the growing number of nominal Catholics who are almost indistinguishable from mainline Protestants.

Regardless of their particular religious tradition, women in all three communities seem to find it fairly easy to separate religious and secular identities into their respective social environments. Secular contexts, such as work or politics, are places where they embrace feminist values and demand full equality with men. Religious contexts, such as church and synagogue, are places where they accept the traditionalist values that men and women have different rights and responsibilities. But what about the home? As we will see in the following chapter, the home is much more difficult to categorize as either secular or religious, and, as a result, it is a place where gender roles are constantly contested.

Chapter 6

But What about the Home?

*Yes, I submit to my husband, but not with big deci-
sions . . . I want my say! Plus I feel like if it's the Lord's
will you're both going to hear the same answer anyway.*

—EVANGELICAL WOMAN

*Some people think that the role of a woman, an
Orthodox woman, is to stay home and put a family—to
be a homemaker. My view is that the role of a woman is
to be an equal partner . . . she is the center force to guide
the family in Yiddishkeit.*

—ORTHODOX JEWISH WOMAN

*That's why I'm not a fundamentalist . . . fundamental-
ists don't have a teaching authority to interpret the Bible
for them, or to help them interpret the Bible. . . . That's
how the church frees you up, 'cause the church believes
in the mind, and you use common sense, and common
sense is that you don't have to obey a man.*

—CONSERVATIVE CATHOLIC WOMAN

IN CONSERVATIVE RELIGIOUS COMMUNITIES, a woman's place is in the
home—or is it? And if it is, what does that mean? The home is clearly
not a secular space where women can largely ignore traditionalist gender norms as they do with respect to work or politics. But neither is
the home an exclusively religious space like a church or synagogue
where women feel compelled to adapt to traditionalist norms. The
home, as we shall see, is a place where gender roles are contested, much
as they are contested in secular homes across America.

From who does the dishes, to who picks up the children from day
care, to who decides whether or not to relocate, men and women everywhere are struggling over who does what in the home. As more and
more women work outside the home, they have less time to take care

of home and children. As more women enter male-dominated professions and gain positions of leadership in the workplace, they are less inclined to accept male authority. Yet most men, especially those in the baby-boom generation, were raised in families where women did take care of home and children and in which the father was seen as the head. It should therefore come as no surprise when studies show that even when both spouses work full-time, women do the bulk of the housework and childcare (Perkins and DeMeis 1996). Neither is it surprising that people fight.

Such tension arises from a disjunction between traditional gender roles and contemporary economic realities. Gender roles in the home can be divided into two parts: family headship (who has authority) and home care (who is responsible for housework and childcare). Judaism and Christianity have traditionally assigned family headship to men and home care to women. Because these role assignments emerged in cultures that did not clearly separate work and home, actual gender roles were more diffuse. If the family farmed, both men and women (and children for that matter) would work the land, with women's cooking and cleaning duties complementing men's responsibilities for herding and slaughtering animals. If the man was a scholar, families might rely on women's income from trade or handicrafts. It was the industrial revolution that separated home from workplace, creating a rigid distinction between the male role of breadwinner and the female role of homemaker. Because the family depended for physical survival on the man, it also became easier to enforce male authority: women were in a very real way dependent on men. Twentieth-century economic trends are shifting these roles once again. The challenge today is that, for most people, home and work are still separate, but women cannot and/or do not want to stay at home and need not submit to male authority.

How should we resolve this challenge? Conservative religions advocate returning to the traditional division of labor, arguing that the community depends on the most efficient use of men's and women's different abilities. Liberal feminists assert that both roles should be equally shared, so that individuals can choose how to develop their abilities. If feminism frees the individual from community restrictions, it can also—as conservative critics point out—undermine community. If both men and women want to express their individual intellectual and creative abilities in their careers, then who will take care of the children? Who will cook and keep the house clean? If both want to be in positions of authority, leading others according to their vision, then who will follow? If you have enough money, you can hire others to follow orders and take care of the home. But most of us must fight it out. And, in fairness, many of us have some level of discomfort with what is increasingly perceived as excessive individualism.

Elizabeth Fox-Genovese (1996) suggests that American women are turning away from the feminist movement because they perceive it as focusing exclusively on women's independence and ignoring women's need to be in relationship with men and children. While most women appreciate feminist efforts to secure women's economic rights (equal access to education and employment), they are more ambivalent about the movement's current focus on sexual freedom (the right to choose abortion and sexual preference). Many women are disappointed with the feminist movement because it has given women access to traditionally male occupations such as business or political leadership without getting men to participate in traditionally female duties such as housework or child care. Perhaps most importantly, feminism has failed to get society to value these traditionally female responsibilities. Conservative religious leaders appeal to that disappointment when they preach that women must make a choice. Either you can be a feminist, which means you'll have more freedom but you will have to work harder and cannot count on anyone to help you; or you can return to tradition, which means you'll give up some autonomy but men will take care of you and you will be part of a community that values women's domestic work.

Most women in the United States do not want to make that choice—not even those in conservative religious communities. Women join conservative religious communities in part because they reject feminist individualism. But the community's traditional gender roles create an inherent conflict because most women want to work and do not want to submit to men. As we shall see, this conflict can create anger and resentment but it can also lead to the transformation of conservative gender roles.

A Tradition of Disagreement

Of the three traditions, the teachings of Orthodox Judaism most clearly differentiate male and female roles. Although Jewish tradition encourages women's employment, particularly if a woman's husband is dedicated to scholarly pursuits, halacha clearly defines home care as a female responsibility. Jewish law exempts women from all positive time-bound commandments, except for three women's mitzvot: preparing the Sabbath loaf, lighting the Sabbath candles, and observing family purity laws—all domestic responsibilities. The exemptions include the obligation to attend synagogue on Sabbath and holidays and are justified as necessary to give women time to take care of home and children. Thus the home is defined as a distinctively female domain, while the synagogue is a male area. Halacha assigns family headship to the man but many Orthodox writers emphasize motherhood more than submission (Frankiel 1990; Kaufman 1993). While some rabbis cite Genesis 3:16 where God tells Eve that her husband "shall rule over you," most defend male headship on more practical grounds: women's responsibility for home care prevents women from acquiring the Jewish learning necessary to head the family.

The clear separation of home as female and synagogue as male domains makes Orthodox Jewish gender roles seem more rigidly traditional than conservative Christian ones. In practice, however, that separation gives women some leverage: if home is the woman's place, she will often be the one who exerts authority there. One way in which the women at Beth Israel use that leverage is by enforcing the family purity laws. To an outsider the purity laws are a potent symbol of women's oppression. A woman is considered *niddah* (ritually impure) during her menstrual period and for seven days after its cessation. During this time women may not enter the synagogue and they may not touch their husbands lest the impurity rub off. At the end of this period they must attend a ritual bath before reentering the sanctuary. Many feminists are angered by what they see as a law that seems to restrict only women by defining their natural bodily functions as unclean. The women at Beth Israel, however, point out that the purity laws apply to both men and women (a man can be niddah if he spills his seed) and argue that a woman's role is different only in that she is expected to enforce the laws. Michelle and her husband sleep in separate beds and refrain from intimate contact for about twelve days each month. "The law restricts *both* men and women from sexual intimacy," she says. "It doesn't mean you're physically impure. It doesn't even mean you're spiritually impure. It just means you're sort of in a different state. . . . I don't have a problem with it." Few of the women at Beth Israel have a problem with being temporarily "different." In fact, several women report that their husbands are more troubled by the purity laws than they are. Ketza admits that she does not strictly maintain the purity laws because her husband doesn't like them. "His feeling is that we both work, and I'm so tired, and we have three kids, and we never do it [have sex] any more. So we shouldn't further restrict ourselves." To the extent that they have a negative impact, then, it is on both partners, not just the woman. Purity laws, in this view, are not a restriction of women but a leadership responsibility. One woman notes that "they are much more to the woman's advantage than men's. They offer women the ability to exercise authority, and women call the shots in terms of deciding when they are ready to have sex again." When women take on this responsibility, it has a favorable impact on their marriage, both improving their sex life and enhancing communication with their husbands. As Miriam put it:

> The difficulties are, you have to restrict your sex life, and that's just not very much fun. The advantages are that when you do have relations, especially like the first time you come back from the mikveh [ritual bath], it's on a very special level and intensity. We've been married almost thirteen years, and sex has always been—I don't see that it's declined as we've been married longer and longer. So I'd say that's a big advantage. And I also think you have to work out your relationship on another level. You can't always kiss and make up. You have to live with each other half a month and not have that option. It forces you to talk things out . . . rather than just going to bed and feeling good about that.

As the women at Beth Israel see it, family purity laws are challenging to both sexes, and actually give women leverage in the marriage relationship. Far from being a sign of women's subordination, these laws encourage a more equal relationship between men and women.

Another way in which male-female separation gives leverage to women at Beth Israel is by designating them as ritual experts.[1] In contrast to conservative Christianity where the central rituals are celebrated in church, some of the most important rituals of Orthodox Judaism take place in the home. It is the woman who prepares for these rituals and who ensures that her family observes the kosher laws, one of the most important signs of religious observance. Because of the centrality of these domestic rituals, many women at Beth Israel interpret spiritual leadership of the family as the mother's responsibility. They often describe this role as a complement to men's leadership in the synagogue. As Marcia put it, "Women have a huge role in the family, that is their shul, the home is, so I don't think men are the head of the household in Judaism, in Orthodox Judaism." Though men often acquire a higher level of religious training, that does not give them more religious authority in the home. Ann, a part-time secretary with two children, points out that "the man gives the Torah to the children, the textual Torah, and teaches them, but the woman is the fire behind the Torah, or something like that, the emotion, the feeling, the love of Torah that you give to your children . . . so I think the woman is the spiritual leader, because most women are spiritual in general." Similarly, Ketza explains that her husband "helps, because he knows more, I guess—you know, because of his Hebrew schooling. But I set the tone, I'm the one who maintains kashrut . . . the level of observance where we are is because of me." She has a point. There are many secular Jews—religion scholars for instance—who are familiar with Talmud but do not keep kosher or observe the Sabbath. Despite Judaism's emphasis on study, what ultimately defines one's Orthodox identity is performance of the mitzvot, and it is usually women, not men, who ensure that the family will follow the most basic religious commandments. The strict separation of male and female domains thus effectively negates male headship. As Ann put it, "the role of a woman is to be an equal partner . . . she is the center force to guide the family in *Yiddishkeit.*"[2]

If the separation of male and female spheres gives women more authority in the family, it also reinforces their duty to care for home and children. Because of Judaism's dietary laws and the many domestic rituals, these duties are far more time consuming than the home care responsibilities of secular or even conservative Christian women.[3] The women at Beth Israel are painfully aware that—even if they are employed—they are the ones primarily responsible for home care. While their husbands will occasionally cook, do laundry, or help the children with their homework, women do the lion's share of daily household chores, and it is the women who adapt their work schedules to the children. Many of the women have cut back their hours at work in order to have more time to look after home and children, and to do the holiday preparations. Not surprisingly, this creates considerable resentment. Laura, a lawyer, admitted, "I'm a believer in partnership between a husband and a wife . . . but the reality is that the woman is still typically the person who worries about how the kids are going to get to school, how they're going to get to this lesson, what the schedule looks like, what are we going to have for dinner, how are the household chores going to be managed—it may vary who's doing them, but they still have to be managed somehow—how all that happens typically falls on the woman. Men just don't tend to worry their little heads about things like that." Laura complains that despite the efforts of the women's movement, men are "still coming home and saying, 'What are we doing for dinner?'" While this is an improvement over "what's for dinner," which implies that somebody else has made dinner, it still leaves the responsibility with the woman. "It's 'what are we doing for dinner, you better have thought about it because I haven't thought about it at all'—as opposed to 'I'm coming home tonight, and I'll make dinner for us.'" Laura's complaint is one that is made daily by millions of American women, most of them not Orthodox Jewish. What makes Laura different from secular women as well as from conservative Christians is that she must not only care for home and children but maintain the dietary laws and prepare special food and ritual implements for the holidays. There are separate sets of dishes and silverware for meat and dairy products which must be cleaned and stored in different places. The house must be cleaned, the Sabbath loaf must be baked, and dinner as well as meals for Saturday must be precooked every Friday before sundown. Before Passover, the house must be *kashered* (a thorough cleaning of all household implements to remove contamination resulting from contact with leavened grain). And special holiday foods must be prepared according to ancient recipes. "I don't know how I manage it," she said. "Particularly around times like Rosh HaShanah, and the whole sequence of holidays and the demands that places on time with preparation and shopping and cooking and organization, having people over, you know. All of that is certainly a major added stress. . . . It also adds tremendous beauty to our lives, and value, but getting there is very, very hard, it really is. So you manage, but by the end of the week, you fall apart. I'm exhausted." Though she values the holiday experience, Laura wishes her husband would contribute more to the work it takes to create that experience. Her theoretical conceptions of gender roles dictate that he should, but her practical experience teaches her that he won't, and, according to Jewish law, he needn't.

How do women resolve such conflicts? They argue with their husbands, of course. More importantly, however, their anger motivates them to challenge the laws that assign responsibility for home care exclusively to women. In doing so, they do not reject halacha but draw on a tradition of disagreement that is built into the halachic process. From the outside, the requirement to live by laws established centuries ago appears rigid and inflexible. Yet the Talmud itself is a record of rabbinical disagreement over how to interpret the law. After the Talmud was completed, questions continued to arise about which halacha was inconclusive or unclear or for which no legal precedent existed. Over the generations, rabbis and scholars interpreted the texts and came up with *responsa* (formal answers to such questions) in order to apply the law to novel situations. These are collected and circulated as part of the larger body of religious jurisprudence. That process is quite democratic since there is no single authority to adjudicate conflicts over gender norms. Legitimacy of a ruling is based on accepted halachic procedures and qualifications for religious leadership that, theoretically, anyone can meet. Although Orthodox Jews look to the consensus or majority opinion of the *gedolim* (the major rabbinical authorities), there are always some rabbis who will come up with different rulings, and it is not that difficult for a woman to find one who will support her. In addition, decisions are made on a case by case basis, which means that exceptions can be made.[4]

To the women at Beth Israel, such disagreement means any ruling is open to question. Indeed, questioning the law and studying Torah to answer ones questions is part of what it means to be a good Jew and is necessary to maintain the Jewish tradition. As Laura put it, "This is a living religion. It is not a dead religion. It didn't stop in the Middle Ages. We continue to grow, and Jewish law throughout the ages has had to deal with social realities and work with them, and figure out what was appropriate within halacha but still appropriate in the society of the time. We are a very different society than we were several hundred years ago, and we should continue to grow with that." One of the ways in which society is different is that most women work outside the home. Given this reality, the women assert that they cannot be held primarily responsible for both holiday preparation and regular home care.

In order to give them time to fulfill their ritual duties (e.g., preparing for the Sabbath or going to the mikveh), many women feel that men should help with all other domestic chores or hire somebody else to do them. "Especially if she is working full-time," Ketza explained, "and if the husband is working full-time too, and they have three or four kids, I mean there has to, you have to have help—otherwise it's never going to get done, and the family's level of observance will suffer." Many women at Beth Israel, including homemakers, have hired outside help to assist with home care. One woman employs a Jewish girl from Russia as live-in help. But she also expects her husband to participate, especially on holidays. "Once my husband walks in the door, he's part of this household, and it's his job. I don't get up and serve him. I don't do things like that, you know. If there's dinner, he'll serve me dinner. We don't have roles like that. I don't feel that only I could have a twenty-four-hour-a-day job and his is only eight hours a day. That's not the way our house is run. He has to go make a living and I'm choosing not to, I'm choosing to be around with the children, but I think that's where it ends." This woman's comparison of the number of hours she and her husband spend on their jobs reflects her assumption that all home care responsibilities ought to be equally shared. When he is out working she will mind the children, cook and clean, and, on holidays, make the appropriate preparations. When he returns, however, he must help.

A more radical reinterpretation of the law is to ask men to participate in performing the women's mitzvot. Just as women can choose to follow the commandments from which they are exempt, men could be encouraged to do the same. Susan, for example, proudly told me how her son was learning egalitarian gender behavior from his parents.

My son and I, the other night, we had a forty-five-minute play session that he totally initiated. We were playing Shabbes, and he is the *abba* [father] and I'm the *imma* [mother] and he put on his *kippah* [headcovering] and he has to make *kiddush* [blessing] . . . and then, I thought this was really cool actually, because he went to get all the food from the kitchen, while I had to sit down. And it's true, my husband does that a lot. "You sit and I'll bring the [food]." I make all the food [for Shabbes] but my husband brings it to the table, and my husband bakes challah. I don't bake challah. So I thought that was nice. He [her son] does see that.

Susan is an exception, as most of the women at Beth Israel do not want to share what they see as their special ritual duty with men. The women's mitzvot impose additional work on Jewish women, but these duties also give women a special role in domestic ritual that is not held by men. Given that women do not participate equally in synagogue ritual, they see asking men to participate in women's mitzvot as upsetting the balance between them.

Whether they ask men to share women's mitzvot, or whether they ask men to do other chores so women have more time to do their ritual duties, Orthodox Jewish do not passively accept home care as their divinely ordained role. Rather, they believe that Jewish law gives them an active part in determining what their roles will be. Judaism, they argue, requires you to question it. Rachel told me that she used to feel guilty for questioning rules she found difficult to follow, things like family purity laws or Sabbath prohibitions. "It's like the director of Hillel told me, he said, 'The day I stop questioning Shabbat is the day I have to worry about doing it.' You always have to question. . . . When you stop asking, you just accept the party line. That's when it becomes a problem because Judaism is a living thing . . . if you stop asking, you're not an active participant anymore." Jewish law is a product of such questions. As Leonora sees it, "when you have a halachic discourse, the decision goes one way or the other, and then the assumption is that's what God intended. I think what God intended was discussion, and probably whether [the decision] turned this way or that is pretty irrelevant. I mean it doesn't bother me if now somebody seems to be turning halacha on its head to get it to go a certain way, because I think that's what halacha is for. That's why the Gemara is so long, you know. They were always turning it on its head." Questioning does not mean accommodating Judaism to the norms of secular society, abandoning laws that seem to conflict with the demands of modern American culture. Rather, it means finding a way to interpret the law to apply to those demands. "Being bound to stay within a framework is a really strong bind on somebody," Leonora explains. "I think that's what the Reform Jews did wrong. Once they said, 'We don't need the framework anymore,' the whole thing fell apart." These women recognize that Orthodox Judaism, while it rejects the kind of accommodation pursued by Reform and Conservative Judaism, has itself adapted to different times and places. While halachic rulings have set strict boundaries for such adaptation, halacha itself has been transformed as it was applied to an ever greater variety of situations. Instead of rejecting the applicability of halacha to contemporary society—as more liberal Jews have done—Orthodox Jewish women use the tradition of halachic dispute to reconstruct Judaism to integrate feminist values.

A Flexible Relationship to God

Like Orthodox Judaism, Evangelical teaching assigns family authority to men and responsibility for home care to women. While the separation of male and female roles is less distinctive, there is more emphasis on male authority. This division of labor is based on a fairly literal reading of scripture, particularly the epistles of Paul. The argument for male headship of the family is draw from Ephesians 5:22: "Wives, submit yourselves unto your husbands as unto the Lord." Although some Evangelical leaders have responded to feminist influences by talking about mutual submission (e.g., Dobson 1982), they continue to designate the man as head of the family. The scriptural basis for female responsibility for home care is less clear. There is nothing in the Bible that explicitly requires women to be homemakers, but Evangelicals extrapolate from passages such as 1 Timothy 5:14, which asserts that "the younger women should marry, bear children, guide the house." Although Evangelical leaders acknowledge that today's economy does not permit most women to be full-time homemakers, they continue to hold that as up as the ideal and argue that women's competition with men in the job market can be detrimental to both the economy and men's self-esteem (LaHaye 1976; Lienesh 1993). The male headship/female home care model is further justified by reference to inherent gender differences which supposedly make men more qualified to be leaders and women more inclined to nurture others.

The women at Victory Church struggle with both aspects of the traditionalist family model. First, there is conflict over home care, particularly for women who work full-time. When I ask these women, "What is a woman's role in the home?" they claim to embrace the homemaker ideal, arguing that in general women should be responsible for caring for home and children, and that their own choice to work outside the home is an exception to the rule. Like Katrina (chapter 1) or Patty (chapter 4), they cite the need for extra income or God's calling as reasons for working outside the home. This confirms the findings of Wilcox (1991) that Evangelical women tend to see themselves primarily as homemakers, even when they are working. Yet when these women return from work just as tired as their husbands, it becomes more difficult to accept primary responsibility for home care. Assumptions of gender difference that assign the bulk of childcare and domestic responsibilities to women then seem unreasonable and are rejected.

Charleen is a good example. Married to a real estate broker, she works full-time as a nurse and has a five-year-old son. When I ask her who should be responsible for home care, she embraces the traditionalist model, asserting that women are more nurturing, more oriented to the details of life and therefore are naturally more inclined to be mothers and homemakers. Like Katrina, she insists that she works only out of financial necessity. "See, my desire is to be home. I mean, since I have got to work, God gave me a great job, but my desire is to be home." Yet the fact that she does work makes it difficult, if not impossible, to fulfill the traditionalist role, and she admits to considerable resentment at the expectation that she should.

> We've been arguing about that [home care] a lot lately, because when you have a full-time job and you come home, you're very tired. . . . I get home and I just barely have enough energy to cook dinner, give Peter [her son] a bath and get him ready for bed. So Jim's at home lately when I get in, and he goes: "So

what's for dinner?" And I go: "Well, you've been home all day, maybe you could've started dinner, maybe you could've done the marketing, maybe you could've cleaned the . . . " His mind is so set that I should do everything even while I have a full-time job! . . . I think when you're married and both parents are working, both people have to take the responsibility for everything.

Though she affirms it in theory, the notion that her natural inclinations make her primarily responsible for cooking, cleaning, and bathing the child seems preposterous when faced with the practical reality of having to work a "second shift." Her husband, she argues, is just as capable of performing those chores as she is, and his refusal to do so is selfish and unreasonable. Taking responsibility for home care does not come as naturally to women at Victory as their church's teaching would suggest.

There is also conflict over family authority. Both homemakers and working women at Victory nominally embrace male headship. Yet in practice, most women do not give their husbands much real authority. Charleen, for example, asserted that "the father is the spiritual head of the Christian family and the wife submits to her husband." Yet when asked if she submits to her own husband, she said: "Yes, but not with big decisions. I mean, there's some things that I don't care about. Just do whatever you want. But, like, going to look for a new place to live or something like that, I want my say!" Charleen clearly rejects her husband's authority in many areas of family life. Other women appear to accept male authority without actually submitting. Marisa thinks "the woman should submit to the husband because it creates peace, but I can tell you something from watching [pastor] Bill and Ann. Ninety percent of the time Ann—things come through for her! . . . I think you should defer to the husband because—I remember this with my own dad!—I go, 'OK Dad, you're right.' And he'd come back half the time and give me what I wanted. It was like, my sister would fight. You'd fight him to the death, and yet believe me, you weren't going to get it. It's when I went, 'OK Dad,' that I got what I wanted." Pastor Jordan's wife was cited by several women to prove that "submission works to our advantage." Yet it is hard to avoid the conclusion that they aren't so much submitting as placating their husband's ego so they will end up getting what they want. Submission to male headship, like taking responsibility for home care, does not come as easily to women as Evangelical teaching would have us believe.

How do the women at Victory Church resolve such tensions? Unlike Orthodox Judaism, where the halachic process explicitly acknowledges the need to adapt scriptural norms to changing times, Evangelicalism asserts that the Bible should be taken literally, providing women with little flexibility to deal with conflict. This may explain why bargaining is such a common strategy at Victory Church: the women follow the rules literally, resolving conflict by focusing on what they get in return. Frustrated with their inability to change the way men and women relate to each other, women who join conservative religious communities may feel that if they accept their traditional role (to care for home and children) then at least they can hold men accountable to perform theirs (to lead and financially support the family). "Women are always the ones who do most of the work around the house—it has nothing to do with religion," was a comment I heard over and over again. If responsibility for home care is simply one of the realities of living in a sexist world, then traditional religious gender norms provide a good way to explain that reality: women do most of the domestic work because God intended it that way. One woman told me that she was "tired of fighting with my husband all the time over who does what" and was considering quitting her job to stay at home full-time. "I can see the wisdom in the way God set it up." By the same token, God expects men to live up to their responsibility as providers. A Christian marriage, the women advised me, protects us in a way secular relationships do not. "Outside of a Christian marriage," Charleen warned me, "the guy wants to be king . . . but they have no standards to run their lives by, they have no accountability before God . . . and so you are going to have enormous problems." Taking responsibility for the home is a good bargain because you can expect your husband to take care of you.

Accepting male headship can also be a bargain. Several women at Victory Church claim that submission has saved their marriage. Tanya, for example, is a homemaker who has been married for ten years. Dressed in a tie-dyed floor-length skirt, her long graying hair hanging loose over her shoulders, she was breast feeding her youngest child as she talked. She confided that she had experimented with various spiritualities before becoming a born-again Christian, and insisted that her marriage would have fallen apart were it not for the Christian submission she learned at Victory Church. "My husband and I had been talking about divorce." But they weren't quite ready to give up on the marriage.

> So we went to the guru, and we had a private meeting with her, and she said: "Well, go ahead and get a divorce if you want. Just don't have any animosity towards each other." And we thought, "Well, that's spiritual counsel?" And a lot of people were getting divorced, so we went to a psychologist, and he was kind of into New Age Eastern religion, too. And Bob met with him, and I met with him, and we met with him together, and he said that I wouldn't be able to fulfill Bob's needs, and so, you know, probably divorce was just the best thing. So my husband filed for divorce. We didn't know what else to do. We thought, "Well, I guess that's it. There's no other way."

Two weeks later, when her husband was out of town, Tanya finally yielded to the repeated invitations of a neighbor in her apartment complex to attend Sunday services at Victory.

> I cried through the whole sermon, and they gave a call at the end, [asking] who would like to accept Jesus as your savior? And I just felt like the curtain was being pulled away, and I just saw the truth, and that Jesus, I needed Jesus. So I raised my hand, and I went to the altar, and I accepted him as my Lord and savior, and I just felt such a peace. I felt a burden lift, and for the first time I felt hope for our marriage, that through Jesus Christ our marriage could be saved. . . . And it was tough, but the Lord would just build up my faith, and I'd get stronger and stronger. And as anger would come up, you know, when we accept the Lord, it's like we fill up with the love of Jesus . . . and so I was able to love Bob more . . . in a way I could never love him before. When anger would come up, I'd just surrender it, literally surrender it to God . . . I was able to forgive Bob, and let go, and just love him in a new way.

Meanwhile, Bob had begun to attend Victory Church as well. He had "started seeing that I really was changing and different," and, after participating in a church-sponsored men's retreat, decided to return to Tanya. As she put it, "I think most of us tend to be selfish and independent and domineering, and God had to change me in those ways, and he had to raise my husband up to be stronger and more the head of the household." In Tanya's view, it was her willingness to submit to God and to her husband that brought her and her husband back together again. For women like Tanya, traditional gender norms of male authority and female submission provided an explanation of what had gone wrong in their relationship and clearly laid out the way to resolve the problem. Told they were faced with the choice of divorce or submission, many women felt the latter made more sense. Submission worked because, in most cases, the marriage was maintained.

Once they decided to submit, Tanya and other women realized that submission is a bargain in other ways. Many argued that in any social organization, be it a corporation, a church, or a family, "somebody has to lead," and that not having to make some decisions takes a big burden off their shoulders. Sandra's comments are typical: "I think submission means a home that works, that has peace and harmony. My judgment is no less acute or good than his is, but it's just that I'm willing to go ahead and give in. Sometimes I think it takes more strength to give in than it does to fight. People say, 'Well, you're weak, you don't stand up to him.' I don't see it that way at all." Tanya and Sandy interpret submission in rather pragmatic ways: they submit because they don't want a divorce, or because they don't feel like fighting with their husbands. They are willing to exchange equal authority for other desirable goods such as a stable relationship. What they lose in autonomy they gain in male responsibility.

Bargaining with patriarchy, as some feminist scholars (Stacey 1991; Rose 1987) have called it, may achieve the practical ends desired by women, but it does not challenge the underlying assumption that responsibility for home care and headship should be distributed unequally. Given the tension that Evangelical women experience with traditionalist roles, bargaining constitutes a kind of resignation to the status quo, a sense that sexism is a reality we cannot change, so we might as well make it work to our advantage. But many women at Victory want more than that. They do not just bargain with patriarchal tradition but also creatively interpret family headship and home care to integrate feminist values. They do so not by rejecting a literal interpretation of the Bible, but by drawing on resources within their tradition to find a new reading. Evangelical theology builds on the classic Protestant notions that the Bible is our only authority (*sola scriptura*) and that we don't need priests to mediate between us and God ("priesthood of all believers"). If anyone can interpret the Bible, then women do not have to rely on specialists (rabbis or councils of bishops) to tell them what its behavioral implications are.[5] And if an individual woman can have a personal relationship with Jesus, she gains considerable leverage over how her role is interpreted, since anything Jesus "calls her" to do will override her church's or her husband's decisions. The outsider may wonder why she doesn't consider a contextual interpretation, which would allow her to disregard parts of the Bible as remnants of a different time rather than as God's will. But Evangelicals, who take the literal truth of the Bible as a given, do not have that option. Instead they draw on other theological concepts that leave the literal interpretation intact.

Several women pointed out to me that "the Bible doesn't say anything really clear about making a woman, you know, having them stay at home." They thus feel free to reinterpret what home care means. Many homemakers do not expect their husband to contribute much to domestic chores so long as he fulfills the traditional role of provider. However, most women do expect men to be involved in child rearing, and they often contrast this new expectation to the more remote role their own fathers played in caring for children. Sandra, for example, explains that "if I worked all day and it was my husband [who stayed] home, I would expect to come home to a house that is somewhat put together. . . . Sometimes he'll work 6:00 A.M. to 2:30. That's an easy day for him, and he'll come home, and I'll ask him if he can help make dinner or vacuum the rug. But on long days I try not to." Tending children, however, is different from cooking and cleaning. Sandra recalls that her father had beaten her mother and had been generally unavailable to the children. It is very important to her that her husband's relationship to her and the children be different. "Just the interaction [with the children] and playing and reading to them, it's important for both of us to do that . . . I want my husband to be able to teach [my son] respect and love for me and for authority and for women." Sandra's last sentence is telling. She uses concepts prized by Evangelicals as means of maintaining a traditional order ("respect for authority") to empower herself ("for me and for women"). Not only does she expect her husband to participate in childcare, but she wants him to help the new generation to be less sexist.

If women reinterpret home care to apply, at least in part, to both men and women, they also reinterpret family authority to be shared by both genders. The women know that parts of the Bible explicitly require female submission. But they also know about other passages that mitigate that requirement. As Stephanie put it: "The other part of the scripture, which people don't always quote, is that it says: husbands, love your wives as Christ loved the church. Well, Christ laid down his life, he gave his life for the church. So it's a mutual thing." Mutual submission is a concept cited by many women at Victory Church. Pamela, for example, is a single mother who works full-time to support her two-year-old son. She complains that people in her church keep trying to set her up with men when she's quite happy being single. She does not believe that submission would have saved her marriage.

> There's a catch there. The women should submit to their husbands, but the husbands are to love you like Jesus loves the church, and Jesus laid down his life for the church. The two become one flesh. You can submit to a man who is taking care of you like he were taking care of his own flesh. I don't think that God calls you to submit to someone other than someone who is loving you like he does himself. When someone is giving to you, esteeming you, and holding you up higher than anyone ever has in your life, then submission would just be a natural response. If you're not getting those things, then of course you would be unable to submit.

According to many women at Victory, they must submit only to men who are willing to return the favor.

Other women assert that they must only submit to a husband's decision if it truly reflects God's will. As these women see it, submission works as follows. All decisions are ultimately made by God, and both men and women must pray to God for guidance. The next step is for both partners to share what God has told them, and then the husband decides what to do. If the wife disagrees with his decision, she may ask him to reconfer with God. Charleen, for example, ends her comment that she wants to participate in making major family decisions by saying: "Plus, I feel like if it's the Lord's will, you're both going to hear the same answer anyway." The implication, of course, is that if you don't hear the same answer it must not be God's will. Many other women at Victory would concur. Julie, for instance, is a homemaker and mother of five who is very involved in her church, teaching Bible study groups and heading the pro-life ministry. She explains that "submission doesn't mean what most people think." A wife should not submit to any decision her husband makes: "She should submit to his prayerful, God-fearing, *wife-considering* decisions." Julie insists that she and her husband make all important family decisions together. If he doesn't agree with her on something, she will ask him to "go pray some more" until they can agree. For women like Julie and Charleen, the authority given their husbands is limited by God himself, who is assumed to agree with the women more times than not. Once again they rely on a concept deeply rooted in the Evangelical tradition—the personal relationship with Christ—to empower women.

The women at Victory Church, then, are not just bargaining with patriarchy but challenging it. They do not passively accept Evangelical teaching that family headship is a male and home care a female responsibility. But they do not reject their tradition either. Instead they find new ways to understand that tradition that are consistent with feminist values. In contrast to fundamentalist rhetoric, which describes tradition as timeless, these women believe that traditions do change over time. As Katrina stated, "Christianity is not a bunch of rules. It's a changing thing." They also recognize that there is considerable room to interpret what a particular role actually means in any given situation. As Patty explained: "I think there's freedom in Christ, and it's taken me a long time . . . to figure out what I really believe." A Christian relationship with God allows for flexibility of biblical interpretation, and defining gender norms in the home is an ongoing process in which the women themselves actively participate.

Saving our Church

Of the three traditions, the way the Catholic Church defines a woman's role in the home seems most adapted to modern society. There is less stress on male headship of the family, and the woman's responsibility for home care is encouraged less directly. In part, this reflects theological differences. Catholic teaching on the family does not rely on a literal reading of scripture but on magisterial tradition, which allows some adaptation to changing cultural values. In part, the difference reflects the heterogeneity of U.S. Catholics. Unlike Evangelical or Orthodox Jewish leaders, Catholic bishops are speaking to a mixed audience of liberals and conservatives and trying hard not to alienate either side.

The result is a mixed message. Catholic teaching on family headship rarely talks about submission. But conservative Catholic leaders do point to Mary as a role model for the selfless giving and nurturing that women should cultivate (Smith 1991; O'Leary 1993; WFF 1994). Catholic teaching also rarely states that women should be responsible for home care. Indeed, pastoral letters by the American Bishops have given working women their blessing, and recent papal documents have emphasized male-female equality and have encouraged men to participate in child rearing and housekeeping (Pope John Paul 1981). Yet Catholic bishops have also stressed the need for the state to provide support for families so that women don't have to work outside the home (NCCB 1980; O'Connor 1986), and the pope has noted that "true advancement of women requires that clear recognition be given to the value of their maternal and family role" (1981:21). Women's place in the home is also encouraged through an absolute prohibition on birth control that is not found among either Protestant or Jewish conservatives.[6]

The mixed message has mixed impact. On the one hand, conservative Catholic women can totally reject the traditionalist concept of male headship of the family in favor of a more feminist understanding of shared authority, and still feel they are obeying church law. On the other hand, following church teaching on birth control puts many women in the position of becoming responsible for home care by default, a position that can lead to considerable conflict.

In contrast to the women at Victory, who at least claim to embrace traditionalist notions of the man being the head of the household, even the most conservative women at St. Joseph's openly reject such ideas. They do not even accept the more limited interpretation of headship, embraced by many Evangelicals, that the man, even if he can't expect obedience from his wife, is responsible for the spiritual leadership of the

Christian family. Instead, many women would agree with Barbara's statement (chapter 1) that it is women, not men, who provide spiritual leadership for the family. Other women would argue that spiritual leadership comes, if at all, from a priest, not one's husband. As Donna put it: "I think that most decisions are not made unilaterally in a good marriage. They are made, like, you both talk and you're changing each other's opinions. . . . I do have a spiritual director, a priest, and I would obey my spiritual director, but I've *chosen* to do that." Men and women, in this view, play different roles, but no one, except for the church and its representatives, can tell a woman what to do.

Like the women at Beth Israel, these Catholic women have no need to bargain with male authority because they don't believe their church gives men that authority. Like the women at Victory, they argue that submission should be mutual. But unlike Evangelical women, conservative Catholics postulate mutual submission as an ideal that is not often reflected in real marriages. In reality, most men and women do not yield to each other, at least not easily, so women must stand up for what they think is right and refuse to submit. As Rita explained, "If you look at that verse in context, it says women are to submit to their husbands and their husbands are supposed to love them as Christ loved his church. That scripture is portraying for us an incredibly beautiful and ideal relationship. . . . but marriage is a complicated and changing relationship, and we can't as women go against our consciences and submit to something we feel is harmful to us." Not only do most marriages not live up to Paul's ideal, but, according to Rita and other conservative Catholic women, times are changing and the Catholic Church is open to such changes. In making this point, the women liked to point out that, unlike some fundamentalist Protestants who take the Bible literally, the Catholic Church is more reasonable and flexible in its interpretation. "That's why I'm not a fundamentalist," Donna told me, "that's one of the reasons I think fundamentalists are—since fundamentalists don't have a teaching authority to interpret the Bible for them, or help them interpret the Bible, they take passages in this incredible way, and do mental gymnastics with them, rather than using common sense. And that's how the church frees you up, 'cause the church believes in the mind, and you use common sense, and common sense is that you don't have to obey a man." To Donna and other conservative Catholics, rejecting notions of female submission becomes a means of distinguishing themselves from conservative Protestants and thereby legitimating a position of conservatism that they know is a minority position in their church. They are saying, in effect, that obeying church doctrine does not make you an extremist, or "one of those fundamentalists." Rejecting submission allows them to maintain traditional assumptions about male-female differences without appearing overtly sexist.

Male headship does not create a conflict for women at St. Joseph's because they do not see it as an official norm of their church. Female responsibility for home care, however, does create some tension. Ironically, it is homemakers who are most troubled about their role in the family. On the surface they appear to accept the traditional responsibility for home care, arguing that while it comes naturally to most women, the Catholic Church does not require it. If the woman chooses to have a career, they point out, the church encourages men to take on home care. The problem for many women at St. Joseph's is that they did not get to make that choice. Rather, being a homemaker is often the result of a different decision: not to use contraception.

Whether or not to obey the church's teaching on contraception is difficult to decide. Take Beatrice, for example, who has a doctorate in French literature and was just beginning her academic career when she had her first child. She admits that, like many Catholics, she was hoping her church would lift its ban on contraception. "When I got married and the question of all these kids coming along—for me it was a terrible struggle, 'cause I was from a more lenient sort of background." She notes that all her "friends were intelligent women, and they decided, even if they were Catholic, that they wouldn't be so stupid as to have a bunch of kids, and they could justify it in many ways, and even Catholic priests were justifying it." Unlike her friends, Beatrice decided to follow the rules: "When Humanae Vitae came out, I decided, well, it's not what I like, it's not what I want, but this is the will of the church." She initially continued to work but realized after her fourth child that continuing her career was not compatible with caring for a growing family. Still determined not to use contraception, she quit her job to become a full-time homemaker. She now has seven children.

Beatrice's case illustrates that the Catholic prohibition of birth control creates a conflict for contemporary women every bit as difficult as that faced by Jewish and Evangelical women. How did the women at St. Joseph's resolve this conflict? The hierarchical structure of the church seems to offer little room for divergent interpretations. Gender norms derive not only from the Bible but also from a large and evolving body of tradition, a product of theological interpretation that is articulated and handed down by councils of higher clergy (bishops) or by the pope who formulates doctrine with them and independently. According to Catholic tradition, the church was founded by Peter at Christ's request, its priests are direct successors to the apostles Christ selected, and the pope is the vicar of Christ on earth. Therefore, the church's interpretation is considered a reflection of God's will, equal in authority to scripture itself. Unlike Evangelicals whose emphasis on the Bible validates individual interpretation, and unlike Orthodox Jews whose halachic tradition is built on disagreement, the Roman Catholic hierarchy formulates norms for *all* Catholics and does not permit dissent.

Catholic women, then, have two choices: obey their church's teaching or disregard it. With respect to contraception, the majority of American Catholic women are choosing to ignore tradition.[7] This constitutes an important difference between St. Joseph's and the other two communities I studied. Once a woman joins Victory or Beth Israel, there is an expectation that she will adopt traditional norms and, if she does, the religious community will affirm her choice. This is not the case at St. Joseph's. The conservative Catholics I spoke to are part of a church that also includes many liberals. Though the proportion of conservatives is larger than in most Catholic churches, there are even more women at St. Joseph's who call themselves liberal or progressive Catholics. Both liberal and conservative women had participated in focus groups that the bishops had organized in preparation for their pastoral letter on women's concerns. The comments of one such woman, Anita, dramatically illustrate the deep divisions between the two groups.

> There were women from all over this area here, and I couldn't
> believe my ears when some of these women were talking about
> how women should be submissive and subservient. They
> believed that everything the church said was gospel and they
> wouldn't question it. And they absolutely believed in no birth
> control, you know, nothing could be done for women, but they

shall have to suffer through it. I was disgusted! In fact, I didn't go back for the second session because I just couldn't believe it. They were putting all of this down as Catholic statistics, you know. "This is what the Catholic women say, what they believe." And I just don't agree!

Anita is, by her own admission, not a conservative, and there are many others like her. With so many women dissenting, there is little pressure from the community to adopt a traditional role. The question for many conservative Catholic women is not just, How can I reconcile my individuals needs (e.g., a career) with the traditional norms of my community (e.g., the expectation that women should care for home and children)? Rather, the question is, How can I make sense of my choice to be a traditionalist in a church full of people who are not? It is in trying to answer *this* question that many women at St. Joseph's reinterpret the traditional role.

One interpretation is that they are saving their church from liberal and secular influences that are threatening to tear it apart. The choice to adopt traditional gender norms, particularly the decision not to use contraception, is a way for conservatives to distinguish themselves from more liberal members of their church. "Dissent from any particular teaching," as Liz put it, "is simply saying 'I'm right and Christ is wrong.' One of the gifts we get is following Christ, his true teachings. . . . The church is not a debate society, it's supposed to be helping you become holy. If you're spending all your time, instead of following the teaching, debating the teaching, then you've lost that gift. I always say to people, 'Well, if you dissent about that, you should be a Protestant.'" Unlike the women at Victory or Beth Israel, Liz is confronted every day with liberal parishioners who disagree with their church's teaching. So is Beatrice. Acknowledging that "there was a whole faction of people after Vatican II who were justifying contraception," she asserted, "I could never bring myself to agree with them, because I realized that if the church is to be the church, we have a head, we have a pope, and that's the crux of the difference between the Catholic belief [and that of other churches], and I wanted to remain true to the tradition of Catholicism, and even though I didn't particularly like it, I had to accept that the pope, for whatever reason, still wanted to see the transmission of life kept sacred." By strictly following the rules of their church, conservative women are maintaining what they see as the essence of Catholic identity.

If adopting traditional norms is a way of saving the church, it can also be a way of protesting the larger society. While that protest seemed to be directed at feminism and secularism, it was also a protest against sexism. Society, according to conservative women at St. Joseph's, is dominated by men who value competition and achievement over caring for others, and it is up to women to change that. Choosing not to use birth control and staying home with your children is perceived as a countercultural act that has revolutionary potential. In the words of Rita:

> One of the most important issues for Christian women is to come to understand their role as women, so that they can speak out intelligently in a countercultural way to the media, to their friends and families, and try to redirect this trend in society to remove for women what's really feminine, because our society is desperately in need of what's truly feminine. Christian women have a wonderful opportunity to make a statement to society by keeping their nuclear family intact, by not living financially inflated lifestyles that are going to require that they go out and work. The children benefit tremendously from a woman who's willing to make that sacrifice—and it's a sacrifice to stay at home, particularly when you're trained to do something, when you have an area that you really enjoy going and working in. One of the most countercultural things a woman can do in this society is have a large family, not use birth control. That's a very courageous statement, and a very unpopular one, even in many Catholic circles.

Rita is protesting against a society that doesn't value women and children. But she also challenges the ethic of expressive individualism promoted by the feminist movement. Her statements contest the traditionalist argument that motherhood and home care come naturally to women. Yet she insists that women adopt these roles. Accepting the church hierarchy as a given, a conservative Catholic woman does not have the option of resolving conflicts by saying—as liberal Catholics do—that the pope is wrong. She cannot—as Orthodox Jews can—find a local rabbi whose interpretation of halacha allows her to do what she wants. Nor can she claim—as Evangelicals do—that God has told her something he hasn't revealed to the church. Instead, the women at St. Joseph's are waiting for the church to change the rules and interpreting that willingness to wait as a sacrificial act that will save their church, and perhaps society as well.

Conservative religious communities—be they Protestant, Catholic, or Jewish—seem to provide a simple definition of gender roles in the home: the woman cares for the home and the man leads it. Yet that definition hides a much more complex reality than most of us are aware of. For one, there are significant differences in how official Evangelical, Catholic, and Orthodox Jewish teaching understands that definition. For another, ordinary women in these communities have been sufficiently influenced by feminism that they contest the traditionalist definition, no matter how it is officially understood. The women at Victory, St. Joseph's, and Beth Israel want more than just a bargain with patriarchy. While they are willing to trade some feminist "rights" for traditionalist "protections," they are also reconstructing the traditionalist meaning of gender in order to make room for feminist values.

Such reconstruction is creative, but it is also a struggle. Indeed, the reader may be wondering about the high level of inconsistency in these women's lives. Why would these women want to live a double life, alternating between feminist and traditionalist roles at work and at church or synagogue? If these women have problems with the traditionalist model of female home care and male headship of the family, why don't they join a community that promotes more feminist values? Or, to phrase the question from an institutional perspective, How do conservative churches and synagogues maintain the commitment of independent, assertive, seemingly feminist women without jeopardizing the institutional order? There are a number of possible answers to these questions which we will explore in the next chapter.

Chapter 7

Understanding Inconsistency

THE WOMEN AT VICTORY, St. Joseph's, and Beth Israel seem to be living with many contradictions. They claim to reject feminism, yet they clearly embrace some feminist values. They want women to have equality and authority at work and in politics, but they are willing to give up on those things in church and synagogue. Evangelical women say a wife must submit to her husband, but almost none of them do. Orthodox Jewish women argue that women can't be rabbis because that would take time away from their main responsibility, the care of home and children. Yet they also insist that domestic work should be equally shared. Conservative Catholics insist on strict obedience to all of the church's teachings, but they criticize fundamentalists for not adapting tradition to changing times. One cannot help but wonder (and people who hear about my research keep asking me about this) how they deal with such gross inconsistencies in their lives. This chapter suggests four possible explanations—cognitive dissonance theory, bargaining theories, the concept of a protean self, and a theory of symbolic boundaries— each of which will be explained in turn.

Cognitive Dissonance Theory

Perhaps the most widely known explanation of how people deal with inconsistencies in their lives is cognitive dissonance theory.[1] Leon

Festinger's classic theory asserts that when individuals act in ways that contradict their beliefs, or are confronted with information that conflicts with their existing belief system, they experience cognitive dissonance. Cognitive dissonance is a state of psychological discomfort that motivates people to change contradictory beliefs and behaviors or to avoid situations and information that induce such contradictions (Festinger 1957). A smoker, for instance, may have convinced himself that the dangers of smoking are exaggerated. When his doctor tells him his lungs look unhealthy, he experiences cognitive dissonance. This may motivate him either to stop smoking (change beliefs and behavior) or to switch to a different doctor (avoid information) in order to reduce the dissonance.

Cognitive dissonance theory is helpful in understanding some of the women in this study. Evangelicals, for example, believe that the husband should have authority in the family, yet few of them act in a submissive way. This may create cognitive dissonance which would motivate them to reinterpret this norm as mutual submission. But there are also problems with cognitive dissonance theory that should give us pause before applying it to all of these women. One problem is that scholars applying the model often rely on written sources which tend to focus on formal norms even though operative norms may be quite different. For example, according to Victory's formal teaching, women should not be heading a church. Yet several women there have founded new churches in surrounding areas—and have drawn nothing but praise from other members at Victory. Female founders of "seed churches" have become the operative norm of the community, so women who violate formal norms do not experience dissonance. The same is true for women at Beth Israel who study Talmud and for women at St. Joseph's who use contraception. Dissonance reduction, in these cases, is built into the tradition and does not occur at all at the individual level.

A second, more significant problem with Festinger's theory is that, because academia puts a premium on logically consistent arguments, scholars have a tendency to assume that consistency is important to everyone. It is not. Robert Wuthnow (1981) has pointed out that classical theories of meaning construction presume a rational individual who strives for a consistent world view, when in reality many people are quite willing to live with some degree of inconsistency so long as their beliefs

and practices provide them with a meaning system that is coherent, especially at an emotional level.

Coherence is a functional term and is common to all people, except the severely mentally disturbed. It simply means that there is some
order to reality. Religious symbol systems often provide such an order.
The system is coherent if it functions as a map that helps the individual
negotiate his/her way through life. The extent to which the map functions effectively varies with the individual using it. For some individuals, a religious order lends coherence to life simply by being there. For
others, however, coherence depends on the internal and/or external consistency of the order. Consistency therefore is a substantive term and is
necessary for some people in order to experience coherence. Many
women in this study did not require a high level of consistency. They
joined conservative Christian or Orthodox Jewish communities because
these traditions provided a system of order that made sense out of their
lives. For many women, that order lends coherence to life because it
sets clear guidelines for behavior. The fact that those rules are not always logically consistent, or that the women's behavior is frequently inconsistent with those guidelines does not seem to matter much.

The women at Beth Israel, for example, are well aware of their need
for a coherent order even when it is not consistently followed. As Rivka
put it, "Part of the problem in the society [is] there's just no guidelines,
you're just kind of running amok," whereas "religion gives you a structure.
Orthodoxy really gives you a very good, complete structure in how to
run your life from A to Z." Another woman at Beth Israel said: "I think
people miss out when you don't have the restrictions, and I'm not saying that it has to be milk and meat restrictions, but I'm saying that
people who don't have something concrete to look at. . . . In our community, you know what is expected of you every day, every month, every year . . . you know what to do and you are not lost." Not being lost
is particularly valuable in a city like Los Angeles. As Ketza explained:
"In a society that is so crazed, and in the city we live in especially, there
is just so much coming and going, no stability, that to have these boundaries really gives you a sense of purpose and a sense of knowing what is
expected of you, and parameters by which to live and instill values in
your kids." Knowing these parameters does not mean you will believe
in all of them. Miriam, for example, acknowledges that she disagrees

with some of the gender norms of the Orthodox Jewish community, yet she appreciates traditional roles because "it takes a lot of pressure off relationships when a certain part of the relationship is accepted as given." Miriam's comment may explain the popularity of recent books such as *The Rules*, which provides explicit and rather reactionary guidelines for dating in the 1990s. Many women today are glad to be rid of traditionalist gender norms, but are confused—and often frustrated— about what to replace them with. The women at Beth Israel talk about "guidelines" and "boundaries"—a map that prevents you from getting lost. You need not always follow the map, but you will feel better if you have one.

Evangelicals expressed a similar need for coherence. Patty said that before she joined Victory church, "I was looking for more of a standard for my life, more guidelines," clear rules for what was right and wrong. Since becoming a born-again Christian, her "life has changed basically in every way . . . a lot more stability. I mean, it's the difference between night and day." Similarly, Katrina told me that before she became a Christian what "attracted me to Jeff [her husband who had been raised in Victory Church] the most was his stability." Yet having clear standards does not mean you will follow them. Katrina admits that she does not always submit to her husband and they fight frequently, but "there's an underlying set of rules that both of you have, that you know you're accountable [for] to God. . . . If you're a Christian, then you're both working on the same goals, and you've got the same book of rules, so it makes a difference." What matters more than following the rules is simply to have them.

Conservative Catholics, by contrast, insist that all the rules be followed. In order to be a good Catholic, one must believe what the church teaches and act in ways that are consistent with those beliefs. It is this consistency that will give coherence to one's life. As Donna put it, strict obedience to church doctrine means that "you have a much more uncluttered life [so] you can enjoy simple things better. I was very confused and unhappy before [when she had temporarily left the church as a teenager] . . . and I am a very happy person now." Similarly, Barbara argued, "It is extremely rewarding to have very little doubt that what I'm doing is right. I know abortion is wrong, and it feels good to know that I'm doing what's right [participating in pro-life activism]." And Rita asserted that, despite the resistance she encounters from more liberal church members, "there's a very good feeling about really following your conscience and trying to be an imitator of Christ, in spite of the guff. There's a kind of squeaky clean feeling that comes from that, and I love it, and it's worth it." This emphasis on consistency reflects the desire of conservative Catholic women to distinguish themselves from the majority of American Catholics who ignore many church teachings. But even conservatives are comfortable with some level of inconsistency. Barbara, for example, believes a good Catholic must obey all church laws, yet she uses contraception and has no intention of changing her behavior. Though Barbara would like to go back in time and argue with Saint Paul about what she perceives to be sexist teachings, she also believes that without the order provided by those doctrines she would not have made it through many of the difficulties of her life. She views the church as a family that gives her warmth and comfort in return for her loyalty and willingness to overlook its flaws. Religion, for her, must not just make sense but feel right. For all of these women, the object of cognitive dissonance reduction, if it occurs at all, is not a logically consistent world view but an emotionally coherent meaning system. For some this means consistency; for others, it does not.

Bargaining Theories

Another set of explanations for how people (and institutions) deal with inconsistency is what might be called bargaining theory. According to this theory, people are committed to one value system (e.g., feminism or traditionalism) but they are willing to compromise on their values if they get something valuable in return. As Ammerman (1987), Davidman (1991), and Rose (1987) have shown, many traditionalist women go out and work because of the extra income it provides. And, as Stacey's (1990) and Kaufman's (1991) research suggests, an independent, feminist woman may marry a traditionalist Christian or Jewish man in return for the stability he provides. Once people begin to bargain, however, it becomes easy to confuse which is their primary value system and which is the one they are bargaining with.

The women studied by Ammerman, Davidman, and Rose are making what I will call a "traditionalist bargain," i.e., these women are really traditionalists who adopt feminist rhetoric only for pragmatic purposes such as higher wages. I do not think there is much bargaining of this kind going on in the communities I studied. If these women are essentially traditionalists, then why did so many of them admit that they worked because they enjoyed it, rather than merely for financial reasons? Why did they express dissatisfaction over their husband's level of participation in domestic tasks? And why were they pushing to expand their role in almost all aspects of religious leadership except for the very top position? To argue that these women adopt feminist rhetoric only so they can make more money to support the family is oversimplified and misleading.

The women at Victory, St. Joseph's and Beth Israel, like some of those studied by Stacey and Kaufman, may be making what I will call a "feminist bargain": they are (or at least were in the past) women with feminist inclinations who are attracted by certain aspects of their traditions. They are willing to give up some of the freedom and equality feminism has wrought in return for tradition's support of marriage and male responsibility. Women who decline church leadership positions in order to encourage men to lead, or who feel submission has saved their marriage, are a good illustration of such a tradeoff. Yet that tradeoff does not mean they have relinquished their feminist inclinations. Recall how Orthodox Jewish women were pushing for bat mitzvahs and Talmud classes for their daughters, or how Evangelical and Catholic women insisted that they already held many important leadership positions. By not challenging male authority in the top positions, these women feel they can avoid putting men on the defensive and gradually gain more power in other positions until eventually they will be allowed to hold the top one too (see Greenberg 1993). They are willing to wait because the sense of meaning and community—coherence—provided by their respective traditions seems a fair tradeoff for the freedoms offered by secular society.

Still, bargaining theory does not explain everything. If so many of these women explicitly reject feminism and fully embrace traditionalist roles (at least in certain contexts) then we can hardly conclude that feminism is their primary value system. The problem with both cognitive dissonance and bargaining theories is that they assume feminism and traditionalism to be mutually exclusive value systems between which women must choose in order to establish a stable, consistent identity. This assumption is based on two seemingly common-sense premises. First, we assume that the women must have some primary identification—either feminist or traditionalist—and that adoption of another identification is merely instrumental to achieve some end. Second, we assume that the purpose of traditional gender roles is to regulate the lives of women so that their behavior conforms to the official order of the community. Logical as they may seem, both of these assumptions may be false.

A Protean Self?

Let us begin by examining the first premise: a "normal" individual has one primary identification and that people with multiple or shifting identities are psychologically disturbed. Though widely accepted, the notion of a single, stable self-identity may be outdated. Psychologist Robert Jay Lifton (1993), for example, argues that the ability to adopt different identities in different parts of our lives is a healthy response to the demands of contemporary life. "We are becoming fluid and many-sided," he writes. "Without quite realizing it, we have been evolving a sense of self appropriate to the restlessness and flux of our time. This mode of being differs radically from that of the past, and enables us to engage in continuous exploration and personal experiment" (1). Lifton calls this mode of being the "protean self," after Proteus, the Greek sea god of many forms. He argues that it arises from confusion, from the feeling that "we are buffeted about by unmanageable historical forces and social uncertainties." Our lives are filled with fear and contradictions. "But rather than collapse under these threats and pulls, the self turns out to be surprisingly resilient" (ibid.). In other words, it adapts. That adaptation is not mere tactical flexibility; rather it represents a new construction of identity. Lifton argues that "the older version of personal identity, at least insofar as it suggests inner stability and sameness, was derived from a vision of a traditional culture in which relationships to symbols and institutions are still relatively intact—hardly the case in the last years of the twentieth century. If the self is a symbol of one's organism, the protean self-process is the continuous psychic re-creation of that symbol" (4).

Although "variation is the essence of the protean self," it does have some consistent features. "Central to its function is a capacity for bringing together disparate and seemingly incompatible elements of identity and involvement . . . and for continuous transformation of those elements." Humor and self-mockery are often used to "lubricate" the lack of fit between various elements of self. The protean self is also characterized by impermanence. Work patterns, community membership, and even human ties and ethical commitments are constantly shifting. Idea systems especially "can be embraced, modified, let go, and re-embraced, all with a new ease that stands in sharp contrast to the inner struggle people in the past endured with such shifts" (5–6). According to Lifton, there are three manifestations of the protean self. It may be sequential, "a changing series of involvements with people, ideas, and activities" over time. It may be simultaneous, a "multiplicity of varied, even antithetical images and ideas held at any one time by the self, each of which it may be more or less ready to act upon." And it can be social, "so that in any given environment—office, school, or neighborhood—one may encounter highly varied forms of self-presentation" (8). In contrast to other observers, Lifton argues that all this multiplicity and fluidity should not be equated with the disappearance of the self. "Proteanism involves a quest for authenticity and meaning, a form-seeking assertion of self. The recognition of complexity and ambiguity may well represent a certain maturation in our concept of self. The protean self seeks to be both fluid and grounded, however tenuous that combination. . . . [It] is a balancing act between responsive shape shifting, on the one hand, and efforts to consolidate and cohere, on the other" (9). The protean self, then, is a positive development.

Although there are forces that oppose this development, Lifton believes it will prevail. "The same historical forces that evoke proteanism—dislocation, the mass media revolution, and the threat of extinction—evoke anti-protean reactions as well," the most prominent of which is fundamentalism. In contrast to the "intellectual and spiritual suppleness of proteanism," fundamentalism claims unfaltering certainty about moral and religious absolutes. Yet fundamentalists, too, are susceptible to various forms of proteanism, as "personal narratives reveal the fundamentalist self to contain much of what it opposes" (160). Indeed, there may be an organic relationship between proteanism and fundamentalism. "In every fundamentalist assertion, there may well be some kind of protean underside, some potential for alternative imagery and symbolization. Correspondingly, every protean exploration may require some protective structuring or even partial closing down of experience" (187). In the long run, Lifton thinks, the protean tide will be stronger. "Fundamentalism, in essence a reactive force, takes on the impossible task of fully controlling the symbolizing process and eliminating its spontaneity and unpredictability. Hence the fundamentalist self feels unable to live up to what is demanded of it," and eventually succumbs to the need to adapt to different times and places.

Lifton's theory makes sense of the apparent contradictions in the lives of conservative Christian and Orthodox Jewish women. Many are attracted to religious traditionalism by its moral clarity and the structure it provides to guide one's daily life. Yet they have chosen communities that allow them to experiment and manipulate that structure to meet their own needs. They are trying to be both fluid, responsive to the changes of our time, and grounded, finding moral certainty in their respective traditions. Since gender is central to one's identity, one's conception of self, the balancing act between fluidity and consolidation is manifested in the construction of gender roles.

The women I talked to are shifting their conception of themselves as women in both place and time, demonstrating all three manifestations of the protean self. Their identity changed sequentially as they moved from nonaffiliation to membership in a conservative religious group. Like Katrina and Miriam, most of the Evangelicals and Jews in this study had been raised in liberal Protestant and Reform or Conservative Jewish homes before they joined a traditionalist community. While most Catholics in this study were raised in the church, they did not identify themselves as conservatives until they were adults and were faced with the decision of whether to obey their church's teaching. It was when Beatrice decided to disregard the advice of her liberal Catholic friends and follow church rules on birth control that "it made me realize that I was trying to be a good Catholic," which, as she sees it, is by definition conservative. The women's self-presentation also shifts in different social environments. As we have seen in the preceding chapters, the women play very different roles and think of themselves in different ways depending on whether they are at home, at work, or in a church or synagogue.

Finally, what Lifton would call simultaneous proteanism, the holding of disparate, often inconsistent conceptions of gender at the same time, seems to be a necessity that arises out of these sequential and social shifts. The sequential shift into a conservative religious community does not mean that these women have left their previous ties behind. Many continue to negotiate uneasy connections to "outside" friends and parents whose conception of gender identity clashes with that of the religious community. The social shifts from home to work to church or synagogue are particularly problematic because they often occur too quickly and repeatedly to adjust the self completely to the new environment. Contrast how Lisa thinks of herself as completely equal to her male colleagues when discussing her job (chapter 4) with her insistence that she is fundamentally different from men when discussing women's role in the church (chapter 5). Both assertions are sincere, and I would argue that both are part of Lisa's gender identity. In other words, neither the sequential nor social manifestation of the protean self would be possible without some degree of simultaneous proteanism as well.

Gender identity, then, is not stable but constantly shifting, not unitary but multiple. The notion that feminism theoretically conflicts with traditionalism is in practice irrelevant. Just as secular or liberal American women must juggle many different roles and do not adopt a consistently feminist identity, so religious conservatives are not consistently antifeminist and are frequently shifting between active, assertive, independent roles that are traditionally reserved to men to more passive, submissive, nurturing roles deemed appropriate for women. To assume that people must have a single, stable gender identity leads us to exaggerate the extent to which different religious conservatives are alike, as well as the degree to which all religious conservatives differ from other American women.

Symbolic Boundaries

The second premise underlying most theories about inconsistency is that the purpose of traditional gender norms is to regulate the activities of women's lives. As Parsons suggested, social institutions maintain order by establishing rules and by socializing individuals to follow those rules even when that involves acting against the individual's self-interest. Recent organizational analysis by Powell and Dimaggio (1991) and Chaves (1994), however, suggests that such rules may have a very different purpose.

These "new institutionalists" draw on the insights of ethnomethodology developed three decades ago by Garfinkel (see Heritage 1984, for an overview). Garfinkel (1967) rejected the Parsonian notion that the social scientist can objectively determine what is in the subject's self-interest. Rather than trying to explain away the subject's actions, he advocated taking a phenomenological approach to research in which what the subject says and does is taken at face value. Based on studies of how people communicate, Garfinkel concluded that social order is not maintained by the socialization of shared patterns, but is constituted in everyday practical interaction. People assume that rules and symbols mean the same things to others even when they don't. Even when person A is given evidence that person B may assign a rule a different meaning, person A will interpret what B is saying to coincide with A's own interpretation. For example, subjects who were instructed to ask advice from experimenters were found to interpret the experimenters' answers to have been motivated by their questions—even when experimenters were responding in a predetermined way. Garfinkel argues that socialization does not effectively create meanings that are broadly shared by different individuals. Rather, people assume shared meanings because they need to make sense of other's actions.

Building on Garfinkel, new institutionalists such as Meyer and Rowan (1977) point out that many social organizations maintain themselves in an orderly fashion despite the fact that their members are not following the rules that supposedly govern the institution. They argue that such organizations often experience conflict between enforcing the rules (which are needed to maintain institutional order) and efficiency (the raison d'être of the institution). Rather than focus on one at the expense of the other, organizations engage in a process that Meyer and Rowan call "decoupling" in which elements of structure (rules) are decoupled from activities (actual behavior of the organization's members) and anarchy is avoided by confidence in each other.

The insights of ethnomethodology and new institutionalism help us understand how the women at Victory, St. Joseph's and Beth Israel—

and those institutions themselves—are able to tolerate a high level of inconsistency in the application of gender norms. Each of these women interprets traditional gender norms a little differently, while assuming that her interpretation is shared by the rest of the group, including the rabbi or pastor. This is particularly evident at St. Joseph's where both liberal and conservative Catholics assume that their interpretation is what constitutes true Catholicism. Compare, for example, Bridget's assertion (chapter 4) that you cannot call yourself a Catholic if you are pro-choice, to the liberal woman's rejection of the bishop's focus group as unrepresentative of Catholics because it included too many women who think like Bridget (chapter 6). Examples can also be found at Victory Church, where some women insist that women should submit to their husbands (even though they often find ways around doing so) while others interpret submission as a mutual act. At Beth Israel, some women argue that maintaining the family purity laws means sleeping in separate beds and avoiding touching their husbands, while others limit the law to a prohibition of sexual intercourse. Since no attempt is made to regulate how these rules are actually followed, everybody can claim to believe in gender norms formulated by papal edicts, or halacha, or a literal interpretation of the Bible, even when the extent to which those rules are actually acted upon varies considerably.

Yet if no effort is made at enforcement, one must wonder to what extent traditional gender norms are even intended to regulate the day-to-day activities of women. I would like to suggest that the function of formal gender norms is not so much to govern women's lives but to symbolize membership in a certain type of religious culture. In other words, the women's (seemingly inconsistent) insistence on male authority has to do with boundaries (see Chaves 1994). While maintaining boundaries is crucial to any religious community, defining those boundaries is increasingly difficult in today's pluralistic society. The patriarchal structure of these traditionalist churches and synagogues constitutes a boundary that distinguishes them from other denominations. In contrast to conservative Christians and Orthodox Jews, most Protestant churches ordain women, and both Reform and Conservative Jews now ordain women and allow men and women to sit together. Maintaining traditional distinctions between men and women is therefore one of the things that makes religious conservatives distinct.

That distinction is very important to the women I interviewed. Many Evangelical women complain that there are too many people out there who call themselves Christian but aren't. As Stephanie put it, "I feel like society out there is trying to tell us that there's not much difference between men and women. Well, I don't agree with that." She continued with what sounded like a description of some of the women in her own church: "There's a lot of Christian women who basically live their lifestyles just as anyone else would in the secular world." Yet she describes hers as a biblical church, and feels that ordaining women is "just not biblical." Evangelical women are similarly upset about gender-neutral language. "That's just totally humanistic and man-pleasing," Tanya complained. "I just think that's the most far-out idea . . . here they call themselves a church" and they are "changing the Bible . . . we're not supposed to change the Bible." According to Evangelicals like Tanya and Stephanie, real Christians, such as those at Victory Church, do not ordain women or use gender-neutral language and joyfully embrace their traditional roles as wives and mothers. It is the liberal churches' attempt to accommodate to the materialistic and selfish demands of the secular world that has led them away from Christianity.

Conservative Catholics, too, emphasize the boundaries between themselves and more liberal members of their church. The abortion issue is often used as a boundary setting device in this context. As Bridget put it, "I don't see how you can claim to be Catholic and still support abortion." While she believes it is acceptable, after thorough study of church documents, to "respectfully disagree" with Catholic doctrine, she complains that the majority of Catholics do not even bother to find out why the church has established a certain rule but simply ignore it. According to Bridget and other conservative Catholics, a good Catholic should follow all the rules of the church except when, after serious dialogue with the church, she decides that doing so would go against her conscience. Those who disregard Catholic doctrine, might as well leave—or, in Liz's words, "become Protestants."

Concerns about boundaries are also voiced by Orthodox Jewish women. Ketza said that when she first heard that Jews were ordaining women as rabbis, "it was OK because it was just the Reform [Jews]. When the Conservatives started doing it, that bothered me. The Orthodox would never [do that]." Marcia expresses similar sentiments: "I'm sorry that Reform and Conservative Jews create their own halacha . . . I mean Reform doesn't even live by halacha . . . they will do whatever they want to do." The biggest challenge for Modern Orthodox women, another woman told me, is "how do we protect the sanctity of Orthodoxy? We don't want to become a Conservative group . . . yet how do we accommodate to changing times?" Resisting women's ordination, like maintaining sex-segregated seating in the synagogue, is an effective way to preserve their Orthodox identity.

But integrationist religious conservatives, such as the ones in this study, also want to distinguish themselves from ultra-traditionalist, isolationist conservatives. Both the conservative Christian and Modern Orthodox women with whom I spoke emphasize how much better off women are in their community than in more conservative ones. Conservative Catholics like to differentiate themselves from Evangelicals by pointing out how ridiculous it is to take the Bible literally. Recall Donna's assertion (chapter 6) that only fundamentalists expect women to submit to men while the Catholic Church has more enlightened views. Referring to her sister, who had converted to an Evangelical church and now submits to her husband, another Catholic woman told me: "That's one of the things that cracks me up with my sister's faith. She is, she's not really, honestly timid, she just behaves that way because the scriptures say that." Evangelicals in turn emphasize how different they are from more fundamentalist Protestants. As Patty puts it, "I really feel for women out there, in churches [where they] aren't allowed to do anything . . . we need to encourage men, but women still need to be encouraged, 'cause I've seen the opposite where they're totally squashed." Similarly, the Orthodox Jewish women I interviewed make a clear distinction between their synagogue, which is modern, and what they term "right wing Orthodoxy," i.e., the Lubavitsher and other Hasidic communities. As Judith notes, "In some synagogues, especially the right winged [sic], women are kind of hush-hushed away. And I don't like that . . . they end up being very submissive, and it's not a healthy feeling." Another woman emphasizes how progressive Beth Israel is compared to Sephardic Orthodox Jewish congregations: "Where my husband comes from, a Sephardic background, I wouldn't even bother to go to shul. They don't have an *eruv* [a boundary within which Jews are allowed to carry things outside the house on the Sabbath], so they can't bring their children, so then they're stuck home with their kids, and they don't leave the house all day. In our synagogue, women feel like they are a part of things. Our rabbi is very open to women's issues, but he's also concerned with halacha." Both of these women insist that while Beth Israel is traditionalist, there are other congregations that are far more traditionalist and much more restrictive of women. In all three communities, then, gender norms have become a symbol of belonging to a particular kind of conservative religious community.

If the function of patriarchal gender norms in conservative religious communities is to a large extent symbolic, the same may be true of more feminist norms in liberal communities. The feminization of American religion that began in the nineteenth century means that women are more involved than men in all aspects of church and synagogue organization. Though this influence may not always translate into power, having a female pastor or rabbi does not necessarily empower other women in the congregation either. As Marc Chaves's (1994) research suggests, American women's support for ordination has been ambivalent for most of this century, at least partly because they are afraid they will have to sacrifice the power gained in other areas for one symbolic position. Once again, we must conclude that women in conservative religious communities are not as different from liberal or secular women as we often think they are.

It is easy to judge the inconsistencies in other people's beliefs and behavior, but all of us live with some level of contradiction. While cognitive dissonance and bargaining theories explain some aspects of the lives of women in conservative religious communities, these models overstate the significance of consistency. The notions of a protean self and of symbolic boundaries help us understand how these women can combine traditionalist and feminist values without compromising their integrity. Neither religious right nor feminist leaders would accept this conclusion, bent as they are on promoting the notion of an antifeminist alliance among religious conservatives. But, as pointed out in chapter 3, incorporating feminist values (norms of behavior) into one's life is not the same thing as supporting the feminist movement (a political entity). The final part of this book will examine how these women feel about that movement and the political issues (e.g., abortion, gay rights) that it promotes.

Part III

No to the Feminist Movement

Chapter 8	Profeminist or Antifeminist?

I HAVE A FEMINIST FRIEND who cannot understand why I wanted to spend two years getting to know women in conservative religious communities. "How could you stand it?" she asked me. "Women like that are actively trying to unravel all the progress the movement has made for us—and for them." When I tell her that many of the women I talked to integrate feminist values into their lives, she is unimpressed. "Then who do you suppose votes for Pat Robertson?" she retorts, "and who sends membership checks to Concerned Women for America [an antifeminist lobby group]?" She has a point. Though ordinary women in conservative Christian and Orthodox Jewish communities are much more open to feminist values than the statements of their leaders would have us believe, they do support those leaders. Indeed, a survey of the women in this study would reveal that the majority agree with their leaders' opposition to the feminist movement.

That does not mean, however, that these women are actively involved in antifeminist politics, or that all of them support the kind of cross-denominational conservative alliance promoted by Robertson or Concerned Women for America (CWA). My friend's comment reveals her lack of exposure to real-life conservative Christian and Orthodox Jewish women. If she spent some time talking to and observing the behavior of these women, she would realize that there is considerable variation among the three communities, both in the degree and the nature of their opposition to the feminist movement. More importantly, my friend ignores the fact that many secular (and liberal Christian and Jewish) women are critical of that movement and, even if they do not actively oppose it, do little to support it. Women in conservative religious communities, as it turns out, are just as ambivalent about the feminist movement as secular American women.

Like secular women, Evangelical, conservative Catholic, and Orthodox Jewish women are not well informed about the feminist movement. They equate it ideologically with liberal feminism, which downplays gender differences and rejects differential treatment of men and women, and politically with the National Organization for Women, which supports complete gender equality, reproductive choice, and gay rights. There seems to be little awareness outside of academia of the diversity within feminism and the fact that some versions of it are quite compatible with religious traditionalism. Given this narrow definition of feminism, women in conservative religious communities resemble secular women in their assessment of the movement's impact. I asked all of the women how they feel about the women's movement and whether they think that feminism has had a positive or negative impact, both on American society generally and on their religious community in particular. Based on their responses to these two questions, women in all three traditions can be grouped into two categories: *profeminists*, who believe that this movement has been good for America and their church or synagogue, and *antifeminists*, who do not. Let us take a closer look at each of these categories and to determine what they reveal about the ideological and political inclinations of ordinary religious conservatives.

Feminism Is Bad for America

Many Evangelicals certainly think so. The majority of women at Victory Church are explicitly antifeminist. Twenty-six out of twenty-seven women think feminism has been bad for America (they do not think it has affected their church). These women blame the feminist movement for almost every social ill, from abortion, divorce, and homosexuality to unemployment. As Charleen puts it, "I think feminism is one of the worst things that ever happened to America." Feminism, according to women like Charleen, is the enemy, a position that sets them apart from secular women. Yet the concerns that lead Evangelicals to this position are shared by a much broader segment of Americans.

Evangelical antifeminists have many complaints about the movement. Perhaps the most common complaint I heard was that feminists are out to reverse gender roles. Most obviously, they want to make women into men. "The danger [posed by feminists] is that women lose their femininity," Ronda explained. "They kind of gird up and go 'I'm going to be just as strong as a man, I'm going to be tough and I'm going to be cutting.' God didn't create us that way. God gave us sensitivity, warmth. And I want to be feminine. I can be a feminine woman and still be as smart and competent as the guy next to me." Less obvious but equally problematic is that feminists want to make men into women. The women at Victory Church feel that feminism has emasculated men, making them irresponsible and increasing homosexual tendencies. As Tanya puts it, "I know men were into the macho thing, and that was off-base, too. But I feel like [feminism] is just getting off in the other direction, and women are just demasculating men . . . our job is to help build up men and encourage them and help them to be the best they can. I think that's why a lot of men are turning homosexual because they aren't getting nurtured by someone, and a lot of women are trying to compete with men and take over. . . . We need to encourage men to be responsible in society and get back to some basic values." There is a sense of nostalgia here: the desire to "get back" to a time when male and female roles were more distinctive. But there is also a sense of frustration with men's failure "to be responsible," i.e., their inability or unwillingness to fulfill their traditional role. That failure is blamed on feminism. "Men just don't seem like men anymore," one woman complained. "A lot, not all of them, but a lot of them are like, they don't want to work, they're just kind of aimless. It seems like courtesy is gone . . . it seems like when I was younger that men used to want to help women. Now it's kind of the attitude, 'Well they can do it for themselves,' because women don't want to be saved anymore. And so men feel kind of lost, like what do I do? I think the feminist movement has robbed women of something, rather than given us something." The argument that the feminist movement has created role confusion mirrors the traditionalist rhetoric of Evangelical leaders: because men and women are inherently different, God has assigned them different roles and separate spheres; when women compete with men, they are interfering with nature and/or challenging God's will and thus bringing doom upon society. But the words of the women at Victory also echo the sentiments of more liberal quarters: leaders in the men's movement, for instance, who hold the feminist movement responsible for a male identity crisis, and secular working mothers, who feel torn between their two roles as breadwinners and homemakers.

Another common complaint is that the feminist movement devalues motherhood and homemaking. Marisa, a single working woman, asserts that "the feminist movement has really damaged a lot of women like my mom, who just was a wonderful mother, and she was always neurotic because she wasn't out being like a killer woman in real estate or a CPA or an attorney." Sandra, a married homemaker with three children, is one of those damaged women:

> I feel when I'm on my husband's truck, there's a fish-sticker on the back, and they see me, and there are kids sitting beside me, they probably think that . . . I feel like people look at us as though we have no brains, all we know how to do is stay home and breast feed our babies, and change diapers, and that's all we're good for, all we're capable of doing. We don't know how the world works, how society works, we're just ignorant. I feel that. I haven't had anybody say it to me, but it's a feeling you get when you're out there. And that bothers me. I'm not ignorant. I'm capable of—I did jobs before. I ran a doctor's office, and I did an excellent job with that. This is just what I chose to do. Whether you're a Christian or not, I think being a housewife today is looked on as being weak.

By insisting that women go out and have careers, Sandra argues, feminists have denigrated their choice to be a homemakers. She feels that raising children takes just as much brains and skill as being a lawyer or a surgeon and is equally, or more, important to the welfare of society, but the feminist movement has led us to overlook that contribution.[1] The devaluation of motherhood affects not just homemakers, Evangelicals assert. By discouraging women from marrying and having children, the movement has harmed career women as well. When they postpone childbearing until after they have established their careers,

Evangelicals argue, women put themselves at physical risk and often find that they cannot have children at all. As Charleen put it: "If [feminism] were so good, why are all these women having babies in their forties when all they wanted was a career?" Another woman comments that "we have a women's movement that has become more masculine than feminine . . . we've opened up a Pandora's box, and we are reaping a bitter harvest. Twenty years later you get women who refused to marry, refused to have children, and now they are in their forties, their clock is ready to be ticked, and they can't conceive, and they've had multiple abortions, and they've ruined their bodies, and they are wondering why they are angry and hurt." Feminism, according to these Evangelicals, has made promises it couldn't keep. Its promises are impossible to fulfill because they go against the laws of nature. Women would be better off if they followed their natural inclination to be mothers early in life and saved their career aspirations until after their children are grown. Such arguments about natural domestic inclination—particularly the depiction of feminists as childless career women—mirror the rhetoric of the religious right. But the concern of Evangelical women that homemaking is no longer a respectable choice is shared by secular women as well.

A third criticism of the feminist movement is that, though it may have started with good intentions, it has become extremist and no longer represents ordinary women. Even the most ardent antifeminists at Victory admit that change was necessary. As one woman put it, "There needed to be some changes. It's not right that men should lord it over women or be treated better than women, which I know that it did happen—that's part of the reason why the feminist movement started." Many women believe that men have been mistreating women and that feminists are justifiably angry about that. "In America today, you see that a lot of men have just kind of left the families," Patty, the school principal, lamented: "I mean we see it here at school. There are a lot of single mothers, some raising four kids by themselves. And I've seen the details of what's happened and what's gone wrong, and in almost all the cases, even in Christian families, the mother is more involved with schooling and trying to get things going . . . and the father, a lot of times, just abdicates the role that he has. Dad took off. It's crazy, and it makes you sad." Sandra, too, holds men responsible for broken

homes and the supermom syndrome which causes women to set standards for themselves that are impossible to meet. "Usually, when you
look at a home that's broken up, it's the man that leaves, it's the father
that abuses the wife or the daughter and abandons them. I think women
have become burned by men and now are trying to do all these things
on their own and are undervaluing themselves because of it." This has
made women angry and resentful. According to Pamela, "There are a
lot of really hurt and bitter women" in the feminist movement. She
told me that she had taken several women's studies courses in college.

> I just remember the discussion groups, there were these women
> who had been devastated. They'd been controlled and manipu-
> lated by men, and most of them had been divorced. I remember
> one woman who had such an impact on me. She said her
> husband gave her money to get a drink at the soda machine
> every day, and she packed a lunch, and one day he came to the
> school—it was amazing that he even let her go to school; I
> don't know how she got past him on that—but he noticed that
> the machine said like forty-five cents. He'd given her five cents
> over a day, and he wanted to know what she had used the
> money for. . . . And she was so full of hurt and had gone
> through so much abuse, that's why she was attracted to
> feminism.

While they blame feminists for many contemporary social problems,
women like Pamela, Sandra, and Patty insist it is men's fault that feminism has emerged in the first place. When men mistreat women, women
have a right to be angry. The feminist movement, at least when it began, had legitimate gripes about a society that allowed men to dominate, abuse, and abandon women.

By contrast, Evangelicals perceive the contemporary feminist movement as out of touch with the lives of most ordinary women. As Tanya
put it, "Women have been put down in different ways, or they haven't
had equal pay for equal jobs. I think it all started over equal wages, like
'I work as hard as Mr. Smith over there and I want the same pay,' and I
can understand that, especially with the education that women had gotten. But I think they've gone to extremes . . . The pendulum, when you
push one way then it swings all the way back, so I feel like that's what's
happening today." If a male-dominated society represents one extreme,

the women at Victory Church feel that a feminist society is equally imbalanced. While it is wrong for men to meet their needs at the expense of women, it is just as wrong for women to fulfill their individual desires at the expense of their children and the rest of society. Because men are ultimately responsible for sexism, imitating them will only perpetuate our troubles, and the deeper problem of society will remain unchanged. That problem, of which feminism is but a symptom, is the selfishness and materialism of modern American society.

Americans, these Evangelicals argue, have become obsessed with fulfilling personal needs and accumulating vast quantities of consumer goods. Compassion for others and concern for the good of society as a whole has been lost in the shuffle of satisfying the "me-generation." Feminism is merely a symptom of this larger social illness. As Katrina put it, "There' a lot of selfishness in movements like that. Like, 'I want to do my own thing, forget about you, I'm more important than you are.' And in God's scheme, it says to value the other person more highly than yourself, and when you do that, it creates your own value. If the feminists heard that, they'd go, 'You mean there's nothing in it for me?' They just want to know what's in it for them." Feminism, in this view, is not an attempt to help the oppressed; rather, feminists, like most Americans, are seeking to enrich themselves at the expense of others. Real concern for society, Evangelical women argue, means putting the needs of others ahead of one's own. Stephanie, for example, admits that her decision to stay home with her children means that their family has less income than if she were employed, but insists that pursuing a career would be putting her interests before those of her children. "Parents must realize that their children need them, and be willing to sacrifice. My husband and I, we're not able to take vacations or buy really nice clothes . . . but that's OK, I really don't mind that. I believe that when we're sixty or seventy years old, having all these kids that we can love, and they can love us back, is more important than having nice cars and pictures of vacations that we took." According to Stephanie, feminists and other secular Americans would not respect her choices. Yet she is convinced that by going against the grain, she is taking a stand for what is right. "You can't look to other people for your approval. That can depress you because there's not that many people out there that think what you're doing is that valuable. You just know in your heart that it is, that you're doing the right thing, and that there will be fruit from it all later on." Identifying the feminist movement with self-ishness and materialism, these women see rejecting it as a counter-cultural act. What they are really rejecting may not be women's rights but the rampant individualism of our society—a concern that is shared by many liberal and secular Americans.

In contrast to what most Americans believe, the women at Victory Church believe the solution to this problem is conversion to Christianity. The way to deal with sexism is not feminist activism but turning to Jesus. Katrina, for example, believes that if more Americans embraced Christianity, then sexism would not be a problem. "If the workplace was a godly workplace, there shouldn't be any discrimination, whether you're black, white, man or woman." Contrary to common perceptions, these women explained to me, the Bible does not legitimate male domi-nation of women but provides a mandate for equality. "People equate the Bible and what is says about submission with how women were treated in America in the past," Pamela argued. "And it just has noth-ing to do with it! Because there's freedom, there's equality in Jesus. You are joint heirs to all his promises. You have a ministry, and you get mar-ried so you can work together for the Lord, and anyone who is abusive or discriminatory, that's wrong. It's not biblical. It's not right." Pamela believes that the feminist movement may have accomplished legal changes, but "the Word is the only thing that can change people's hearts. Period." She compares the women's movement to the Los An-geles riots following the Rodney King trial. "Remember the riots, people were angry, people exploded, and they had a right to. I could see how they had just been held down for so long they had to got forward, and they made that statement, but now what do we do? The only thing that's going to heal them is the Word. Period. So the gospel is really the only movement there is that's going to bring change from the inside, not just from the outside." According to Pamela, feminism, like so many other social movements, only addresses the symptom, not the cause of oppression. Because people are basically selfish, they will always be tempted to dominate and take advantage of others. Secular movements may prevent people from acting on this urge, but they cannot elimi-nate it altogether. Only Christ can induce such a transformation. According to Evangelical antifeminists, it is Christianity, not feminism, that will liberate women.

Conservative Catholic antifeminists are in many ways similar to Evangelicals, though they are fewer in number. St. Joseph's Church is almost evenly split between pro-and antifeminists, a split that mirrors the division between liberal and conservative Catholics. Seeking to separate themselves from liberals, many of whom are profeminist, conservative women are self-consciously antifeminist. Almost all of them feel that the feminist movement is bad for America and bad for their church. Yet the reasons they cite for this opinion reflect concerns that may be shared by liberals and sometimes even resemble arguments made by radical feminists.

The primary complaint, as at Victory, is that feminists are trying to eliminate natural gender differences. Because of the feminist movement, Beatrice asserted, women "have no definite role now, and they can't take pride in the things that come naturally, like having kids, that's not something you'd necessarily take pride in anymore." Similarly, Donna admitted, "I don't like feminists" because "I think there's an element of radical feminism which says there's absolutely no differences between men and women . . . instead of trying to appreciate femininity, what it means to be a woman, and the good things, they tend to want to blur all the lines between men and women." Unlike Evangelical antifeminists, conservative Catholics do not seem concerned that feminist efforts to eliminate gender differences will increase the rate of homosexuality or make men less responsible. Instead they fear that such efforts will make *women* less responsible and increase the abortion rate. Beatrice, for instance, asserts that feminism encourages women to deny their female selves. "I've known many women from India and from other cultures, and that's what I like and respect about them, that they have a much deeper perception than we do of the role of nature in their own lives, in our own bodies." By losing touch with their biology, women are losing their innate sense that abortion is wrong. "There's natural feelings women have that children are good, that a baby is good, that every woman who looks at a baby feels that it's good. If we lose that it's really dangerous, and we're sort of getting to that point." The problem, according to conservative Catholics, is not that feminism makes men weak but that it makes women destructive. The women's emphasis on female biology may reflect Catholic teachings on natural law, but it also mirrors feminist arguments. Donna's comment about radical feminism illustrates how misinformed many women are about the feminist movement. Radical, to her, simply means more extreme in the effort to deny differences. She is not aware that more radical feminists actually celebrate gender differences.

A second criticism I heard from many Catholic antifeminists is that feminism devalues motherhood and homemaking. In contrast to Victory Church, this was a particular problem for young conservative women at St. Joseph's, perhaps because so many of their peers are liberals who have postponed motherhood in order to pursue a career. Jill, who is single and working, believes that the feminist movement has made it difficult for young women to choose a traditional role.

> Women are confused. I mean, just in my own personal life, when I think about getting married, I have to decide: How much do I contribute to the income of the family? Do I work and have children? That's a great burden . . . but if I just stay home—see, *just* stay home!—and take care of my kids, that's a lesser position. . . . They're considered less of a person, "Oh, she's just a mother." . . . you're pretty much written off socially, and I don't like that. I think motherhood is a beautiful thing, and it should not be something you're ashamed of and that you feel you have to do on the side. And I think the women's movement has done that, so that now women feel like they *have* to climb the corporate ladder, you have to prove yourself, otherwise you're less intelligent. That's the way you prove yourself is by competing against men. No! I don't have to compete against men to be intelligent.

Jill feels that the feminist movement has failed to broaden women's choices; instead it has simply reversed the narrow range of options that are available to women. While a woman of the 1950s felt she had to be a homemaker, a woman of the 1990s feels compelled to have a career. If career women of the past were considered less feminine, homemakers of the present are seen as less intelligent, unable to cope with the realities of the world. Those realities, according to Jill, are still being defined by men. By refusing to be measured by those definitions, a woman who chooses motherhood over a career is actually taking a stand for women. Jill's assumption that homemakers of the past had more status than they do today reflects the nostalgic rhetoric of the religious right. At the same time, her rejection of a world defined by men is a radically feminist argument.

Like Evangelicals, Catholic antifeminists believe that the women's movement started out for the right reasons but has become far too extreme to be useful anymore. Bridget, for example, believes that "it started out with what appeared to be good intentions. I think it started out trying to equalize some things that—I mean they really discriminated! You don't pay one doctor $100,000 a year and the other $50,000 just because she's a woman . . . but now I wonder if that was just part of a ruse to get people behind them to do more radical things." Among feminism's more radical demands is the right to have an abortion. "By allowing abortion, you just start loosening things up. I mean, the man who wants to have an affair, if he knows he can get his secretary to have an abortion, he has no moral compunction or any kind of motivation to not hop into bed with her. . . . So sexual harassment could be worse now than it ever was before." Like her antifeminist counterparts at Victory Church, Bridget does not want to go back to the times when society tolerated overt gender discrimination, and she sympathizes with the anger that feminists directed against such oppression. Yet she, too, feels that feminists have pushed too far in the opposite direction, and have ended up harming rather than helping women. Similarly, Beatrice admitted that "at first I thought it [feminism] was a good thing. When I read Betty Friedan's book, I thought 'Oh my gosh, this is right. Women shouldn't stay home and think about floor polish all day. She's perfectly right.' And I thought it would have a good result, and in a way it has, but in another way—we're in this bad stage right now because by denigrating the home we are harming women more than we're helping them." Beatrice first encountered feminism in college and acknowledges that the women's movement has had a positive impact on American society, particularly in encouraging women—herself included—to get an education and enter various professions previously closed to them. Twenty years and seven children later, however, she doubts whether the changes wrought by feminism were worth the price. Like Evangelicals, Catholic antifeminists use the image of a pendulum swing to describe their sentiments about the women's movement. As one woman put it, "You hold the pendulum too tight at one end, and when you let go, it goes to far the other way, and it has to work it's way back down. We had to break away from being held too far on one side. And it's quite natural that it's going to go too far on the other side before it comes back to where it belongs." This woman takes a rather philosophical view of social change, arguing that reform movements come and go, but nothing really changes. "I can look through history and find nothing different. It really is almost like a cycle of social issues that come and go, and come and go." Having raised five children by herself, she appreciates some of the benefits feminism has brought to women, especially fair lending laws and affirmative action programs that ensured her a job. Yet, like Bridget and Beatrice, she feels that the movement has gone too far and that ultimately no social movement can eradicate the human tendency to dominate each other. Sexism, to Catholic antifeminists, is a real problem, but the women's movement is not the best way to solve it.

Indeed, the women's movement itself is part of the problem. Like Evangelicals, conservative Catholics see the movement as an outgrowth of excess individualism in modern society. Feminists, like most Americans, selfishly compete for more and more material goods without any regard for how this might affect the community. But unlike Evangelicals, the women at St. Joseph's blame this excessive individualism on male domination. Thus Rita's deepest criticism of the movement is also an affirmation of feminism:

> I'd like to make a comment about being a feminist . . . the modern feminist movement, the feminist movement as we know it, emulates masculine qualities, masculine virtues and masculine values. It is *not* feminist, in that it does not emulate what's feminine. And I've always been frustrated and confused as to how someone can call themselves a feminist and then go out about trying to make themselves as masculine as possible, by trying to compete in the same job market as men, the same way, which was never something I admired, by defining reproductive freedom as meaning limiting or abolishing the whole notion of having children, by saying that reproductive freedom has to include annihilating one's child in order to

compete. And that's what the feminist movement tells us, that if we're going to compete in the job market, a woman has to be able to deny her reproductive nature by, if birth control doesn't work, by abortion. This is *not* to me what feminism is about. Feminist means really emulating what's feminine, what is womanly, what is distinctly female, and taking those qualities and elevating them in society—so that they're acknowledged as equally important to what's masculine, so that motherhood isn't seen as a second-rate thing, motherhood is seen as what it really is: one of the most important jobs anyone could ever embark upon. . . . That's why I admire Mary. Mary was a woman who had a child against the odds. She wasn't a single mother, but she was technically an unwed mother who could have lost her life and said yes anyway. That's really something I admire. Mary was a feminine woman, and yet she really packed the wallet. She had tremendous influence over her child, her husband, she is respected and emulated in the Catholic church. The Catholic church has one of the most positive feminine role models in existence on this planet, and I consider *that* to be feminist!

On the one hand, Rita employs clearly antifeminist rhetoric, insisting that women are essentially different from men and elevating motherhood to one of women's highest callings.[2] On the other hand, she departs quite radically from the patriarchal model in suggesting that Mary should be admired because she rejected the sexist values of society and risked becoming a single mother. Though she rejects the feminist movement, Rita does not accept male-dominated society. She believes the world would be a better place if it were transformed according to feminine values because women are more likely to counter the rampant individualism of modern culture.

Although Rita believes that Mary provides an excellent role model for such a transformation, she does not advocate conversion to Catholicism as a solution to our social problems. Like Evangelicals, conservative Catholics are eager to point out that their religion is not antifeminist. Donna, for example, asserts that "the pope came out with encyclicals about women which are fairly open to some of the elements of feminism . . . and women are legitimately given more roles in higher echelons of the church." She and Rita feel that there is much within the Catholic tradition that elevates and empowers women. But, unlike Evangelicals, they do not advocate—and nobody at St. Joseph's does— that Christianizing America is the best way to liberate women.

In contrast to Victory and St. Joseph's Church, only very few women at Beth Israel are explicitly antifeminist. I found four women out of twenty-seven who feel the feminist movement is bad for America and even worse for Judaism. Their reasoning is very similar to that of conservative Christian antifeminists. Like Evangelicals and Catholics, Jewish antifeminists complain that feminism devalues motherhood and homemaking and tries to make women into men. Rivka's views are representative. "In general I don 't find the feminist movement has done anything positive," she told me. "I don't feel it's like a very positive movement. My sister was always like a feminist. So I grew up with that. She was ten years older than I was, and she was definitely the bra-burning type, you know? She was really a staunch feminist. And she got married last year at thirty-nine. I thought for sure she'd never get married." According to Rivka, her sister's involvement in the women's movement encouraged her to suppress what made her different from men, her ability to be a mother, until it was almost too late to change her mind. Feminism, in this view, limits rather than expands women's options and oppresses rather than empowers women.

Like Christian antifeminists, Orthodox Jews acknowledge that early feminists had legitimate gripes, but feel that the movement has gone awry. "They probably did start out with good intentions," Rivka admitted, "but then they got a lot of radical people involved and it really started to veer off the path. . . . I think in a lot of ways it has really hindered women's progress, because people don't like radical, on either end of the spectrum." Rivka's comments echo the feelings of women at St. Joseph's and Victory Church that the pendulum of change had swung too far in the other direction. Of course women should have equal educational and employment opportunities, of course they should receive the same pay as men. But the contemporary women's movement, according to Rivka and other Jewish antifeminists, has gone far beyond such goals to become extreme and therefore unrepresentative of and even harmful to most women.

But what do these women mean by harmful? In contrast to their Christian counterparts, the main problem for Orthodox Jewish antifeminists is not that feminism encourages women to have abortions or men to become homosexuals, but that it challenges Jewish tradition. As Rivka put it, "I think it's really rocking the boat in a boat that just doesn't need to be rocked. It's been fine for thousands of years. No one's had a problem with it. These roles have been the roles that everyone's had, you know, everyone's mother, grandmother, great-grandmother, all the way up the ranks, and no one seemed to have a problem." Rivka complained that it is feminism "that has bred a lot of the dissatisfaction" among women in Orthodox communities, because "feminist women look at an Orthodox woman's role as very suppressive [sic]. I don't feel suppressed at all! But obviously other women do, otherwise they wouldn't be out there fighting to change our traditions"—or, worse yet, leaving Orthodox Judaism. She and other antifeminists are well aware that their tradition is a tiny minority within what is already a minority religion in the United States. What makes them a minority is most people's desire to adapt to the larger culture. Such adaptation must be resisted if Orthodoxy is to survive and grow. Because feminist demands for a change in traditional women's roles are merely another symptom of adaptation, feminism must be rejected. Given this high level of minority consciousness, it is no surprise that antifeminists at Beth Israel do not advocate mass conversion to Orthodox Judaism as a solution to the problems of sexism in America. Their concern is not feminism's impact on society, but its challenge to the survival of an already endangered tradition.

I'm Not a Feminist, But . . .

Concern for the survival of tradition is a common one in the Orthodox Jewish community, and several Orthodox writers have commented on the threat that feminism represents to that tradition. I was therefore surprised to find that the majority of women at Beth Israel are explicitly profeminist. While they, too, express concerns about excessive adaptation to secular culture, they believe that the overall impact of the women's movement has been positive, not only for American society but for the Jewish community as well.

In contrast to antifeminists who tend to take women's legal equality for granted, profeminists give the feminist movement full credit for changing the status of women in American society. Marcia, a college professor, thinks the feminist movement

> has been stupendous, really wonderful. It's just been fantastic, bringing things to consciousness—that we were always there. . . . There was a time when women would graduate from prestigious law schools, they had been on law review, and they would come out and there were no jobs. Nobody would hire them. That doesn't happen now. It's almost inconceivable to think of it, but that's the way it was, and it was the women's movement who brought this out. They've done a lot of stupendous things. Look at the press: the bra-burning made them look ridiculous, but I remember on radios and TV, all these women jokes and mother jokes—gone!

Unlike antifeminists who look to the past as a time when mothers and homemakers were respected, Marcia recalls that they were not only devalued but denied the option to choose an alternate occupation. Vicky, a lawyer, also appreciates the progress women have made since her mother's generation. "I think it did an awful lot in raising women's consciousness, everyone's consciousness. And enabling women to get out of the house. I mean, my mom always worked, she's a professor . . . but they were considered real trendsetters for their day. She was like one of three women professors at her college. So for me it was the norm growing up with a working mom, but that was by no means the norm for the late fifties and early sixties." By the time Vicky went to law school, many faculty and almost half the students were female, and double-income couples had become the norm in American society. Though she likes her work, she does not want to be a trendsetter and is glad she did not have to face the challenges her mother did when she decided to pursue a career.

It is not just career women who appreciate the accomplishments of the women's movement; homemakers do as well. Michelle, for example, has chosen to stay home with her children. Yet she feels that "there was a whole generation of women that really felt that they had no choice and no options and could do nothing except be at home and watch soap operas and be Suzy Homemaker. . . . I don't know if it was the movement as much as economics that forced so many women into the workplace, but I think the movement certainly is responsible for letting them know that they don't just have to be secretaries, they can be bosses, they can be anything they want to be. That's very positive!" According to homemakers like Michelle, feminism is positive because it bolsters women's self-esteem and broadens their choices. While they believe that many women work out of economic necessity—and they appreciate the fact that they themselves don't have to—these home-makers argue that the feminist movement allows working women to see their jobs as a career, rather than a temporary source of supplementary income, and therefore to seek employment that is personally fulfilling which in turn increases the quality of their lives. According to most women at Beth Israel, the overall impact of feminism on American society has clearly been positive.

Indeed, many Jewish profeminists believe that feminism has not come far enough. "I don't think [the women's movement] has done everything it has set out to do," Vicky told me. "I mean there's certainly still gender discrimination, there still isn't equal pay for equal work." Marcia, too, feels that "the world is still run by men and it's an all-boy network. Take a woman who has worked in an office for five years, is excellent, does great work but she isn't promoted. The young junior executive comes in, and the world is open at his feet. It's just a different world for him than it is for women. It's because men rule the world, and I don't think it's fair but it is so." Similarly, Laura, a mother and lawyer seeking to become a partner in her firm, notes that "there is still a glass ceiling in many respects, especially for women with young children. There are still a lot of issues that employers have difficulty dealing with." She feels that businesses "still need to go much further in the kind of flexibility that is needed for both parents in terms of childcare," and that schools should "hold PTA meetings in the evenings as opposed to during the day." According to Laura, feminism may have been successful in forcing legal changes that prevent overt discrimination against women, but it has yet to change the underlying attitudes that continue to maintain women's inequality and that are harmful to both women and men. In contrast to antifeminists like Rivka who believe that, having achieved legal equality, the women's movement no longer has a reason to exist, profeminists like Laura, Marcia, and Vicky insist that much of the feminist task still remains to be done.

Yet despite their support for the feminist movement, these women criticize some of the same things that antifeminists complain about. Like antifeminists, profeminists lament that feminism has degraded mother-hood and homemaking. Michelle, for example, asserted that "the only way a woman can be equal is to be on a man's terms. And as a result of that, there's a lot of women in their forties who want nothing more in life now than to marry, to have a partner and have children, to start a family. They have spent so much of their lives learning how to be so fiercely independent and to achieve in business that they are no longer capable of needing—they're so independent, they don't need someone else." Michelle, who earlier expressed her appreciation for the women's movement, here sounds much like Charleen at Victory Church, who, as the reader will recall, feels that feminism is one of the worst things that ever happened to America. Similarly, Laura, who insists that femi-nists should push for still further changes, echoes the words of antifemi-nists when she talks about the women's movement's impact on society's perception of motherhood. Laura claims that when she took almost a year off from work after having her first child, she realized just how chal-lenging motherhood is. Contrary to feminist perceptions, "there is noth-ing wrong with being a housewife. God knows I work twice as hard when I'm a full-time mom and housewife as I do when I'm employed. It's a twenty-four-hour job, and that's to be respected. That's promot-ing the best, the betterment of our society in the most tangible way, and that's raising good citizens, you know, good human beings in a world that is becoming more and more chaotic and dangerous." Like the antifeminists introduced earlier, this profeminist believes that most femi-nists do not appreciate the valuable social contribution that stay-at-home mothers make to our society.

Many Jewish profeminists also agree with antifeminists that the women's movement is trying to eliminate male-female differences. Naomi told me that she herself had been very involved in feminist poli-tics. "I used to work for the women's center up in Portland, Oregon, I was the education coordinator, and I led a 'Take Back the Night' march and wrote for a feminist newspaper and organized speakers and work-shops." She feels that feminists have done a lot of positive things, but "they have inadvertently downgraded the positive things that women provide, their role as nurturers, their role as mothers. They try to smooth over these differences between men and women . . . and I think that basically we need to have more separation between men and women rather than less." Naomi contrasts feminist efforts to erase gender differences with Orthodox Judaism's separation of male and female roles which she sees as beneficial to both sexes. Thus she argues that women's limited role in the synagogue allows men to feed their egos by being leaders, while it permits women—especially overworked women like herself—to attend services late and leave early without feeling guilty. Dana expresses similar views. She is grateful for the feminist movement's efforts to end discrimination based on gender differences: "It shouldn't be that women are always the ones at home. Men can't have babies, but they *can* raise them." Yet she is critical of what she perceives as a feminist effort to eliminate those differences: "I think men and women are different, and I think that we require different things. . . . I don't think women should try to imitate men or vice versa." Dana and Naomi both support the women's movement, but they feel that in order to be successful it needs to change its focus from imitating men to affirming women.

Like antifeminists, several profeminists at Beth Israel feel that the women's movement has become too radical and is no longer representative of the concerns of most American women. Laura believes that "ten years ago, twenty years ago, feminism was critical to the advancement of women" and that "often we have to offer a radical extreme" to reach people on the other side "who are so conservative—you have to swing way over to the other side just to wake them up." Unfortunately, "I think the radicalism still continues within much of the women's movement. For instance, the National Organization for Women, I get their literature, and I'll throw it right in the trash. I think they have not been able to adapt to the change in realities of where women are at today. They are still way to the left when they don't *need* to be that far left anymore. . . . They have remained entrenched in the stands that they were in twenty or thirty years ago, and now *they* are the ones refusing to move, just as the conservatives refuse to move. . . . I think the majority of women are much more in the middle." Laura and other women feel that the contemporary feminist movement is too concerned with reproductive choice and gay rights and is not doing much to change the problems faced by working mothers such as themselves. As Laura puts it: "A lot of these issues [espoused by NOW], I'll just say to myself 'This does not represent me.'" In pushing for gender equality, Jewish women argue, feminists ignore the reality that most women have children. Whatever their legal rights in the workplace, it is women who get pregnant, go through labor, give birth, and nurse a child. By glossing over those fundamental differences between the sexes, the women's movement has unwittingly harmed many women. Thus Susan, a mother of three who teaches full-time at a Hebrew day school, blames feminism for imposing a double shift on many working women: "Yes, we have created a lot more options for ourselves. There are a lot more things for us to do, but I think men stayed—with all this liberation they are still stuck to the few choices they had before. So now, besides being the mother and the housekeeper and the caretaker, we can also have a full-time job. Well, gee thanks, who's great idea was that? That's really what feminists have created, a society of women trying to be superwomen, and it is just not possible!" Laura, too, feels that women are overburdened. "If a woman gets a call from school that her child is ill, she—not her husband—is generally the one that needs to go home." She believes that feminists should be pushing to create alternative options for women—not to merely give them the same options as men. Leonora would agree.

> What I don't see in this country is a sort of basic acceptance
> that, yes, women are going to be in the work force and, yes,
> they are going to have children, and, yes, you're going to have
> to make accommodations, and, yes, it's going to cost you
> economically. That's life. I think it's much easier for women to
> work in Israel because there it's so accepted that women are
> mothers, that there are part-time jobs, that women need that. I
> was just reading this book by a Jewish feminist, and she writes
> as a criticism of Israel that 60 percent of the women in the
> work force have part-time jobs. See, I see that as the way that
> women can *survive* having jobs and children

The comments of Leonora, Susan, and Laura reflect a deep disappointment in the promises of the women's movement. As much as they would like to make more money, they also want to be with their children. As much as they expect their husband to participate in child rearing, these women have come to accept that mothers will do more. To come to terms with that reality, they have turned to traditional roles that affirm that women's connection to children is primary. They expect the women's movement, in turn, to accept that connection as a starting point before pushing for any further changes. To the extent that the movement denies that connection, Jewish profeminists, like antifeminists, see it as out of touch with the needs of most ordinary women.

Jewish profeminists, then, are actually quite ambivalent about the feminist movement. That ambivalence is most intense when they consider the movement's impact on the Orthodox Jewish community. On the one hand, profeminists at Beth Israel assert that feminism has encouraged some positive changes in their tradition, such as allowing women to study Talmud. Feminism "has challenged us to be more creative," Dana told me, "and I think that's healthy, because when religion gets stagnant, there's no growth and that's when people get turned off." Ketza, daughter of a rabbi, agrees. "The women's movement created a lot of questioning within Orthodox Judaism, and some of that is good. People like Debra [Rabbi Feldman's wife] who have kept their maiden name, that would have never happened fifty years ago. And women having their own careers. That's just not what Orthodox Jewish women did." Questioning and changing, according to these women, is what keeps a religion alive.

On the other hand, they are afraid that too much questioning can be harmful. They feel that many aspects of Orthodox Judaism do not need to be changed because, unlike secular American society, the Jewish community has generally not oppressed its women. Thus Marcia insisted that "women always had a place of respect in Orthodox Judaism. Orthodox men don't tell jokes about their mother-in-laws or their wives. They don't use foul language. They don't use sexually suggestive language. They don't do obscene things, they don't make obscene gestures to women in the streets. A lot of things on a day-to-day basis that the women's movement addressed, they don't exist in Orthodoxy, it was never an issue." American society, she asserted, needed the women's movement a lot more than Orthodox Judaism did because the former was far more sexist than the latter. Similarly, Naomi pointed out,

> Orthodox Judaism takes into consideration and deals best with
> the differences between men and women. We still see unbeliev-
> able amounts of rape, incest, abuse. It's not getting better. All
> the feminist awareness and all the feminist groups, and it's not

getting better. I think the separation that we have in Orthodoxy provides a healthier response to these types of problems.
There should be separation, there should be modesty. We
shouldn't have relations before marriage. It should not be
encouraged. . . . There's been sexual tension from when God
created the world, you can't erase that. Making things equal
doesn't erase these inherent tensions that exist.

While Naomi agrees with many of the women's movement's goals and
even believes that some of them can be incorporated into the Jewish
tradition, she feels that feminists can learn from Orthodox Jews because
Judaism has resolved many of the problems facing the larger society.
Judaism, according to this argument does not need to be changed because it already *is* feminist.

Though Judaism and feminism need not be at odds, the latter can
be a serious threat to the former. Despite their support for feminist challenges to tradition, Ketza and Dana are wary that change may go too
far. "The thing that is so attractive about Orthodox Judaism," Ketza told
me, "is that what we are doing, and presumably the way our children
are being raised and the schooling that they are getting, is the same as
in generations past. It is a tradition, you know. This was going on for
centuries." She cites the example of another synagogue where they have
started adding the names of women (Sarah, Rebecca, Rachel, and Leah)
to the names of the patriarchs (Abraham, Isaac, and Jacob) during the
Amidah. "That was one of the things that got us to leave that shul,
because you can go into any shul around the world and that central
prayer is the same anywhere. And you start screwing around with that
and changing it, then it's like closing a chapter on history. It's like you
are going to write your own now. I want to keep that connection to
the past." While Ketza supports changes that leave the basic structure
of the synagogue service intact (e.g., separate rituals for women or girls),
she rejects those that seek to transform that structure (e.g., giving
women a more active role in community rituals). Feminist additions to
tradition are acceptable, but changes of tradition are not. The line between changes and additions is a fine one, and profeminists are often
confused about where to draw it. Because "we do not know how women
are going to reconcile feminist views and their role in the Orthodox

community," profeminists at Beth Israel err on the side of caution. Though they affirm the need for such reconciliation, they would agree with antifeminists like Rivka that feminism is a product of the larger society and that conceding to feminist demands is a form of adaptation that threatens the survival of the Orthodox community.

Profeminists at St. Joseph's have different concerns. Among conservative Catholics, support for the feminist movement is exceedingly rare. I could find only one woman who identified herself as conservative and who can be characterized as profeminist: Barbara. As we have seen in preceding chapters, Barbara's personal experience with gender discrimination has led her to support the feminist movement, arguing not only that its impact on society has been positive but that continued activism is necessary to protect women. Yet like profeminists at Beth Israel, Barbara is critical of the movement as well: "I think the women's movement has made a lot of women like me feel not quite as important as the female lawyer or judge or doctor and all those—fine, if that's what they feel they're called for, do it, but don't stand there and tell me you're better than me—because that's what they do, because you're not! I think the women's movement has contributed to making the role of motherhood and wifehood seem not quite so important, and I think that's wrong because it's very important." Barbara would agree with antifeminists that the movement ignores real gender differences, devalues motherhood and homemaking, and has become too extreme to represent most ordinary women.

Like Jewish profeminists, Barbara is ambivalent about the impact the feminist movement has had on her church. On the one hand, she thinks it is positive because the movement got the church to be more inclusive of women, for example through the use of gender-neutral language in parts of the Catholic liturgy. On the other hand, she feels her church does not need any further changes. Arguing that women at St. Joseph's already have plenty of power, she lamented that "it's hard trying to be a liberated woman in a world that says Catholic women are put down. I don't feel put down. I don't feel put down by the church. I feel put down by *them*, the liberated women who think I'm being put down by my church." Barbara knows that many liberal women in her church would disagree with her, and she believes these women have been negatively influenced by feminists. She argues that feminists are creating unnecessary divisions, particularly in their effort to get women ordained. Though she is sympathetic to the idea of female priests, she fears that such a change will tear her church apart. Women like Barbara do not fear, as do profeminists at Beth Israel, that the feminist movement threatens their community's survival. The Roman Catholic Church, after all, is the largest Christian denomination in the world. Rather, they are afraid that the movement may induce "another Protestant Reformation," forever dividing their church.

The women at Victory Church, by contrast, seem more concerned about the feminist impact on society than on their church. I was able to locate very few women who felt that the feminist movement is good for America as well as for their church. One exception is Karen. A lawyer and divorced mother of three boys, she articulates the Evangelical profeminist position particularly well. Like profeminist Catholics and Jews, she feels that the women's liberation movement was a necessary response to the oppression of women. She praises the achievements of feminism in society as well as in Evangelical communities and insists that sexism persists and that further changes are necessary. Yet Karen, too, criticizes the movement for seeking to eliminate gender differences, devaluing motherhood and homemaking, and being led by extremists who do not represent ordinary American women, particularly with respect to the issues of homosexuality and abortion. Her comments on the latter two issues are worth quoting in full because they resemble so closely the statements made by antifeminist Evangelicals. Karen believes that the secular feminist movement is led by lesbians: "We saw it from the beginning . . . the lesbians made it clear right then and there who was going to take charge of the women's movement. These are injured and hurt people. They are not my enemy, but we're just not touching those people at all with the Gospel . . and I really believe that God— that we are going to hear about it." Just as she fears God's punishment for feminist efforts to legitimate homosexuality, Karen believes God must set an end to the feminist massacre of children: "I think that abortion is murder. I am honestly afraid of a curse to come over our nation that won't be lifted, a curse from God, 'cause I think God absolutely abhors any injustice of that kind. When you have somebody who's utterly helpless to defend themselves, and you have a society that not only permits but promotes the abuse of that person—there is a God in heaven, and we will hear from him eventually." Reading only these two statements, one would conclude that Karen rejects the secular women's movement as much as the most ardent antifeminists in her church. Like those women she associates the movement with homosexuality and abortion and believes that it is Christianity, not feminism, that will ultimately liberate women. Yet Karen is not an antifeminist. Despite her misgivings, she insists that the overall impact of the feminist movement has been positive and supports its continued activism, not only in the secular society but within the Evangelical church. What bothers Karen is that there is no room in the movement for women such as herself.

Karen's strong opposition, not only to reproductive choice but also to gay rights, make her different from the Catholic and Jewish profeminists I interviewed. While Catholic profeminists also oppose abortion, they usually support gay rights, and Orthodox Jewish profeminists do not seem to have strong feelings about either issue. What also makes Karen unique is her deeply held conviction not only that feminism is fully compatible with Christianity, but that churches should take the lead in promoting women's liberation in the larger American society:

> I believe the women's movement is a direct result of the church
> dropping the ball. I believe the church was to spearhead
> women's liberation, but they didn't do it. I think God's plan was
> for the church to spearhead equality. I believe that Abraham
> Lincoln was led by God, and that we saw a great thing happen
> with slavery ending, but somewhere along the line, the church
> dropped the ball with women. And whenever the church does
> not fulfill its mission and it falls to the side, Satan picks up the
> banner, and *he* moves with the movement under *his* banner.
> That is why we've seen so much lesbianism, that's why we've
> seen abortion, that's why we have an abortion problem—
> because if the church had spearheaded the women's movement
> and influenced women, instead of the world influencing
> women, then we would've been teaching them God's prin-
> ciples, and we wouldn't have lesbianism—which is really just a
> rejection of men, and finally women just saying "I'm just
> completely fed up, I don't want anything more to do with
> you"—and the abortion thing. . . . Instead of the church
> impacting society, society has impacted the church. And

> Christian women have been awakened to the inequality and
> the injustices [in the church], not because of godly women
> speaking out from the word of God, but because women on the
> outside have spoken a word of truth, it's truth but it's cloaked in
> so many other untruths. . . . Oh yeah, we dropped the ball, this
> was not the way it was supposed to have been.

Karen's comments contrast sharply with those of profeminists at St. Joseph's and Beth Israel. Both Catholic and Orthodox Jewish support-ers of the women's movement see the source of that movement as secular and believe that changes in their community are a spill-over effect of changes in the larger society. Karen, by contrast, insists that feminism originated in Evangelical Christianity and has spread from there to secu-lar American society. She blames the extremism of the secular move-ment on the church which has abandoned its mission of fighting for equality. To the extent that feminism is incompatible with Christian-ity it is because Evangelical leaders have lost interest in defining what feminism should be about. If Evangelicals once again become involved in the women's movement then it can promote the kinds of changes that God intended for this country. Karen's rhetoric reminds us of what Robert Bellah calls "civil religion," a term he coined to describe the patriotic myths and rituals that affirm the belief in America as a cho-sen nation with a special destiny (Bellah 1967). While civil religion uses biblical language, it is not tied to any particular religious denomi-nation and is frequently cited by both liberals and conservatives. Karen here expresses a kind of Evangelical feminist civil religion that identi-fies both women's liberation and the spread of Christianity with the mission of America. While profeminists like Karen are rare at Victory Church, her comments are significant because they reflect a worldview that is unique to Protestants.

The Politics of Ambivalence

The relationship of conservative Christian and Orthodox Jewish women to the feminist movement is far more complex than one would expect. Both the religious right and feminist leaders like to think that women in conservative religious communities actively oppose the feminist movement and that this is a significant reason why they joined a conservative tradition. In reality, however, the women I studied were deeply ambivalent about the movement. Not only did all three communities contain both pro-and antifeminists, but upon close examination there is not much difference between the two categories: antifeminists do not want to live without the changes the movement has wrought, and profeminists are still critical of many aspects of the movement. Moreover, the women who fall into each category are not necessarily those one might expect. Many working women, for example, are antifeminists, while a number of homemakers are profeminist.

Conservative Christian and Orthodox Jewish women's ambivalence about the feminist movement resembles the feelings of many American women, especially younger ones. As Elizabeth Fox-Genovese (1996:31–32) has pointed out, "Polls show that women's issues—equal pay for equal work, sexual harassment, day care, and shared responsibility in marriage—have mass support." Yet "only about a third of American women are willing to call themselves feminists," and the proportion of college women is "fewer than one in five." Her research demonstrates that secular women express many of the same criticisms of feminism as the religious women in my study. Supporters of the feminist movement complain, with some justification, that many of these women take their improved status for granted and notice only the supposed downsides of feminism: it's failure to acknowledge and appreciate real gender differences, its devaluation of motherhood and homemaking, and its extremist leaders. Feminist activists also point out that they have continued to promote the kinds of changes that all American women (including those in this study) care about, for example, legislation that would allow both male and female workers to spend more time with their children. Unfortunately, such "family friendly" activism does not get as much media attention as feminist efforts to secure abortion and lesbian rights, issues that religious conservatives oppose and even liberal and secular women have mixed feelings about. Until feminist leaders convince them otherwise, many American women, like the religious women in this study, will not feel represented by the feminist movement.

Ironically, women in conservative religious communities— antifeminists in particular—actually resemble some of the most radical secular feminists today. Debra Kaufman (1991) has noted the similarities between radical feminists and the newly Orthodox Jewish women she had studied, and I believe her observations are applicable to conservative Christians as well. Both radical feminists and religious conservatives celebrate gender differences. For both groups, "women represent a special source of strength, knowledge, and power." Just as radical feminists believe that "men see the world from a dualistic viewpoint, rationally attempting to analyze and exploit nature, while women trust their intuitive mode of knowing," conservative Christian and Orthodox Jewish women "claim that there are natural differences between the sexes, and that women's superior moral sensitivities arise from their greater intimacy with the everyday physical world" (152). Finally, religiously conservative women, like radical feminists, have argued that this is a man's world that should be reformed according to women's values.[3]

Kaufman argues that "the fundamental distinction between the two" is that "radical feminists have politicized the reproductive sphere, believing that it determined how economic production as well as other forms of culture are organized" while Orthodox Jewish women have "no analogous understanding of the politics of sexuality" (153–154). I would like to suggest an alternative interpretation. Many women in this study understood only too well that the American economic system is centered around the needs of men. Women had to deny their reproductive nature in order to compete with men in the marketplace on male terms, either by having abortions or by not giving their children the care that they deserved. The women in this study *were* politicized by this understanding. Not only did most of them support increasing the number of women in politics, but they were adamant about electing candidates that cared about women's issues. To them, caring about women's issues meant supporting a woman's inherent desire to nurture her child rather than abort it. It meant restructuring the workplace in such a way as to allow women to have a career *and* care for their children. While radical feminists seek to free women from the burdens of reproduction (through contraception, abortion, and perhaps in the future through technology), conservative religious women want society to affirm and support their reproductive nature by freeing both men and women from inflexible work arrangements.[4] Their political standpoint clearly differs from that of radical feminists, but they are politicized just the same.

Their deep ambivalence about the feminist movement is common to all three groups in this study. However, there are also important differences. There are far more antifeminists at Victory church and St. Joseph's than at Beth Israel. Among antifeminists, Evangelicals are upset that feminism discourages male responsibility, making men into homosexuals, while Catholics feel feminism discourages female responsibility, causing more women to have abortions. Jewish antifeminists, by contrast, are more concerned with the impact of feminism on Orthodox Judaism than either of those issues. Among profeminists, both Jews and Catholics express some doubts over whether their religious communities should accommodate feminism, the former because they fear for the survival of Jewish tradition, the latter because they fear further division in their church. By contrast, it was a profeminist Evangelical who insisted that feminism originated in her community and that it is, or should be, her church's mission to spread feminist values to the rest of society.

How can we explain these differences? One reason is education. Jews as a group tend to be more educated than Evangelicals or Catholics. Since the communities I studied reflect these broader patterns and since support for feminism correlates positively with higher levels of education, it is not surprising that Beth Israel had the most profeminists, while Victory Church had the least. A second reason is numbers. Another researcher could probably find an Orthodox Jewish congregation that was less supportive of feminism than Beth Israel, and an Evangelical congregation that was more supportive of it than Victory Church, but it is also true that historically Evangelicals, by sheer numbers, have been in a better position than Orthodox Jews to oppose a broad cultural movement such as feminism. Neither of these reasons, however, explains the particular concerns of pro-and antifeminists in each community.

A more narrow focus may provide some insight. As we shall see in the next chapter, the differences between Evangelical, conservative Catholic, and Orthodox Jewish perceptions of the feminist movement are even more pronounced when we examine their responses to two key feminist political issues: reproductive choice and gay rights. This makes sense, since for many women the feminist movement is a rather nebulous entity, while abortion and homosexuality are more concrete issues that are subject to specific political decisions in which they can become actively involved (at the time of this research, for example, Congress was debating the question of gays in the military). All of the women in this study oppose both abortion and homosexuality, but they do so for very different reasons, and their willingness to take political action to express their opposition varies considerably. Examining these differences will help us gain a more nuanced understanding of the relationship between religious conservatives and the feminist movement.

Chapter 9

Conflict with Secular America—Abortion and Homosexuality

Homosexuals, abortionists, feminists and humanists . . .
their goal for the 1990s is the complete elimination of
God from American society.

— JERRY FALWELL, 1993[1]

THE YEAR I BEGAN this research, President Clinton was creating a furor among conservatives by proposing to end the ban on gays in the military. As of this writing, anti-abortion activists are threatening to disrupt the Republican convention if a tolerance plank is inserted into the party platform. Reproductive choice and gay rights have become key symbols in what is widely perceived as a culture war over American values. That war is not just about reconciling secular and religious values but about balancing individual rights with the needs of the community. Giving women the choice to reject a child after it has been conceived challenges the traditional assumption that motherhood is the primary role God has given to women. Designating homosexual relationships as a legitimate alternative lifestyle questions the traditionalist view that men and women are fundamentally different and that God has assigned them different roles. Accepting homosexuality and abortion, then, means we can no longer take for granted that women will take care of children. It is partly for these reasons that liberal feminists have championed, and religious conservatives have opposed, both reproductive choice and gay rights. The feminist movement, represented by organizations such as NOW, has spearheaded the liberal position in the culture war, which insists that choosing who to sleep with or when to have a child are part of an individual's right of free expression. The religious right, represented by organizations such as the Christian

Coalition, has become the standard-bearer for the conservative position which resists such expression as a threat to community.

It is not at all clear who will win this war. During the Reagan years, it seemed that Christian conservatives had managed to halt—if not reverse—feminist progress. But now that the FDA has approved the French abortion pill and increasing numbers of corporations are granting benefits to partners of homosexual employees, the religious right's effort to oppose abortion and homosexuality has acquired a new urgency. As feminist efforts are succeeding, religious right leaders are beginning to see the need to reach beyond their traditional Evangelical Protestant base to include conservative Catholics and Jews as well. How successful have they been in this effort? One way to find out is to ask conservative Christian and Orthodox Jewish women how they feel about abortion and homosexuality and the movements to oppose reproductive choice and gay rights. The answers I got from the women in this study suggest that the religious right leaders still have a way to go in building an effective cross-denominational alliance. While Evangelical, conservative Catholic, and Orthodox Jewish women all see abortion and homosexuality as a problem, their perceptions of what *causes* that problem and how to *resolve* it are very different.

Christianizing America

The women at Victory Church firmly believe that having or performing an abortion and engaging in homosexual activity are grave sins. They are therefore understandably concerned about what they see as an "epidemic of homosexuality" and a dramatic rise in the abortion rate. The main cause of this increase in immorality, they believe, is a lack of accountability. Abortion and homosexuality are only two of many social problems in modern American culture that are the result of people not being held accountable for what they do. Fathers leave their children without supporting them, criminals don't go to jail, drug addicts receive public assistance, politicians make empty promises, homosexual teachers seduce innocent school children, and women who have casual sex can simply eliminate the product of those encounters. Not being held accountable for our sins is the disease of modern society.[2]

Although Evangelical women talk about respect for life, a far more

prominent theme in their discussion of abortion is moral accountability. Today's women are more promiscuous, they argue, because abortion
allows them to avoid the consequences of their sin. As Ronda put it,
"If you're going to be going out and sleeping around and not marry
and violating God's principles, then you need to be responsible for the
outcome. If you set out on that path, then you need to take full responsibility for the results." Economic considerations such as being
unemployed, lacking a husband to support the child, or needing to fin-
ish school are dismissed as factors a woman should have thought of before she got pregnant when she made the decision to have sex. Although
they are willing to allow abortion in cases of rape and incest, these
women believe that the pro-choice lobby exaggerates the incidence of
those exceptional cases in order to keep convenience abortions legal
for all women. Says Ronda: "They use all those theoretical cases, and
they'll give us the real gut-wrencher of the child who was raped by her
father, but usually it's not those situations, those are a small percent-
age. When you think about abortion, the greatest demand for that is
basically teenagers. Promiscuity. Fornication. Most abortions are basically for people who don't want the inconvenience."

Consensual sex, unlike rape and incest, is a woman's choice for
which she "must account to God." The fact that women are *not* held
accountable and are actually encouraged to "murder their children" is,
in the eyes of many Evangelicals, a symptom of a diseased society.
Katrina summed it up succinctly: "Abortion isn't the issue. It's a symptom of the disease of society. It's just one of many things that is wrong."

The solution to the problem, therefore, is not just to ban abortion
but to reform the moral structure of American society. Almost every
time I attended Sunday services at Victory Church, Pastor Jordan would
inveigh against the failure of liberals to enforce morality and the need
for conservatives to re-Christianize society. He would be pleased to know
that most of the women in his church agree with him. As citizens of a
society that permits what they consider to be an immoral act, most
Evangelical women feel it is their Christian duty to change that society. Many women are active in the pro-life movement, and most vote
on their conviction. While interviewing women at Victory, I was repeatedly asked to sign anti-abortion petitions, and had to explain over
and over again that political involvement was not appropriate to my

position as a researcher. In one conversation, I sat at the kitchen table minding the children, while Sandra was at her desk stacking index cards for a pro-life letter-writing campaign. "Part of the problems we have today," she told me, "are a result of the church retreating and not taking an active stand on social issues. The churches are the only ones that cry out for morality, so when we retreat, then morality retreats, and society is going to suffer." Sandra has been arrested for picketing an abortion clinic, yet that only strengthens her commitment. She believes that most people are naturally selfish and inclined to fight for their individual rights. The role of religion therefore is to counter selfishness and "lead people to take responsibility for each other and hold each other accountable for what we do." According to Sandra and other women at Victory, it is the duty of all who call themselves Christian to promote such responsibility.

One way to promote responsibility is through the kind of political activism Sandra engages in. Yet political activism alone is not sufficient, according to these women, because responsibility can ultimately not be enforced by law. Many women point to the rising rate of crime in American society as an indicator of the failure of the legal system to solve our most pressing social problems. Responsibility, they argue, is a voluntary characteristic that comes from being taught the right values—Christian values. America was founded as a Christian nation and the problems we have today are a direct result of the secularization of society. As Katrina put it, "Abortion is wrong, but so are a lot of other things, and I think what we have to dwell on as Christians is not the abortion issue, or this, or that, but it's the people. If people have a relationship with God, they're not going to get an abortion. They're not going to beat their wives, mistreat their children, if they have a relationship with God that's working. And that's what we have to deal with . . . we need to get these people saved." Katrina does not picket abortion clinics nor organize letter-writing campaigns to her senator. Rather, she focuses on evangelization. Every person who becomes born again as a result of her efforts will come to embrace a pro-life position and therefore represents another step in the direction of reforming society. Because each convert can bring yet another person into the fold, she is confident that the pro-life movement will grow exponentially and will eventually constitute the majority view in this country. In short, whether through political activism or through evangelization, the way to resolve the abortion problem is to expand Christian values to the rest of America, to "bring people to Christ."

A similar line of reasoning is applied to homosexuality: the women at Victory Church believe that homosexuality is a societal disease that results from a lack of moral accountability and can be cured by conversion to Christianity. In this view, God has set moral rules that everyone should follow, including the prohibition of homosexuality. As Jennifer puts it, "Our country was founded on a lot of good Christian principles, and that's one of them—I mean God says homosexuality is an abomination, and I agree with that." The problem is that society no longer expects people to live up to those rules, a failure in enforcement that has resulted in moral laxity and degeneration. Charleen, for example, relates a conversation she had with a coworker about whether homosexuality should be accepted as an alternative lifestyle. "Don't tell me this is OK! The Bible says—and I just read this to my boss yesterday 'cause her brother-in-law is homosexual—it says in Leviticus that when a man sleeps with a man as with a woman, it's an abomination to God. Now that pretty well clears it up. . . . To think that there are so many gays and lesbians now being leaders in our government, it makes me sick!" The presence of openly homosexual persons in government positions, she continues, sends the message to our society "that promiscuity and perversity is acceptable." To Charleen, the issue is simple: if the Bible says homosexual behavior is sinful, then it should not be tolerated.

Homosexuality, to these women, is not genetic, but a moral choice. Even women who know gays personally do not see homosexuality as a legitimate alternative lifestyle. Sandra, for example, told me, "I had a brother who was a homosexual, died of AIDS, so all I see is it being something that damages people and destroys. . . . I don't think it's natural, not what God created men to be. The whole thing that it's just in the genes, that you don't have a choice and that you are homosexual by birth, I think it's just a big lie." I was told that Lisa had been a lesbian before she was "born again." She admitted, "I still have some friends that I had before. They're homosexual, and they live a homosexual lifestyle, and I love them dearly but I can't accept their lifestyle anymore, whereas before I accepted it. But now I can't accept it, and I let

them know that." These Evangelical women insist that unlike a person who is black or female, homosexuals are not born that way. Thus
Lisa believes her attraction to women had to do with the insensitivity
of men in her life. "My friends tell me, they tease me, that I'm brain-
washed. . . . I really want to get married now. I didn't want to get
married for many years. I just didn't like men. I didn't like their posses-
siveness or their masculinity. I mean the real macho types, yuk, it still
detests me [sic] when I think about it. But I guess that's why . . . most
of my friends were gay. Because there was a really sensitive side to them
that I could get close to." Though she isn't interested in dating anyone
at Victory Church, Lisa hopes that some day she will meet a "good
Christian man." When I asked Sandra why she thought her brother was
gay, she blamed it on bad family relationships. "I had four brothers and
he was kind of the one who was different. He wasn't that much into
sports. He liked to cook and became a very good chef in San Francisco."
Those feminine attributes led her father and brothers to abuse him.
"And then when my father left, my brothers carried on that hostility
towards him, so I think that was the beginning of it . . . maybe he was
trying to find something that he lost in these relationships with men.
That's the only way I can reason it away." As we were talking, Sandra's
three-year-old son walked into the room—proudly wearing his sister's
clothing. Sandra was visibly distraught. "The pediatrician assures me it
is just a phase," she said, laughing nervously. Sandra acknowledges that
her brother was different from the beginning—but she has convinced
herself that it was her family's response to that difference, not something inherent in her brother, that made him become a homosexual. If
only he had received the right kind of nurturing, he would have turned
out "normal." If only he had found the right church, he might have
chosen to change his ways.

Because they see it as a choice, the women at Victory Church believe that homosexuality can be cured by conversion to Christianity.
Having changed her ways, Lisa now comes to terms with her former
life by attempting to reform her gay friends.

> My friend, Randy, has come to me and said that he wanted to
> have a change. And it wasn't because I went to him all the
> time and said, "Randy, you're going to go to hell. You're going

to burn for life." But I would talk to him, 'cause he'd call me and tell me about his boyfriend problems. And I'd say, "Well, you're never going to be happy, 'cause it's just not a natural lifestyle." I think it's a choice. Because if it was biological, then that means God created them that way. And God is a loving God, there's no way he'd create anyone in a way that they could not be loved and accepted for who they are—and homosexuality is not something that people love and accept.

Lisa admits that gays are discriminated against, yet she does not expect the discriminators to change. Instead, she thinks she can change homosexuals by converting them to her religion.

The women at Victory Church feel that conversion can be encouraged by passing appropriate laws. Just as the lack of stiff penalties has increased adolescent drug use, so society's tolerance for gays and lesbians has increased the incidence of homosexuality. If the law "held gays accountable for their perverse behavior," they would be more motivated to seek help. More than half these women feel that gays should not be protected by equal rights laws. They oppose lifting the ban on gays in the military (which was a big issue in the media at that time) and are adamant that schools should have the right to not hire gay teachers. "I wouldn't want a gay person teaching my kids," Katrina told me. "Because most gay people are very outspoken about what they do. If they kept it to themselves, then that would be fine, but the people I've known that are gay are openly gay and make no bones about it. There's no way I want someone like that teaching my kids, or being near my kids. So I guess that's discrimination. I don't want homosexuals teaching. That's part of the reason my kids are not in public school, that's a big reason, 'cause of the morality that they teach, or lack of it, that homosexuality is OK. It's not OK! Not simply because it's perverse and disgusting, but because God says it's not OK." Public institutions should reflect public values, and the majority of the public, Evangelicals insist, is Christian. The secularization of our schools, the government, and the military, therefore reflects the disproportionate influence of secular minorities on our legal system. Louisa, whose husband is in the military, said that homosexuals "are a very powerful lobby in the American government, and if they get into the military, there are going to be a lot of other things. If the ban on gays in the military is lifted, then you've got the issue of homosexual marriage, because they want to legalize marriage between homosexuals as well, which means that they are going to have the same rights to pensions and health care as heterosexual couples." Many women fear that prohibiting employment discrimination against gays will result in the extension of gay rights to other areas of life, or worse yet, result in quotas that may force people to hire homosexuals. As Stephanie puts it: "Once you start passing all these laws, they don't know when to stop, and the next thing you know, they're wanting to let homosexuals teach our children and all that. It's like, where does it all end?" The only way to end it is for Christian women like themselves to become active in opposing homosexuality. Whatever method is employed, political activism or evangelism, the women are convinced that success is assured—not only because God is on their side but because the rest of America once shared their views and has only recently been led astray. It is their task, they feel, to bring America back to God.

Empowering Women

The women at St. Joseph's would disagree. While conservative Catholics, too, condemn abortion and homosexuality as sinful, they have a very different view of what causes these problems and how they should be solved. For the women in this church, the main problem represented by abortion is not that women are not being held accountable but that they have lost touch with their female bodies, their natural biological selves. Life is sacred, and the natural female response is to want to nurture that life. Beatrice, who has seven children, argued that "women have to get in touch with their biological selves again. They are trying to deny that, which is a very strong part of us, and I think that's going to be key. . . . To kill your own child, with whatever rationale, a woman should feel that is wrong. It's really a contradiction of something so basic, that that's going to hurt her terribly. . . . So it's really up to women to keep that alive, the sacredness of life. It is up to women because men aren't going to do it. They don't have that sense. It's not within their body." Beatrice's focus on the body and on what is natural reflects the influence of Catholic sacramentalism and of natural law theology. It also suggests a feminist concern: the awareness and appreciation of woman's body. Indeed, many women at St. Joseph's responded to my abortion questions by raising feminist themes. They argue, for example, that having children is "a special gift" that women contribute to society, but that, like many other female contributions, it is not valued as equal to the achievements of men. They feel that feminists' desire to be equal to men has led them to buy into patriarchal norms that ultimately devalue women: if a woman wants to compete in the job market, she must "deny her reproductive nature by—if birth control doesn't work—by abortion." They believe that the moral deterioration of American society derives in part from male domination and "an overemphasis on masculine characteristics and contributions such as competition and economic achievement." Yet they also hope that, while more and more men have become obsessed with material production, women's biology can keep them in touch with the sacred: the creation of life itself. The rise in the abortion rate, therefore, reflects not a moral laxity in women but alienation from their own bodies and their lack of power in a sexist system.

From this perspective, the fight against abortion becomes a movement to empower women. For conservative women at St. Joseph's, abortion must be banned not to hold women accountable but to create a society that truly values women. Rita sees her position as head of her church's right to life group as "truly feminist" because she is getting society to respect "what is womanly, what is distinctly female": motherhood. Similarly, Barbara suggested:

> I think women are going to do more to end abortion than men.
> People seem to think that [ending abortion] is a violation
> of women. The new Supreme Court nominee said "to keep
> women equal we must keep abortion legal." I have no idea
> where they connect [that to] being equal to men. Men are not
> allowed to kill people, why should women be allowed to kill
> people? I don't understand that at all, and I think women are
> going to end this. I don't think men are. When women begin to
> realize, "This is not my body being flushed down the toilet, this
> is somebody else's," and when women who already believe that
> realize, "My voice is important," then change will come.

Many women at St. Joseph's feel that they, not men, must assume leadership of the pro-life movement. Yet despite their feminist rhetoric, the solutions they propose are even more conservative than those of Evangelicals. Evangelicals focus on the woman's choice to have sex—and therefore are willing to make exceptions for victims of rape and incest who did not have a choice. Catholic women believe that what caused the pregnancy is irrelevant; what matters is that God has given her a child and that because of her female biology she should want to have that child. Conservative Catholics have adopted the feminist language of women's empowerment, but they also insist on a biological determinism that is incompatible with feminist principles.

Conservative Catholics' use of feminist language reflects their awareness that a growing number of women in their church are supportive of reproductive choice. In contrast to Victory Church, conservatives at St. Joseph's regularly interact with large numbers of liberal church members. As my interviews with liberal Catholics revealed, there are deep divisions over gender issues. While St. Joseph's has one of the most active pro-life committees in Southern California, the church also has a feminist Bible-study group and a vocal movement to place more women in church leadership positions. Although conservatives insist that a few disgruntled feminists are misrepresenting the views of most Catholic women, they are also afraid that a growing number of women are listening to those feminists. In order to enlist these women for the pro-life cause, conservatives are repackaging it as a feminist effort. Whether or not such repackaging will work, it suggests that what concerns conservative Catholics as much as, if not more than, the secularization of America is the liberalization of their own church.

Conservative Catholic women voice similar concerns in their discussion of homosexuality. Although opposed to homosexual relationships, they are aware that many other women in their church support tolerance for gays and lesbians. Just as they do not want their opposition to abortion to be interpreted as antifeminist, conservative women, especially younger ones, do not want their opposition to homosexuality to be labeled as intolerant and reactionary. As one woman, who insisted on remaining nameless, put it, "I believe that [not having an] abortion, that's a divine decree, and [the prohibition against] homosexuality—though I'd probably get slammed in the face if I said this in a mixed

crowd—I believe that's a divine decree too. Practicing that type of behavior is wrong. I mean, that's really hard for me to say because in this
day and age that's so conservative, but that's what I believe for myself."
I asked this woman what she meant by "mixed crowd": homosexuals
and heterosexuals? Catholics and non-Catholics? "No," she responded,
"just, you know, people in my church." Her perception that others would
disagree with her reflects a dilemma faced by many conservative Catholics that is not an issue for Evangelicals: conservative Catholics are a
minority within their own church. Their most immediate struggle is not
with the secular society but with liberal Catholics.

Perhaps because of their interaction and dialogue with more liberal church members, the women at St. Joseph's were more sympathetic
to homosexuals than the women at Victory. For conservative Catholics, the problem with homosexuality is that it is unnatural. Bridget,
for example, asserted that "it goes against everything in nature. It's not
a normal activity. I don't think you can fault people for what they think
is their psychological make-up, so homosexuals are OK, but if you
choose that lifestyle, if you say, 'OK, this is what I am going to do,' instead of 'Why is this? Can I change it?' then it's a problem." Similarly,
Beatrice doesn't "think it's a sin if you have that orientation, but if you
openly practice it, I think it would be. Again it goes back to what is
natural . . . so I would consider somebody who pursued that as a lifestyle
to be going in the wrong direction." Homosexuals in this view are not
so much lacking in morality as they suffer from psychological problems.
Some women believe those problems are acquired. Liz who claims to
have done some research on the subject told me that "it's a disorder.
Books that I've been reading emphasize that it's primarily a personality
disorder that comes from deprivation of love from a male, or a female
if you're a lesbian, usually from the parents, the same-sex parent. And
it's a desire to compensate for something missing in that relationship."
Other women feel homosexuality is an orientation you are born with.
Although unnatural, the physical attraction to a member of the same
sex is something the homosexual cannot control. Whether their orientation is acquired or inborn, many conservative Catholic women feel
homosexuals should be pitied, not condemned.

Discriminating against gays and lesbians will thus not solve the
problem. In contrast to Victory Church where most people oppose gay

rights legislation, most conservative Catholic women I interviewed believe that homosexuals should be legally protected against discrimination. Mary's view is typical. "If there's a problem with them, that they
are going after someone at the office, then maybe it should be dealt
with. But if I found out that the woman I work next to was a lesbian,
it wouldn't bother me 'cause I know where I'm coming from. So probably we should not kick them out [of the military] unless it's a serious
problem. . . . Everybody's going to have to deal with their own morals
on that. The homosexual deserves a job just as much as the regular guy."
St. Joseph's youth minister takes a similar position: "I don't think homosexuals should be immediately kicked out of the military, because
they're probably good soldiers too. They are just living out different tendencies that a lot of people won't agree with, but I don't think that's
going to make them less of a hard worker." If homosexuality is a physical or mental—rather than a moral—problem, then punishment will
not work. Just as alcoholics or handicapped people cannot be fired unless their disability interferes with their performance on the job, so homosexuals should be protected by equal opportunity legislation.

This insistence on legal equality does not mean that conservative
Catholic women accept homosexuality as an alternative lifestyle.
Though they assert that a person should not be discriminated against
if someone finds out he or she is gay, most women think homosexuals
should "stay in the closet." Thus the youth minister modifies the tolerant position she took earlier by saying: "I think it's OK if homosexuals
are in the military, but I don't think it should be open. I think their
private life should be kept to themselves." Bridget is much more critical: "Homosexuality is a sexual perversion, OK? I don't think we want
to go around broadcasting our perversions to other people, not more
than rapists would want to broadcast theirs. I don't equate homosexuals with rapists, but, you know, a perversion is not something you're going to be proud and happy about, or that we should be going, 'Gee, it's
OK, it's OK if you're perverted.' Homosexuality, if it's there, OK, live
with it, but you don't advertise it, and you don't encourage it." Women
like Bridget tolerate homosexuality but they don't accept it. Though
they insist that homosexuals should not be punished for their orientation, these women do believe homosexuals should be encouraged to resist their unnatural urges.

The solution to homosexuals' problems, the women argue, is not to pass laws that discriminate against them but for the church to help them gain control over their bodies by encouraging celibacy. Pointing to the Catholic tradition of celibate priests and nuns, conservatives claim that living a life of abstinence is not unreasonable. "From my point of view," Donna asserted, "a homosexual should not practice their homosexuality. And that's what the church is presenting, that there should be no prejudice to that orientation . . . and the fact that there are priests and nuns, we've always had a celibate clergy, for fifteen hundred years at least, so we see nothing wrong with—I guess we have a belief that a person can live a whole life being celibate. It's not to say it won't be hard, but it won't take away from your happiness if you're balanced." Most conservatives at St. Joseph's see homosexuality, like alcoholism, as an addiction to destructive behavior. Just as Alcoholics Anonymous counsels total abstinence as the only means of overcoming one's addiction to alcohol, so these women argue that sexual abstinence is the only way to constructively deal with a homosexual orientation. While abstinence is difficult—both for the alcoholic and for the homosexual—it is certainly possible and need not diminish the quality of one's life experience. When I asked Mary, who has been divorced for twenty years and has never remarried, if she felt that homosexuals should be abstinent, she responded "Yes, but so would I, 'cause I'm not married either. So it doesn't bother me. If I can suffer, they can, too." She laughed. "I'm still alive. I'm not dead with my feelings, but I don't go chasing around men. You live a life of abstinence. It can be done." To conservative Catholics, the fact that priests, as well as monks and nuns, are celibate but can live a fulfilled life refutes any argument that requiring abstinence is unfair to homosexuals. Indeed, the women see becoming a member of the clergy as a valid alternative for homosexuals and others who will not marry to contribute meaningfully to the larger society. The recognition that some of the priests and nuns in the community are individuals who have chosen this alternative may explain why conservative Catholics are relatively tolerant of homosexuals compared to the Evangelicals in this study. "We have to learn to deal with it and make it work," the youth minister told me, "because we're all going to be living together for a really long time, and we can't pretend homosexuals don't exist. . . . We are going to have to compromise somehow." According to these women, the church provides a caring rather than a punitive solution to homosexuals' problems, a solution that uplifts and empowers rather than demeans them.

Protecting Judaism

For the women at Beth Israel, abortion and homosexuality present an entirely different problem. Like their conservative Christian counterparts, Orthodox Jewish women feel that having an abortion or engaging in homosexual activity is sinful, an "abomination to God," that is justifiably prohibited in their community.[3] They, too, believe that the incidence of abortion and homosexuality has increased and see that rise as problematic. Yet Jewish women do not agree with the Evangelical or Catholic diagnosis of what the problem means and what should be done about it.

The women at Beth Israel are well aware of the *halachic* restrictions on abortion. Although Jewish law is theoretically not as strict on abortion as Catholic or Evangelical teaching, it does in effect prohibit abortion in the majority of cases. Rabbis have permitted abortion to protect the physical and mental well-being of the mother as well as in cases of abnormal or defective fetuses. However, such cases are considered exceptions to the general rule that abortion—and certainly abortion on demand—is wrong. Aborting a child because the mother is poor, unmarried, or still in high school is not considered acceptable by most Orthodox rabbis. "Abortion," the women told me, "is prohibited by Jewish law—in most cases, anyway." Several Jewish women praised their tradition for allowing exceptions to this rule that conservative Christians would not allow. According to Leah, a marketing executive at a large corporation, "the Jewish view on abortion is so far ahead of most other religions, forget it, it's light-years away from Catholicism . . . and there's a lot of good things about that. If [the pregnancy] is going to make the woman crazy, if it's going to push her over the edge . . . her decision, all the choices remain in her hands." Yet Leah acknowledges that an Orthodox woman is unlikely to choose abortion. For one, the rabbi would not allow an abortion for many of the cases in which American law permits it. For another, like Evangelicals and Catholics, most women at Beth Israel believe that life begins at conception and that having an abortion is killing your child. "You can see it at three weeks," Michelle said. "There's no question that's not a mass of cells together, you can see little hands and everything, it's definitely a baby." Similarly, Susan said, "I hate when people say 'It's my body, I can do whatever I want.' If you want to say, 'It's my life and I can't have a child in my life,' that's true. But don't talk about it like it is your arm or your leg or your nose." Clearly these women feel abortion is wrong and they fully accept their religion's restrictions on it.

I was therefore surprised to find that almost all of the Orthodox Jewish women I interviewed are pro-choice. "I think [abortion] should be available," Cecelia told me. "The fact of the matter is that people don't have the sexual restrictions that they did fifty or sixty years ago . . . and the byproduct of that is that people are conceiving and becoming pregnant, and I'm not sure I can see what can be gained by someone giving birth to a child that they didn't want to have. . . . I'm not saying that everybody should have abortions, but what about the handful of people who absolutely can't afford it, or are in high school or whatever, and are just forced to have this child that they don't want and probably aren't going to treat very it well after the fact . . . I don't think there's anything good about that." Similarly, Michelle noted that despite all the prevention efforts, teenagers "don't care what you say to them. They're going to spit out babies faster than they're chewing gum. . . . I would much rather see the money being spent on abortion clinics than have to deal with all these unwanted babies." Michelle and Cecelia take a rather pragmatic approach that accepts increased sexual promiscuity as a given and sees abortion as the most efficient means of solving a host of social problems, such as teenage pregnancy, single motherhood, and welfare dependency. Thus they fully support existing legislation that permits abortion on demand.

How do we make sense of this? If these women feel that abortion is murder and accept their rabbis' prohibitions against it, then why do they insist on keeping abortion legal, regardless of the circumstances of the pregnancy? The answer is that Orthodox Jewish women believe that their own values do not apply to American society at large. As Naomi put it, "Abortion is prohibited by Jewish law, but I don't think it should be illegal for other people. That's a strictly religious question." Over and over again I was told that Jewish law does not apply to the rest of society. As Michelle pointed out: "The majority of people out there in the world are not Jewish, and those who are Jewish, the majority are not observant Jews, so they obviously don't adhere to the same standards that I do . . . I can't tell them, 'This is what the Torah says, that you can't have an abortion.' That's not going to mean anything to them." Just as Orthodox Jews do not expect other Americans to follow the laws of kashrut or obey the Sabbath prohibitions, so they think it is not reasonable to expect non-Jews—or even non-Orthodox Jews—to respect halachic rulings on abortion.

The problem underlying the abortion debate therefore is not a lack of accountability, nor a disregard for women's biology, but a question of religious freedom. For women at Beth Israel, limiting the applicability of Jewish law is grounded in a deep concern for the separation of church and state. As Laura explains, if we considered limiting abortion to cases of "rape, incest, health issues—how do you define that? How do you define health issues? Mental health? Physical health? Endangering the baby? Endangering the mother? Where do you—where is the line drawn, and, more importantly, who is there to draw it? Who are the people who are going to say this is acceptable and this is not acceptable? I don't want somebody like Pat Robertson or even the pope telling me when I can have an abortion and when I can't." To Laura, maintaining a woman's right to choose abortion "comes down to a separation of church and state." Though she feels that abortion is wrong in most cases, she fears that making common cause with conservative Christians to outlaw abortion will end up subjecting her community to a Christian government. Because they want to limit state interference in Jewish affairs, most Jewish women are not inclined to join a conservative alliance that seeks to legislate what they consider to be a religious matter.

Their position on homosexuality is backed by a similar line of reasoning. While women at Beth Israel believe it is wrong for an Orthodox Jew to engage in homosexual practice, most women feel that the Jewish prohibition of homosexuality does not apply to secular society. "I think that they should let homosexuals into the military," Miriam told me. "I don't think that's a problem . . . but halacha and homosexuality, that's a big problem." Similarly, Vicky draws a distinction between her Jewish and non-Jewish homosexual friends. "This one guy, since he's not Jewish I don't have a problem in terms of my religion versus his practices, but the other guy is [Orthodox] Jewish and . . . I mean it's just not permitted, it's an abomination in the Torah." Finding out he was gay did not change her friendship with the first man, but caused a serious rift in her relationship with the second man. A similar experience was reported by Leah: "I work with somebody who is gay and Jewish, who left any form of Jewish community when he came out . . . I don't have any answers for him. But it's another thing if they are not Jewish. Now we are talking civil rights! I'm an American. . . . Live and let live." Leah feels pity for her gay coworker for having no choice but to leave his religious community if he wants to openly express his sexual orientation. Yet she does not go so far as to criticize the halachic prohibition against homosexual activity. While supporting this prohibition within the Orthodox community, she insists that for non-Jews expressing one's homosexual orientation is a matter of civil rights. Her perspective is not unique: in contrast to Evangelicals and conservative Catholics, most Jewish women I interviewed believe that openly gay individuals should be allowed to enter the military as well as become school teachers or adopt children. As is the case with abortion, the women at Beth Israel make a clear distinction between the rights of homosexuals in the Jewish community and in the secular society.

This compartmentalization of morality into "what is right for us" versus "what is right for the rest of society" does not come easily. Most women at Beth Israel are deeply ambivalent about homosexuality. Take Laura, for example. When I first asked her about homosexuality, she said: "I don't think that is how people should be. I don't think that it's a real healthy lifestyle. Would I be happy if my kids, if one of my children turned out to be gay? No! I would be very upset about that. So I do make—there is some judgment to make that says no, this is wrong, there is something wrong with this picture, this is not how society grows and flourishes, you know." Laura here indicates that there is something unhealthy and immoral about homosexuality and that it does lead to social decline. Yet only a few minutes later, she told me, "There are plenty of children now—and more and more—of gay couples that need to be . . . we need to give some recognition that this is an alternative lifestyle, that this is, that there is nothing bad about it, because you don't want kids growing up feeling ashamed of who they are and what they come from." She has now completely reversed her previous position, accepting gay couples—with children, no less!—as a fact of life and indicating that there is nothing wrong with their lifestyle. Laura's contradictory statements reveal that she has not resolved the tension between Judaism's prohibition and society's tolerance of homosexuality. Other Orthodox Jewish women are similarly ambivalent. Almost all believe that homosexuality is a permanent genetic trait rather than a sexual preference that can be changed. Yet this belief conflicts with their conviction that homosexuality is an abomination to God. "I have a problem," Naomi admitted. "One of the problems I have in Orthodox Judaism is, I feel that people are born homosexuals, so why is it that God, if he is a compassionate God, would have prohibitions and [say] that it is a sin? I don't know how to answer that question." Neither did Leonora who told me that "as a scientist, the more I read . . . it's really a genetically determined thing. So I just can't think that way, that it's an abomination. But I don't think it's a lifestyle choice either." The women are also torn between their conviction that homosexuality is incompatible with Orthodoxy and what they perceive to be an excessive condemnation by the Orthodox community of actual Jews who are gay. Rachel told me,

> I feel like if I say yes [it is an abomination], then I'm homophobic, and if I say no, then I'm not being honest with myself. I do think it's an abomination. . . . There is something about it to me that is just not right. I bought that line, I'm married, I have children, I believe it works . . . but I think the part that I have a problem with is condemning people as Jews. I see the struggles that people who choose that life go through . . . feeling excluded and feeling isolated and feeling oppressed. It's an abomination to God. Yeah, that's the party line I have to toe for the community that I live in, and I hate it. I don't like it because it excludes a lot of people.

Rachel's fear of being labeled homophobic indicates that she has to some extent embraced the feminist argument that homosexuals should be accepted by society. Yet she also accepts the norms of Orthodox Judaism which indicate that homosexuality is wrong. To Rachel, the fact that homosexuality is sinful does not mean gays and lesbians should be excluded from the Orthodox community. Rather, they should be accepted and tolerated like other sinners whose wrongdoings will ultimately be forgiven or punished by God. The unwillingness of her community to even discuss the matter makes her resentful and angry. Like Leonora, Naomi, and Laura, Rachel struggles with the conflict between secular and Orthodox Jewish perceptions of homosexuality. For Orthodox Jewish women this is a conflict that remains largely unresolved.

While they accept the religious prohibition of homosexuality within their own community, the women at Beth Israel insist that American law must protect the rights of all citizens, including homosexuals—and Jews. Homosexuality, like abortion, ultimately raises questions of religious freedom—a natural concern for a religious minority. Throughout history Jews have learned to survive by keeping to themselves. Frequently persecuted, they nonetheless often achieve financial success and are not unfamiliar with the antisemitic charge that "Jews are taking over America." Perhaps as a result of that experience, they have learned to preserve their religious freedom by not interfering in anyone else's. Orthodox Jews *are* opposed to homosexuality, but the possibility that they will join with conservative Christians to legislate their opposition seems remote.

Divided We Stand

Leaders of the religious right still have a way to go in establishing a broad-based, grassroots, antifeminist alliance that can fight what they see as the twin evils of abortion and homosexuality. Even if they agree with their leaders that these practices are sinful, ordinary women in Evangelical, Catholic, and Jewish communities differ in how they feel such sin should be dealt with. Evangelicals believe sin is on the rise (i.e., the incidence of abortion and homosexuality have increased) because individuals are not held accountable for their actions. This lack of moral accountability is a direct result of the secularization of society; the solution therefore is to Christianize America. Conservative Catholics, on the other hand, see abortion and homosexuality as signs that modern society has alienated us from what is natural: a man's attraction to the female, and a woman's longing to care for a child. In order to reach out to liberal Catholics, conservatives are repackaging the pro-life and antihomosexual stance as empowering to women and

to gays and lesbians. Not once did I hear a conservative Catholic suggest that America needs to be Christianized. The problem for conservative Catholics is not so much the secularization of society as the
liberalization of their own church. For Orthodox Jews, finally, the rise
in sin in the larger society is not a major concern for their community.
Non-Jewish Americans have always behaved in ways that violate Jewish law; the fact that they do so more now than in the past only confirms Jewish women's conviction that they made the right choice to
join the Orthodox community. The specter of a Christian America, to
these women, is far more frightening than living in a sinful society, an
experience they've grown quite accustomed to anyway. Abortion and
homosexuality, in short, mean something very different for different religious conservatives.

These differences between women at Victory Church, St. Joseph's,
and Beth Israel are not unique to these particular communities but reflect broader variations among conservative Protestants, Catholics, and
Jews that are consistent with the findings of other researchers. For example, a national survey conducted by the Princeton Religion Research
Center (1989) found that Catholics are more tolerant of homosexuality than Protestants. While numerous studies have documented conservative Protestant involvement in national abortion politics, Ingersoll
(1993) has noted that Evangelicals recently added homosexuality, which
they perceive as connected to the feminist agenda, to their list of top
political concerns. Ted Jelen's (1984) analysis of national survey data
found that Catholics are most likely to oppose abortion on "right to
life" grounds (an argument based on natural law), while fundamentalist Protestants oppose it because "easily available abortions seem to render sexual promiscuity less costly or risky" (a moral accountability
argument). While conservative use of feminist language may be unique
to St. Joseph's, conservative Catholic concern about the liberalization
of their church is not. As Appleby (1995:327) points out, "Conservative Catholics agree that the most powerful threat to Catholicism comes
from within," from feminists and liberal clergy and laity. Davidman and
Stocks' (1995) article comparing fundamentalist Christians and Hasidic
Jews confirms my finding that the minority status of Orthodox Jews
makes them less interested in transforming society. Similarly,
Wertheimer (1993) asserts that Orthodox Jews have not been particu-

larly involved in the political efforts on either abortion or homosexuality but have long been concerned with protecting their religious freedom. As the many examples in this book have shown, ordinary women in conservative Christian and Orthodox Jewish communities are not the same.

Why are these women so different from each other? It is my contention that the differences I found reflect not only theological variations but long-standing socio-political divisions based on the diverse history of Protestants, Catholics, and Jews in America. In order to understand both theological and historical differences, let us turn to the final chapter of this book.

	Understanding
Chapter 10	the Differences

AMERICA IS A DIVERSE PLACE, but it is not as polarized as some of its leaders would have us imagine. Gender roles are being contested, but the players in the contest have overlapping loyalties and it is not at all clear who will win. The woman who attends the Orthodox synagogue in my neighborhood, or the Evangelical woman who handed me a Bible tract at the mall, or the Catholic woman who carried her "It's a Baby, Not a Choice" placard in front of city hall—all these women may be subject to official gender norms that are different from my own, but the roles they actually play are quite similar. It is more likely than not that we all work outside the home, and we all face the challenge of balancing work and family, of negotiating responsibilities and authority with men in our lives. Chances are they have all, to some degree, integrated feminist values into their outlooks. More importantly, these women—though all religious conservatives—are quite different from one another. It is true that most religious conservatives, including ordinary women, oppose the feminist movement and the political issues (such as reproductive choice and gay rights) that it promotes. But, as we have seen in the last two chapters, women in conservative religious communities are actually rather ambivalent about the feminist movement, and abortion and homosexuality mean something different to different religious conservatives. These differences are no coincidence but are grounded in deep theological and historical divisions between Evangelicals, Catholics, and Orthodox Jews.

Theological Differences

You will recall that the women at Victory, St. Joseph's, and Beth Israel conceptualized abortion and homosexuality as entirely different problems: for Evangelicals they represented problems of moral accountability, for conservative Catholics violations of nature, and for Orthodox Jews issues of religious freedom. These different conceptualizations are not unique to the particular communities I studied but point to important theological differences between the three traditions.

Evangelical women's emphasis on moral accountability reflects a characteristically Protestant emphasis on moralism: the designation of a strict code combined with the expectation that anyone who violates the code deserves to be punished. Albanese (1981) has pointed out that such moralism, rooted in Puritan Calvinism and the Holiness tradition, is a prominent characteristic of American Protestantism, and that it was only when liberals became more lax on personal morality issues that conservatives became visible as the ones who carry the moral torch. Different conservatives emphasize different parts of that Protestant heritage. Fundamentalist Presbyterians and Baptists draw more heavily on the Calvinist strain brought here by the Puritans in the colonial period. Calvinism emphasizes the essential powerlessness of humankind: God has already elected those who will be saved and those who will be damned. At the same time, Calvinism also emphasizes the importance of this-worldly activism: the best way to serve God is not by retreating into a monastery but by disciplined work at one's calling. Lacking direct influence over their salvation, Puritans looked to hard work and moral discipline as signs that they were among the elect. The result was a rather rigid code of personal morality that was enforced by punishment or exclusion. Pentecostal and charismatic Evangelicals are more heavily influenced by the Holiness tradition, initially brought here in the eighteenth century by Methodist founder John Wesley. Holiness churches emphasize perfection in behavior which they believe should flow naturally from becoming a Christian. The first step in this process, the born-again experience, begins with the believer acknowledging her personal sinfulness. The next step, sanctification, begins when the believer accepts Jesus Christ as personal savior and gradually rids her life of sin. The result of this emphasis on sinlessness is a moralism just as strict and often as punitive as that of the Puritans (Lawless 1988).

While liberal Protestants have moved away from such moralism, Evangelicals are proud to carry on what they see as "our country's tradition of Christian values." Both abortion and homosexuality are, according to the women at Victory Church, prohibited by the Bible, but they realize that, given our legal system, they cannot expect all Americans to abide by biblical rules. Instead, they argue that the law must encourage moral accountability.[1] If abortion is legal, they insist, women can engage in random promiscuity, and can simply get rid of the consequences. If homosexuality is accepted as a lifestyle, then men can avoid their responsibility of caring for families by having sex with other men. The women do not define whose morality they are talking about, but assume a consensus grounded in biblical values. Their suggestion that the feminist movement's support for reproductive choice and gay rights fails to hold individuals accountable for their actions is thus a characteristically Protestant response.

Conservative Catholic women, by contrast, seem unconcerned with moral accountability and discuss abortion and homosexuality in terms of what is natural for the human body. This response makes sense in the context of Catholic theology. The practice of confession in order to obtain forgiveness may mitigate against the kind of punitive moralism evident at Victory since it presumes that even Christians are prone to sin. The church's teaching about natural law helps explain the women's emphasis on our physical nature. The concept of natural law goes back to Thomas Aquinas, who argued that God's will is revealed not only in the Bible (as many conservative Protestants insist) but can also be discerned by human reason through the observation of nature. Because God created nature, our physical body and its natural inclinations reveal God's will. Human nature has three basic inclinations: preservation and conservation of our being; procreation and training of offspring; and seeking the truth about God and living in community (McBrien 1981). From observing these inclinations, we can derive basic moral rules, some of which are specified in the Bible (e.g., the condemnation of homosexuality), others which are formulated by the church (e.g., prohibition of abortion).

It is therefore no surprise that St. Joseph's women would conceptualize abortion and homosexuality as a problem with nature. What is more surprising is that they also draw on a more liberal interpretation of natural law, the seamless garment ethic, formulated by Cardinal Joseph Bernardin of Chicago. This ethic calls for consistent support for the sanctity of life in all situations, and requires Catholics to fight not only against abortion, but against the death penalty and euthanasia, and for economic support of poor women and children. The acceptance of this ethic explains why women like Barbara seem liberal on welfare (she wants it maintained) even while they are ultraconservative on abortion (she does not want exceptions even for rape and incest). All actions, according to these women, should promote life. Abortion and homosexuality are wrong because they prevent reproduction, the natural outcome of sex. To suggest that, by promoting reproductive rights and gay rights, the feminist movement encourages unnatural acts and distorts God's order is a characteristically Catholic response.

Orthodox Jewish women, finally, did not much care about moral accountability or what is natural. Their conceptualization of abortion and homosexuality as issues of religious freedom reflects a theological emphasis on the election or chosenness (*bechirut*) of the Jewish people. Election is central to the Jewish covenant: God has a special relationship with the Jewish people which requires that they follow his laws. Observing the law will bring rewards, but observing Jewish law also sets you apart from the rest of the world. Ever since Christianity became the official religion of Rome in the fourth century, Jews have been a minority religion in Christian society. Protecting their right to observe the law has thus been central to the survival of Judaism.

Even today, the notion that Jews are a chosen people, subject to separate laws, continues to be an important means of maintaining the tradition. Until the eighteenth century, most Jews actually lived in separate communities; they did not vote in the countries where they lived, and conflicts involving Jewish people were resolved internally in Jewish courts. Jews gradually became more integrated in European societies as those societies became more secular. Reform Jews responded to this integration by adapting to secular society. They interpreted the

Torah as a product of history, so that some of its requirements are no longer applicable today. Orthodox Jews, by contrast, want to be part of society without becoming secular. While Orthodoxy requires Jews to live by the Torah, adhering strictly to all of its regulations, it allows Jews to live a portion of their lives in the secular world so long as that does not violate the norms of Torah. For example, Orthodoxy requires Jews to study Torah but they may also acquire a secular education. Jews, then, may take on secular responsibilities in addition to, but not instead of, their religious ones. The burden that this imposes reinforces the understanding that they are chosen. This concept of election was clearly reflected in how the women at Beth Israel understood abortion and homosexuality. Following halacha, as they saw it, is difficult, and cannot be expected from most people in this society. What is more important is to ensure that Jews will always have the right to follow it. To suggest that Jewish women have no problem with allowing reproductive choice and gay rights in American society, so long as feminists don't try to mess with Jewish law, reveals their understanding of Orthodoxy as exceptional and separate from the world.

It could be argued at this point that although Evangelical, Catholic, and Orthodox Jewish women have different theological reasons for opposing the feminist movement, their common opposition may lead them to temporarily set aside those differences. Their theological differences, however, are reinforced by historical divisions which are much more difficult to overcome.

Historical Divisions

It is tempting for sociologists to ignore history, to see current contradictions faced by conservative religious women as unique and influenced only by current events. But if we look at history, we see that traditional gender norms have always been a source of tension, and that historical experience forms part of a heritage/memory that shapes identities and attitudes today. It would be particularly tempting for me to ignore history because so many of the women in this study are adult converts to conservative religion. It could be argued that since Evangelical, Catholic, or Orthodox Jewish history is, strictly speaking, not these women's past, that history has no bearing on their interpretation of and response to present conflict. I would like to suggest, however, that these histories do affect even the new members of conservative religious communities because the beliefs and practices and, most importantly (at least for this study), the gender norms of each community are shaped by a particular historical context. These norms are mediated to members of the community through the teaching of laws and rules that are justified by reference to the past and through the telling of stories about the past. By embracing those rules and learning the stories, women who join in a sense "acquire" the history of that community.

Whether they had been raised within the tradition or became members as adults, the women I interviewed had learned to interpret their present situation in light of the community's history. For example, in explaining why working outside the home was consistent with Orthodox Jewish norms, Marcia asserted that "Jewish women have always worked" and gave examples of women in the early-twentieth-century immigrant community. In illustrating her argument that God sometimes chooses women to be religious leaders, Stephanie pointed to Aimée Semple McPherson, founder of the Foursquare Gospel Church, to which Victory Church is related. Similarly, in order to demonstrate that traditional Catholic gender norms do not oppress women, Jill told a story about Dorothy Day. The women learned this history from their pastor's or rabbi's sermons, from books and magazines promoted by their community, and from study groups they attended. For converts to traditionalist religion, appropriating their new community's history was an important way of demonstrating their full membership in the group.

For many of the women I interviewed, part of the appeal of conservative religion was the idea of being part of a community that *has* a distinct past, a history with which they can identify. In the case of many Evangelicals, appropriating that history meant confirming or sharpening their identity as Americans as the norms of their community were seen to reflect the original intentions of America's founders (see, for example, the comments of Katrina and Karen in chapters 8 and 9). In the case of Orthodox Jews, appropriating history usually meant a clearer identification as a Jew. For many Jewish women in this study, the decision to become religiously observant followed a trip to Israel motivated by a college-age search for identity (see Miriam's comments in chapter 1). Most Catholics in this study had been raised in the church. However, for those who were not, becoming a Catholic was closely tied to the appeal of being part of the oldest church in Christian history. As Jill put it, "I really like the idea of belonging to a tradition that can be traced all the way back to the Apostles of Christ." Adult converts to traditionalist religious communities can and do acquire their tradition's history. They draw on that history directly when they tell stories such as those mentioned above, and indirectly when they employ their community's particular interpretation of the world, an interpretation which has been shaped by historical experience.

A Christian America[2]

If joining a traditionalist religious community means, at least to some extent, appropriating its history, then a study of that history may help explain the diverse ways in which Protestant, Catholic, and Jewish women in this study respond to feminism. The history of these communities in America differs in important ways. Although members of all three groups have been present in America since colonial times, my historical survey will begin in the late nineteenth century because it was during this period that conservative Protestants formulated a distinct identity and that large numbers of Orthodox Jewish and Catholic immigrants entered the American scene. We will look first at Evangelical women because it was Protestants who had the most power in shaping the public culture to which both Catholics and Jews had to adapt and because it was fundamentalists who most clearly formulated an antifeminist ideology. There are two factors that uniquely shape Evangelical women's experience: (1) conservative Protestants' loss of mainstream status in the early twentieth century, contributing to the development of a rigidly antifeminist ideology, and (2) the reestablishment of Evangelical power through the New Christian Right in the 1970s and 1980s, reviving the hope of Christianizing America. These factors have a distinct effect on how contemporary Evangelical women come to terms with feminism that differentiates them from conservative Catholics and Jews.

In her recent book, *Fundamentalism and Gender*, Margaret Bendroth argues that the key to understanding present-day Evangelical attitudes about women is their forbears' loss of mainstream status at the beginning of this century. Today's Evangelicals are considered conservative, while liberal Protestants are designated as mainline. In the nineteenth century, however, beliefs and practices that we today associate with conservatism, such as literal interpretation of the Bible, were part of the mainstream. Various innovations—scientific (e.g., theories of evolution), theological (e.g., higher criticism of the Bible) and socio-economic (e.g., industrialization and urbanization)—caused a split within Protestantism, between those who embraced these changes (modernists) and those who rejected them (fundamentalists). The split led to an extended battle which was fought out within major Protestant denominations, especially among Baptists and Presbyterians, and which the conservatives eventually lost, as symbolized by their public humiliation in the Scopes trial (the 1925 trial that gave the issue of biblical teaching versus the teaching of evolution in public schools nationwide publicity). Unable to stem the rising tide of modernism both in the larger culture and within their churches, many conservative Protestants left their denominations to form independent fundamentalist churches that, at least temporarily, withdrew from active participation in society.

Evangelical antifeminism is directly related to that loss of direct cultural influence. According to Bendroth, the roots of fundamentalist antifeminism lie in the simultaneous feminization and liberalization of religion in the late nineteenth century. Unlike Catholic and Jewish immigrants, fundamentalists were not natural outsiders. "Nearly all of the movement's early leadership was white, male, middle-class, well-educated and Protestant . . . making their livelihood in a social institution that was predominantly female in membership and, fundamentalists believed, in its watered-down doctrine" (6). Identifying liberalism and secularism with femininity and feminism, fundamentalists emphasized masculine language and gradually developed a distinctly antifeminist theology.

Protestant leaders who opposed liberalizing and secularizing trends in Christianity did so at a time when Protestant churches were numerically dominated by women and the Victorian cult of domesticity had assigned men a relatively passive role in religion. Victorian ideology had restricted women to the home but at the same time elevated them as morally superior to men. The home was seen as a safe haven from the rough and immoral world of industrial capitalism in which men had to compete to earn a living. It was up to women, through their greater moral sensibilities, to exercise a moderating influence on men and to guide children to become moral adults. Women's greater morality also rationalized an increasing role for women in the church and in social reform, which contributed to the first wave of feminism that culminated in women's suffrage. In an attempt to appeal to men, fundamentalists reversed the Victorian formula and elevated men as the upholders of morality and religion. Christian manliness meant replacing the language of penitence and surrender with an emphasis on victory and power, and forging a link between revivalism and the masculine business world. In short, the late nineteenth-century urban revivalism of Moody and others was decidedly masculine in message but not necessarily antifeminist.

A coherent antifeminist rhetoric did not emerge until after World War I when fundamentalists had gone on the defensive, following the Scopes trial. At a time when women had won the vote and flappers symbolized a new feminine freedom, the fundamentalist doctrines of biblical inerrancy and dispensational premillennialism expressed the conviction that the defense of traditionalist Christianity was incompatible with women's emancipation. To fundamentalists, the fact that women's arguments for greater power relied on nonliteral, thematic reading of the Pauline epistles clearly demonstrated the necessity for a literal reading of the Bible, and the rising status of women in society was proof that the world would degenerate prior to its immanent end. Women, in this view, were to have no authority, either in the church or at home. In practice, however, women's roles were not as restricted as this rhetoric would suggest. Although most fundamentalists were not economically disadvantaged, they were a minority religious group that depended on women to further institutional growth.[3] Thus many fundamentalist women did work outside the home, particularly in domestic and foreign missions.

Bendroth argues that despite their outsider status, fundamentalists seem to mirror mainstream cultural patterns. Like American women in general, fundamentalist women increased their participation in the labor force in the years before and during World War II. But during the cultural turn toward domesticity in the 1950s, fundamentalists urged women to retreat to their preordained roles as submissive helpmates and encouraged men to fill the positions the women vacated. The Victorian family was brought back, only this time without the elevation of women who were allowed only limited moral authority within the home.

Following World War II, fundamentalists began to move out of their self-imposed exile and into the mainstream. Beginning in the 1950s, the neo-evangelical reformation encouraged greater openness to secular thought and gave conservative Protestants greater respectability.[4] The rise of neo-Pentecostalism in the 1960s and 1970s also lent legitimacy to Evangelicals. Except for their emphasis on the gifts of the spirit, neo-Pentecostals share much of the same theology as Evangelicals, as well as their conservative social and political orientation, and are today generally seen as part of the Evangelical movement (Paloma 1982). Because neo-Pentecostalism arose among middle-class people in mainline churches, it enhanced the perception that Evangelicalism was becoming mainstream (Quebedeaux 1983). Finally, Evangelicals were aided by leaders like Billy Graham who was able to define a middle ground and forge common goals between competing Evangelical groups as well as formulate a Christian message that had broad mainstream appeal (Hatch 1992).

In the 1970s and 1980s Evangelicals were experiencing phenomenal growth, and, more importantly, became politically active.[5] The response of politicians and the media to the New Christian Right reinforced Evangelicals' sense of power and bolstered their conviction that it was not only necessary but possible to re-Christianize America. The reestablishment of Evangelical power had an important effect on conservative Protestant women. Because the New Christian Right was to some extent motivated by opposition to feminism (Conover and Gray 1983), conservative Protestants became identified as antifeminists (a label that as we have seen may or may not reflect the sentiments of ordinary Evangelical women). And because of the perceived size of the conservative Christian constituency, Evangelicals could argue that their gender norms should be normative for all American women.

These two themes in the Evangelical movement—the early development of a strong antifeminist ideology and the emergence of the New Christian Right—shape the way in which the women at Victory respond to the feminist movement. From a historical perspective it makes sense that there were far more antifeminists at Victory than in either of the other two communities, and that the most virulent antifeminist statements I encountered came from Evangelical women (e.g., Charleen) who blamed feminism for every social ill, including violent crime. It also makes sense that many Evangelical women (e.g., Karen and Katrina) feel responsible for solving what they see as "the problem of homosexuality and abortion" by Christianizing America—a response that was not found among either Catholic or Jewish women. While conservative Catholics and Orthodox Jews have jumped on the religious right bandwagon, they are not similarly identified with antifeminism, and do not have the power to shape the norms of the nation as a whole. It is their historical conviction that "we are America" that distinguishes Evangelicals from Orthodox Jews and conservative Catholics and shapes the way they respond to feminist influence in society.

A Divided Church[6]

The relationship of the Catholic Church to American culture is quite different from that of Protestants. Two factors that uniquely shaped the experience of conservative Catholic women are (1) their immigrant/ working-class status in the early twentieth century, which resulted in a more liberal political orientation and a more ambivalent attitude towards feminism than their Protestant counterparts; and (2) the Second Vatican Council which resulted in a division between conservatives (who oppose it ramifications) and liberals (who support them) and led many Catholics to conclude that anything can change.[7]

While Catholics had always been a presence in America, they became far more visible in the late nineteenth and early twentieth century when large numbers of Catholic immigrants from southern and eastern Europe came to the United States. The first massive wave of Catholic immigration occurred before the Civil War, beginning with the Irish in the 1840s, and followed by the Germans. A second, even more massive immigration wave toward the turn of the century brought Catholics from Italy and Poland to American shores. A third wave of Catholic immigrants from Latin and South American countries began in the late twentieth century and is still ongoing. Although large numbers of Mexicans "entered" the country through territorial acquisitions by the United States, still greater growth in the Mexican American population arises from contemporary immigration patterns. Because they came from many different ethnic backgrounds, it is difficult to generalize about Catholic women. Nonetheless, if one surveys the history of some of the largest groups (Irish, Italian, Polish, and Mexican Catholics), some broad patterns do emerge.

As immigrants struggling to adapt to the United States, Catholic women tried hard to meet the standards of Victorian womanhood, but many of them did not succeed. McDannell (1989) argues that the Victorian concept of the "Catholic lady" and mother as center of the home and as foundation of Catholicism was created by the Irish middle class, who monopolized the clergy and lay leadership, and thus was able to set the standards for gender norms. Yet due to class and ethnic differences, the Victorian ideal was modified or ignored by most immigrants. Although most of the Irish were not middle class, even working-class Irish women were more likely to adopt the Victorian ideal than other Catholic immigrants. In part this was because they spoke English and thus were more exposed to the popular media which peddled that ideal. In part, it was because Irish women, far more frequently than other immigrants, worked as maids, which gave them daily contact with middle-class women whom they then tried to emulate. Because Irish Catholicism centered upon the church, the Victorian ideal of women as moral exemplars allowed the Catholic woman, like her Protestant counterpart, to expand her role there.[8] Italian and Mexican Catholicism, by contrast, centered around the home, where women practiced devotions to Mary and various saints at domestic shrines. Because the anticlericalism of Italian and Mexican men meant they participated little in the domestic religion perpetuated by their wives, religion was primarily a female occupation, albeit for different reasons than in the Victorian model.

The main obstacle to meeting Victorian gender norms was the economic necessity for immigrant women to work. In the late nineteenth century many women, particularly the Irish, worked as domestic servants, while others, especially Italian women, did piecework from their homes. By the early twentieth century, a disproportionate number of Catholic women were working in the factories of the garment industry. Most were young and married and recent immigrants. Wage earning undermined traditional roles of women staying at home and also induced the use of birth control (Kenneally 1990). In addition, working got Catholic women involved in the labor movement, which soon became a "good Catholic cause" that provided them with unprecedented leadership opportunities in the public sphere (Campbell 1989).

The outcome of this conflict between Victorian norms, old-world traditions, and economic imperatives was a reformulation of gender norms that had an ambiguous effect on Catholic women. While many immigrant women were forced to work outside the home, they retained considerable power within it. For the Irish, the separation of spheres in America which placed women in control of the home undermined the patriarchal structure of European Catholicism where the father ruled over an extended family. In the case of Italian Catholics, the Victorian notion of "woman' s sphere" contributed to the creation of a public patriarchy/private matriarchy in which mothers were the guardians of morality, with the power to define who belonged and who didn't, while fathers retained the power to define the role of the good woman as limited to marriage, children, and suffering. The dual demand to exercise power while appearing powerless meant that women's power was often exerted indirectly and manipulatively, and as a result was generally resented (Orsi 1985).

Catholic women hung on to these traditional gender norms longer than Protestants (Kenneally 1990).[9] Yet they did not develop the kind of coherent antifeminist ideology that emerged among conservative Protestants. Their response to early twentieth-century feminism was ambiguous. The fact that the suffrage movement, the most visible feminist organization, was led by middle-class Protestants, made many Catholic women feel ambivalent about it. Most Catholic women were working class and the feminist rhetoric of political equality did not seem to address economic concerns such as workplace safety and higher wages. Moreover, given their experience with anti-Catholic nativism, many Catholic women saw Protestant reform efforts as attempts to protestantize them and were therefore reluctant to participate. Support for feminism derived from Catholic women's participation in labor activism. While Catholic women were not prominent in the suffrage movement, many were leaders in the labor movement who were able to convince unionized women to support suffrage as a means for improving work conditions (Kenneally 1990; Weaver 1985). Opposition to feminism came from Catholic clergy (including some liberals like Cardinal Gibbons) and lay leaders, the majority of whom vocally opposed suffrage until just before the Nineteenth Amendment was passed (Campbell 1989).[10] It is unclear to what extent the leadership influenced ordinary Catholic women. In the end, most of them did support suffrage but probably more for practical than for ideological reasons.

As subsequent generations of Catholics left their immigrant status behind, they became increasingly similar to mainstream Protestants. Catholic women shared the general pattern of increasing labor-force participation during World War II and returning to domesticity during the 1950s. In the 1960s, suburbanization, rising levels of education and income were all signs that Catholics were moving into the middle class, and the election of John F. Kennedy showed that they had been accepted as part of the mainstream. This emergence from "ghetto-Catholicism" and accommodation to cultural values of individualism and choice led many Catholics to question authority in ways they had never dared before (Hoge 1981).

The Second Vatican Council seemed to affirm these developments by emphasizing both cultural adaptation (e.g., performing the Mass in the vernacular rather than Latin) and democratization (e.g., allowing more lay participation in church administration). Interestingly, lay responses to Vatican II have been expressed most vocally in terms of women's issues. The majority of more-liberal Catholics welcomed these changes and were surprised and disappointed when Humanae Vitae reaffirmed the traditional Catholic prohibition on birth control in 1968 (Greeley 1990). More-conservative Catholics seized on birth control and abortion as symbols of their opposition to further change, and became politically active in the anti-ERA and pro-life movements. The impact of Vatican II on the role of Catholic women was profound. On the one hand, it opened the door to adapting to feminist ideas. On the other hand, it engendered a backlash by conservative Catholics who saw feminism as a symbol of all that was wrong with the church. As conservatives resist further changes and liberals push for more, American bishops are put in the unhappy position of having to write regulations sufficiently vague to minimize offensiveness to either party.[11] All Catholics are left with the impression of a weakened church in which anything can change and change is often rather arbitrary.

The historical experience of conservative Catholic women, then, differs significantly from that of their Protestant counterparts. Unlike Evangelicals, Catholics did not lose a position of cultural dominance—they never had it. And unlike conservative Protestant women, who are riding the crest of the Evangelical resurgence, conservative Catholic women in America find themselves a minority in a divided church. It is telling that although the church is the most visible opponent of the feminist effort to promote abortion rights, the only woman ever nominated to be vice president of the United States (Geraldine Ferraro) was a Catholic—and pro-choice. While their position might be compared to that of fundamentalists in the Protestant divide earlier this century, Catholic conservatives are not free to leave and are forced to remain a countercultural movement within a largely liberal majority.

These historical patterns shape the way conservative Catholic women respond to feminism today. Antifeminists at St. Joseph's were fewer in number than at Victory Church and less virulent in their attacks on the movement. They also appeared self-conscious of their lack of power or right to shape the dominant culture. Several women asserted that most Protestants don't really understand what Catholicism is about; Evangelicals in particular were resented for "spreading false stereotypes about Catholics." The sense of being a historical outsider was also reflected in Catholic women's reluctance to expand their religion to the rest of society. As we have seen in chapter 9, conservative Catholic women did feel their country was in need of moral reform, but unlike Evangelicals they did not feel it was necessary for all Americans to become Catholic or even Christian. The women's comments also reflect the rift in the Catholic Church since the Second Vatican Council. Recall Anita's disdainful comment about conservative Catholics or Beatrice's frustration that most Catholics ignore church teaching on issues such as birth control (chapter 6). Conservative Catholics' understanding that they do not speak for most women in their church combined with residual suspicion of Evangelicals may make it difficult for such women to organize effective resistance to liberalizing trends both within their own community and in the larger society.

Jewish Survivalism[12]

The history of Orthodox Jewish women parallels that of Catholic women during the immigrant era of the early twentieth century; but those similarities recede in the latter part of this century. Two factors that uniquely shape the history of Orthodox Jewish women in America are (1) their immigrant experience, which (as in the case of Catholics) resulted in a more liberal political orientation and an ambivalent attitude to feminism; and (2) the Nazi Holocaust and the Six-Day War in Israel, which have induced an intense concern with Jewish survival which conflicts with feminism in various ways.

There have been Orthodox Jews in America since colonial times, but they became far more visible in the late nineteenth and early twentieth century when large numbers of eastern European Orthodox Jews came to the United States. Until that time, the largest number of Jewish immigrants had been Reform Jews of German origin (Blau 1976). It was these Jews, most of whom by the turn of the century had worked their way into the middle class, who set the standards of womanhood to which all Jews tried to adapt. Like middle-class Irish Catholic women, upwardly mobile Reform Jewish women accepted the Victorian model as a sign of assimilation and modernity. However, as in the Catholic case, the more recent Eastern European immigrants have had trouble living by that standard.[13]

Eastern European Jewish gender norms contrasted starkly with the Victorian ideal. Partly because restrictions on many occupations limited male wages, and partly because of a cultural tradition that idealized the scholar husband who is financially supported by his wife, Eastern European Jewish women were actually encouraged to work outside the home.[14] In late-nineteenth-century Russia, for example, 28 percent of families had a female breadwinner. Not only did women work, but many were also active in the European labor movement, particularly the Bund. Bund socialism was more accepting of women's education and gender equality than other institutions of its time, and it provided important leadership opportunities for Jewish women (Glenn 1990). Moreover, Jewish idealization of the scholar did not encourage the macho models foisted on men in the United States. Thus Eastern European women seemed masculine and their men feminine by American standards (Baum 1976).

Old-world traditions were not the only reason why Orthodox Jewish immigrants had trouble with the Victorian ideal. As in the case of Catholics, economic necessity forced most Jewish immigrant women to work for wages. Partly due to the mandate to provide religious education for boys and partly to adapt to the Victorian standard of domestic wives, girls usually worked to support the family, and daughters often became the primary breadwinners. While 73 percent of single women worked, "Jewish immigrant wives had a lower rate of labor force participation than all other groups of married women, immigrant or non-immigrant" (Glenn 1990). Yet married women too contributed to family income by conducting business within the home, doing piecework and running stores or boarding houses (Baum 1976).

A major employer for Orthodox Jewish women was the garment industry. Unlike Catholics who saw domestic service as protective, Jewish immigrants viewed it as demeaning and most of their women worked in the factories rather than as maids. Moreover, while most Catholic immigrants came from peasant backgrounds, Jewish women came with industrial work experience and skill in needle work which enabled them to be promoted more quickly (Glenn 1990). Their strong numerical representation in the factories combined with their (or their mother's) experience with socialism in Europe made it inevitable that Jewish women would respond to employment discrimination and poor working conditions by joining the labor movement. Participation in union activities, in turn, provided them with important leadership opportunities in the public sphere that belied the domestic boundaries set up by Victorian norms.

As in the case of Catholic women, the outcome of this conflict between the Victorian ideal, old-world traditions, and economic imperatives was a reconstruction of gender norms that both benefitted and harmed Orthodox Jewish women. On the one hand, Orthodox women managed to combine the best of both worlds. Women's social role in the United States was more exclusively domestic than in eastern Europe, but Americans idealized womanhood, so Orthodox Jewish women in America could maintain the old-world tradition of women's work while rejecting the moral inferiority of women (Glenn 1990:6). On the other hand, as eastern European Jewish women more successfully integrated the American model of total domesticity (especially in 1950s), the characteristics that had helped them survive in the *shtetl* as well as in immigrant America became the targets of ugly stereotypes, and the old-world ideal of the strong, competent woman was transformed into the caricature of the domineering Jewish mother (Baum 1976).

Even though their actions often contradicted the Victorian ideal, most Orthodox Jewish women did not see themselves as feminist. Like immigrant Catholic women, the response of eastern European Jewish women to early-twentieth-century feminism was ambiguous. The fact that the suffrage movement was led by middle-class Protestant women made many working-class Jewish women feel ambivalent about it.[15] Like Catholic women, they were more concerned with improving work conditions in the factories than with women's political equality,[16] and antisemitism on the part of Protestants further limited cooperation with them.[17] Support for feminism derived from Jewish women's participation in labor activism. Although Orthodox Jewish women, like Catholic women, were not prominent in the leadership of the suffrage movement, labor discrimination and sexual harassment drove many to support suffrage as a means of improving working conditions. In addition, their experience as labor leaders led them to support suffrage as a means for expanding the public roles available to women (Kuzmack 1990). Education also increased Orthodox Jewish women's receptivity to feminism. Although poverty often limited female education (as poor people kept their boys in school while the girls worked to support the family), it did not stop women from educating themselves. More Jewish women attended evening school than any other immigrant group (Glenn 1990), and by the 1920s, a disproportionate number of Jewish women were enrolled in colleges and universities, often at the urging of their mothers (Baum 1976). Opposition to feminism came from Jewish religious leaders. Because Jewish suffrage activists tended to be middle-class Reform women, most statements on the subject came from Reform rabbis, who like the Catholic clergy, initially opposed women's suffrage, but came around to supporting it shortly before it was passed. It is unclear to what extent the rabbis influenced ordinary Orthodox Jewish women. Like their Catholic counterparts, working-class Jewish women ended up supporting suffrage but more for practical than ideological reasons.

Eastern European Jewish immigrants differed from Catholic immigrants in that Jews came to stay on a permanent basis (Glenn 1990), a fact that created considerable pressure to adapt to American culture. As subsequent generations of eastern European Jews left their immigrant status behind, they too moved into the middle class. Yet in stark contrast to Catholicism, Orthodoxy remained marginal despite its upward mobility. Respectability came from adaptation, and Orthodoxy's emphasis on proper practice made it more difficult for Jews to adapt than for Catholics who could keep their beliefs to themselves. Thus the pressure to adapt generally resulted in membership losses for Orthodox Judaism. The desire to hold on to their constituents intensified the debate begun in Europe between the Modern Orthodox who felt that Orthodoxy was compatible with modern life in an increasingly secularized society and the Traditionalist Orthodox who felt that it was not. Modern Orthodox rabbis, trying to prevent their congregants' defection to Conservative Judaism by softening the demands of Orthodoxy, initially seemed to prevail. Yet during and after World War II, traditionalist immigrants fleeing the Nazis provided more hard-line leadership for Orthodox Jews, beginning a gradual shift to the right (Wertheimer 1993).

Wertheimer argues convincingly that the Six-Day War in 1967 inaugurated a shift from accommodation to survivalism among U.S. Jews, a trend that greatly enhanced the stature of Orthodoxy. While the Nazi Holocaust led American Jews to identify with the collective insecurity of all Jews, it was the Six-Day War that converted American Jewry to Zionism and intense identification with Israel. The event not only increased political activism for Jewish causes (e.g., lobbying for military support of Israel and freeing Soviet Jews), but transformed Jewish education (Orthodox schools now use the Sephardic pronunciation of Hebrew popular in Israel, and Jewish teenagers now commonly spend a summer there) and increased concerns about intermarriage. The concern with Jewish survival had important implications for how Orthodoxy responded to modern feminism. On the one hand, the need to maintain Orthodoxy as a primary carrier of Jewish culture provided a powerful argument against feminism, because feminism demanded significant changes in Jewish practice. On the other hand, the continued switching of Orthodox Jews to Conservative Judaism created pressure to enhance the religious involvement and education of women.

The experience of Orthodox Jewish women resembles that of Catholics during the immigrant era but departs significantly in the second half of the twentieth century when the Jewish experience more closely resembles that of Protestants. While the major Catholic event of the 1960s, Vatican II, seemed to legitimate Catholic liberals, a key event for Jews in the 1960s, the Six Day War, legitimated conservative trends in Judaism. As in the case of Protestants, the events of the 1960s and 1970s led to a loss of religious commitment among liberal Jews (both Reform and Conservative) who were identified with the establishment, while Orthodoxy acquired new legitimacy and prestige.

What makes the Orthodox Jewish experience different from that of both conservative Protestants and Catholics in America is the fact that Jews have always been and probably always will be a minority. For Jews, moreover, minority status is not a factor peculiar to the American experience. Since the onset of the Diaspora, Jews everywhere have been a minority religious group, and as such have been subject to both Jewish laws and customs and those of whatever state they happen to reside in. Since emancipation ended the social isolation of Jews, they have had to deal with the dilemma of choosing between the economic and social benefits of integration and the desire to uphold Jewish law. Resolving this dilemma has resulted in what might be called a "habit of compartmentalization": following Jewish law and custom as it pertains to family and synagogue, and accommodating secular law and custom in other areas such as the workplace.[18]

On the one hand, this habit of compartmentalization has made Orthodox Jewish women more accepting than their Christian counterparts of feminist influence in the larger society. On the other hand, compartmentalization reflects an intense concern with the survival of Orthodox tradition which makes Jewish women particularly wary of feminist influence in their own community. Although Jews and Christians in this study were equally conservative in their conceptions of the proper role for women in church or synagogue (see chapter 5), Jewish women were more likely to work outside the home (see chapter 4). I found more profeminists at Beth Israel than at either Victory or St. Joseph's (see chapter 8) and none of them, not even the antifeminists, were interested in opposing reproductive choice or gay rights in the larger society. Yet both pro-and antifeminists sought to limit the movement's influence on Orthodox Judaism. To these women, feminism was a threat to the survival of their tradition.

The concern for the survival of Jewish tradition, for unity in the Catholic Church, and for a Christian America, are very different reasons to oppose the feminist movement. While theological differences may be temporarily set aside to pursue a common political goal, the divisions between Evangelicals, conservative Catholics, and Orthodox Jews go beyond theological disagreements and are rooted in longstanding differences in their relationships to American society. Overlooking these differences only serves a small political elite: liberal feminist activists who need an enemy and religious right leaders who want to appear stronger than they actually are. It is probably no coincidence that most of the evidence for a potential cross-denominational conservative alliance comes from conservative Protestants; after all, the concept of such a moral majority mirrors the Evangelical self-understanding that they are representative of America as a whole. But overlooking these differences leads to dangerous stereotypes and an exaggerated sense of polarization in American culture. One of the most important things I learned from doing this research was that the women I studied were in many ways quite similar to me, a secular feminist. Other American women, too, strive to reconcile the variety of often-conflicting roles they play at home, at work, and in other social environments. Like the women in this study, many nonconservative, nonreligious women are ambivalent about the feminist movement while at the same time yearning for a society in which women's contribution is more highly valued.

It is time to think about cultural conflict in new ways: yes, religious conservatives *are* in conflict with feminists, but that conflict reflects an ambivalence that is shared by many secular Americans. Moreover, the central conflict is different for different religious communities. For Evangelicals it is a conflict over the shape of American culture, for conservative Catholics a battle over the future of their church, and for Orthodox Jews a struggle for the survival of their tradition. By listening to the voices of ordinary women rather than to the rhetoric of feminist or conservative religious leaders, we come to see the complexity and diversity in the traditionalist religious worldview.

Appendix A

Survey and Interview Questions

Reprinted below is the demographic survey administered to women in this study, as well as the interview guide I used in my conversations with them.

Demographic Survey

1. Age: _____
2. Occupation: _____
3. Marital Status (circle one):
   —never married
   —married
   —divorced or separated
   —widowed
4. Children
   —how many? _____
   —age range? _____
5. Education (circle highest level completed)
   —high school
   —attended college
   —bachelor's degree
   —graduate or professional degree
6. Household Income (circle one)
   —under 20,000

—20,000 to 39,999

—40,000 to 69,999

—70,000 to 99,999

—100,000 plus

7. What religious denomination were you raised in?

    _____

8. When did you become an Evangelical Christian/Catholic/Ortho-
    dox Jew? (circle one)

    —as a child

    —as a teenager

    —as an adult

    —through marriage

9. How long have you belonged to this church/synagogue? _____

Interview Questions

1. Tell me about yourself

    —your childhood (place of birth? parents and siblings? religious
    upbringing?)

    —your education and work experience

    —your current family situation (married? children?)

2. Briefly, how/when did you become a conservative Christian/ortho-
    dox Jew?

    —what was the reaction of family and friends?

    —why did you join this church/synagogue?

3. Tell me about your life as a conservative Christian/orthodox Jew

    —since you committed to your faith/observance what aspects of
    your life (friendships, relationships with men, career plans) have
    changed and which have remained the same?

    —on a daily basis, are you mostly in contact with other Christians/
    Jews?

    —who are your closest friends?

    —what does being a good Christian/Jew mean to you?

    —are there things about which you have questions?

    —what do you think are the most important issues facing conser-
    vative Christian/orthodox Jewish women today?

4. What roles should women play in American society?

—do you think it is a good thing when women go into tradition-ally male occupations like engineering or the military?

—do you think America would benefit if more women were elected to political office or promoted to leadership positions in business corporations?

—do you think gender discrimination/sexual harassment is a real problem?

—do you support laws mandating equal rights for (or prohibiting gender discrimination against) men and women?

5. How do you feel about women's role in the church/synagogue?

—do you think women should be pastors/priests/rabbis?

—how do you feel about the use of gender-neutral language in church/synagogue services and literature?

—how do you feel about changes in women's role? (e.g., female lec-tors and cantors in Catholic church; women's Talmud study and prayer groups in Orthodox synagogue)?

—Jews only: how do you feel about the mechitza?

6. What do you feel are the proper roles for men and women in the Christian/Jewish family?

—do you consider the man as the head of the family?

—should the man have final say in family decisionmaking?

—do you feel you should submit to/obey your husband? what does this mean? can you give examples of how this plays out in your daily life?

—do you feel a woman should stay home with the children while the husband supports the family?

—does your husband help with child-rearing/domestic tasks?

—homemakers: how did you feel about quitting job/career?

—working women: how do you manage job and kids?

—single women: are you looking to (re)marry? What would you look for in a man?

—Jews only: do you (married women)/do you plan to (single women) cover your hair and practice the family purity laws? what does this mean to you?

7. Social issues

—how would you assess the impact of the women's movement on American society?

—has the women's movement had any impact on Christianity/Judaism?

—how do you feel about abortion? birth-control?-how do you feel about homosexuality?

—have you taken action on either of these issues?

8. Overall, what would you say are the most difficult or challenging aspects about being a conservative Christian/orthodox Jewish woman in today's society? Which are the most rewarding?

Glossary of Hebrew and Yiddish Terms

The spelling of the words below is based on Ashkenazic and Sephardic pronunciations of Hebrew words as they were used by the women at Beth Israel.

abba—father; daddy.

Agudat Yisrael—"Unity of Israel"; Jewish party and lobbying organization that promotes the policy perspectives of Orthodoxy.

aliyah—going up; in the synagogue, the process of going (or being called) up to the Torah.

Amidah—the central prayer in the Jewish services, read in silence.

Ashkenazi—eastern European Jewish.

ba'alat (pl.: *ba'alot*) *teshuvah*—"person who returns"; woman who adopts Orthodox Judaism as an adult.

bar/bat mitzvah—"son/daughter of the commandments"; an adult with religious responsibilities; a ceremony in which a thirteen-year-old boy/girl is initiated into religious adulthood.

bechirut—chosenness, election.

bimah—center stage from which prayers are conducted.

challah—braided Sabbath loaf; the taking of the dough portion when baking this bread.

chazzan—cantor; person who chants the service.

chuppah—marriage canopy.

daven/davening—to pray/prayer.

devar Torah—a brief talk on a Jewish theme, often the content of the weekly passage of Torah.

eruv—boundary around an Orthodox neighborhood.

frum—traditionally observant.

gadol (pl.: *gedolim*)—"great person"; giant in Torah scholarship; halachic authority.

Gemara—commentary and discussions on and a supplement to the Mishnah; together with the Mishnah, forming the Talmud.

get—Jewish bill of divorce.

halacha—Jewish law.

halachic—pertaining to Jewish law; legal; orthodox.

Hanukkah—the eight-day Feast of Lights.

imma—mother; mommy.

kashering—ritual cleansing process that removes contamination due to unintentional violations of dietary regulations.

kashrut—the kosher laws that regulate the dietary behavior of observant Jews.

kiddush—ritual blessing over the wine, part of the Shabbat meal.

kippah—headcovering worn by Jewish males; also yarmulke.

mechitzah—partition in an Orthodox synagogue that separates the women's section from the men's.

mikveh—ritual bath.

minyan—quorum of ten men needed for Jewish communal prayer; prayer service.

Mishnah—oral law, composed in six orders or divisions which were originally taught orally, then codified, edited and committed to writing in the early third century; together with the Gemara, forming the Talmud.

mitzvah (pl.: *mitzvot*)—commandment; good deed.

Mussaf—additional Amidah.

niddah—menstruant; state of ritual impurity resulting from menstruation.

onah—"season;" the husband's obligation to have marital relations with his wife.

Pesach—Passover.

Purim—Feast of Esther; festive, playful holiday in early spring commemorating the victory of the Jews over the wicked Haman who plotted to eradicate them.

Rosh HaShanah—Jewish New Year.

Sephardi—Spanish or Portuguese Jewish.

Shabbes, Shabbat—Ashkenazic and Sephardic pronunciations (respectively) of the Hebrew word for Sabbath (both forms were used interchangeably at Beth Israel).

Shabbaton—special weekend Shabbat program with meals, singing, lectures, and discussion.

Shacharit—morning service at the synagogue.

shiur—study group.

shofar—ram's horn, sounded on Rosh HaShana and at the end of the Yom Kippur service.

shomer mitzvos—Ashkenazic pronunciation of Hebrew word for one who observes the Jewish commandments.

shomer Shabbes—Ashkenazic pronunciation of Hebrew word for one who observes the Sabbath.

shtetl—small, tight-knit, bounded community in which Jews in premodern Europe lived (in eastern Europe, the shtetl persisted through the nineteenth century).

shul—Yiddish for synagogue.

Simchat Torah—the festival celebrating the conclusion of the annual cycle of Torah (Pentateuchal) readings.

Sukkah—temporary dwelling outside the home in which the Jew resides during Sukkot.

Sukkot—the eight-day festival of booths.

taharat hamishpacha—laws of family purity governing sexual relations between wives and husbands, especially laws pertaining to niddah and mikveh.

tallit—four-cornered, fringed prayer shawl; in Orthodox shuls it is worn by married men.

tefillah—prayer.

tefillin—phylacteries; leather straps connected to a box containing sacred scrolls that observant Jewish men wrap around their arms and head for their weekday morning prayers.

tichel—headcovering worn by married Jewish women.

yarmulke—Yiddish word for kippah, headcovering worn by Jewish males.

yeshiva—institution of Jewish education.

Yiddishkeit—Judaism; Jewish way of life.

Yom Kippur—Day of Atonement.

Notes

Chapter 1   Stories of Ordinary Women

1. For scholarly treatments, see Danzger (1989), Davidman (1991), and Kaufman (1991) on Judaism, and Weaver and Appleby (1995) on Catholicism. For examples of media coverage, see Gittleson (1984) on Jews, and Arnold (1987) on Catholics.
2. The study was conducted in the greater Los Angeles area. However, to protect their privacy, individuals, organizations, and locations have been given fictional names.
3. According to Orthodox tradition, married women are required to cover their hair, though some Modern Orthodox Jews dispute this tradition. There is no dispute, however, that married women must observe the family purity laws, which require a separation of husband and wife during and for seven days after her menstrual period (for further details, see chapter 6).
4. There are over forty retreat centers associated with the Catholic Church in California, more than in any other state. Centers are often run by religious orders whose members provide counseling and spiritual direction during the retreat (Alexander 1993).
5. It is for this reason that I decided against the use of "composite portraits" which have become increasingly popular in ethnographic and sociological research. Composite portraits are fictional characters that combine characteristics which the researcher found to be typical of a group but that are usually not all present in one individual. While such portraits are useful in highlighting group characteristics, they also create the misleading impression that the group is filled with typical individuals.
6. Officially lay leaders, these women fulfill all pastoral duties except for sacramental functions for which a rotating priest is responsible.
7. The Promise Keepers movement may be a symptom of such changes.
8. Davidman and Stock (1995), an insightful article comparing family values of fundamentalist Christians and Hasidic Jews, is subject to these limitations.

Chapter 2   The Rhetoric of the Elite

1. Both LaHaye and NOW are quoted in Hunter (1991:181).
2. MS Magazine, January/February 1991:76. Similarly biting criticism can be found in some essays in Christ and Plaskow 1989 and in Goldenberg 1987. Women who join conservative religious communities are, from this perspective, lacking in self-respect (see Dworkin 1983).

3. Sources of statistics: Chronicle of Higher Education (August 29, 1997:23); Bureau of the Census, Statistical Abstract of the United States (1993:185); Fox-Genovese (1996:114, 123); Simon and Danziger (1991:46–47, 69–76).

4. Liebman (1983c) asserts that Orthodox Judaism remains an immigrant religion: the bulk of Orthodox Jews are first generation Americans, while most Conservative Jews are second generation, and most Reform Jews belong to the third.

5. Of these, 489 were in the United States and 57 in Canada.

6. Several commentators (Greeley 1990; Johnson 1982; O'Sullivan 1993; Weaver 1985) have noted a rightward shift in Catholic leadership and have argued that conservative lay people have benefitted from this shift.

7. For example, Jewish opposition to ERA was motivated mainly by concern for its impact on sex segregation in Orthodox day schools.

8. Quoted in "Befuddled by Women," *Time*, November 30, 1992:23.

9. Greeley shows that while political orientation (Republican or Democrat) does not correlate significantly with Catholic conservatism, sexism does (70 percent of conservative Catholics think women ought to subordinate their careers to those of their husbands).

10. Over the last century, most mainline denominations have begun to ordain women. A woman was ordained in the Methodist Protestant church in 1880. Some Congregationalist, Unitarian, and Disciples of Christ women were ordained in the early twentieth century. United Methodists and United Presbyterians both gave full ordination to women in 1956. In 1964 the Southern Presbyterians followed the Northern example. Women were ordained in the Lutheran Church in America and the American Lutheran church in 1970, in the Free Methodist church in 1974, and in the Episcopal church in 1976 (see Hargrove 1985; Hardesty 1984).

11. Accounts of the history of conservative Protestant feminism can be found in Bendroth 1993, Fowler 1985, and Hunter 1992, but Bendroth is by far the most comprehensive source.

12. Hardesty called for the formulation and declaration of a progressive stand on women at a Thanksgiving workshop in Chicago in 1973, where "a distinguished group of 53 Evangelicals met to draw up a progressive social agenda," but even reform-minded Evangelicals were opposed to Hardesty's proposal and only passed a watered-down version (see Fowler 1985:21; Bendroth 1993:122).

13. When the EWC voted to "recognize the presence of a lesbian minority" at the July 1986 conference in Fresno, several prominent members resigned and started a new group: Christians for Biblical Equality. EWC has since lost about 50 percent of its membership. Now that CBE pushes for women's equality in Evangelical churches, some EWC members feel they should focus on minority and social justice issues (reported in *Christianity Today*, October 3, 1986:40–43, and September 2, 1988:43–44).

14. Accounts of the history of Catholic feminism can be found in Farrell 1991, Kenneally 1990, Kennelly 1989, and Weaver 1985, the last of which I found to be the most useful.

15. Though many Protestant churches had admitted women to the ministry by 1970, the Catholic church didn't really have to address the ordination issue until Anglican bishops ordained women in the early 1970s, which moved Vatican officials to vigorously oppose it.

16. The name reflects their argument that "we are the church," a feminist interpretation of Vatican II's new designation of the church as "the people of God."

17. Weaver argues that the nuns' coming to feminism was natural. Their high level of education and the bonding they experienced as a women's community would make them receptive to feminist ideas, and "their outsider status in the hierarchical church gives them insider status in the women's movement" (107).
18. For example, the general American emphasis on education after the 1920s meant that Catholic schools had to have qualified teachers to compete. Thus nuns, who traditionally staffed these schools, were encouraged to acquire advanced degrees.
19. I found the most comprehensive accounts of the history of Jewish feminism to be those of Lerner 1977 and Fishman 1989. However, neither of them contains much information on Orthodox Jewish feminism.
20. For example, many Christian feminists were critical of Israel. Even more hurtful to Jewish feminists was the argument that Jewish patriarchalism had sullied what otherwise would have been purely egalitarian Christianity.
21. For descriptions of the controversy this generated in the Jewish community, see "Women Tell Off Their Orthodox Rabbis," *Jewish Post & Opinion*, January 26, 1983, and "Orthodox Women are Running Their Own Sabbath Services," *The Jewish Week*, March 23, 1984.
22. There are interesting parallels between this case and Shannon Faulkner's experience with the Citadel, a military college in South Carolina.
23. Various explanations have been offered, including that men have more precepts to perform and therefore a greater potential for reward, and that, in order to be a man, he must suppress his feminine traits and the prayer therefore refers only to those traits that are undesirable in a man. For further examples, see Spero 1973.

Chapter 3   *Three Conservative Religious Communities*

1. The Charismatic movement is an outgrowth of Pentecostalism which was born at the turn of the century when revivalists in the Holiness tradition began preaching that the born-again experience is followed by a state of sanctification that is signified by the expression of gifts from the Holy Spirit. For a good history, see Anderson 1979, Paloma 1982, or Quebedeaux 1983.
2. Although there has been some debate about how the terms "conservative" and "liberal" should be defined, the categories employed here are consistent with commonly used research indicators (see Cuneo 1988; Greeley 1991; Hunter 1991; Weaver and Appleby 1995).
3. According to the Talmud, a man takes or acquires a wife through sexual intercourse with her, a financial gift, or a contract. The traditional Jewish marriage ceremony, which takes place under a chuppah (canopy), formalizes the marriage.
4. Los Angeles has the second largest Jewish community both in the United States and in the world. Although the Los Angeles Jewish population is younger and has a higher intermarriage rate than other major Jewish centers (New York, Chicago, Philadelphia), the relatively high level of education and income of Jews reflects broader national patterns. According to a recent demographic study of the Los Angeles Jewish population, Jews (both males and females) were better educated than non-Hispanic whites (Jewish women were 50–60 percent more likely to have graduated from college than non-Jewish women); those higher education levels were accompanied by higher Jewish representation in professional occupations (Phillips 1986). While similar data on Los

Angeles Catholics and Evangelicals is not available, a look at national surveys may provide some comparative perspective. According to a recent national poll conducted by the Gallup organization, Catholics are replacing Protestants as "the new middle class." Catholics constitute 26 percent of the population, compared to Protestants who constitute 56 percent. Yet 26 percent of college graduates and 26 percent of those who attended at least some college are Catholic, compared to 53 percent and 52 percent who are Protestant. Similarly, Catholics represent 30 percent of those with incomes over $75,000, 30 percent of those with incomes between $50,000 and $74,999, 27 percent of those with incomes between $20,000 and $49,999, and only 23 percent of those with incomes under $20,000. By contrast, Protestants represent 48, 55, 57, and 60 percent of those categories, respectively (PRRC, March 1993). Evangelicals in particular tend to be clustered at the lower end of the income scale (PRRC, April 1993).

5. I use the term "Hispanic" rather than "Latino" because the former is the term employed in the communities themselves. It is estimated that the vast majority (about 80 percent) of Hispanics in the United States are Catholic. According to a 1994 study conducted by the Life Cycle Institute at Catholic University of America, the average American diocese is 7 percent Hispanic; the archdiocese of Los Angeles is 36 percent Hispanic. California Evangelical churches, too, often have a significant proportion of Hispanic members. According to recent studies (see Roof and Manning 1994 for an overview), about 20 percent of the Hispanic population in the United States identifies as Protestant, and Evangelicals are among the most effective in attracting Hispanic Americans to their congregations.

6. Modern Evangelicalism, or Neo-Evangelicalism as represented by the National Association of Evangelicals, split from fundamentalist Protestantism over precisely this issue of involvement in the world (Marsden 1987). It is mainly Evangelicals such as Jerry Falwell, and not fundamentalists, who have become politically active in the New Right (Marty and Appleby 1992). Similarly, Modern Orthodox Judaism was founded in nineteenth-century Germany by Samson Raphael Hirsch who believed that traditional Judaism was compatible with life in the modern world. His approach was institutionalized in the United States by the founding of Yeshiva University which trains Orthodox rabbis but is committed to educating its students in secular knowledge as well (Davidman 1991).

7. Good examples of more isolationist conservatives are the fundamentalist Christians described by Ammerman (1987) and the Lubavitcher Hasidic Jews described by Davidman (1991). In contrast to the congregations discussed in this study, members of these communities actively avoided contact with the outside world, e.g., by seeking employment from other Christians and Orthodox Jews, by not watching TV and reading only Christian or Jewish periodicals, and by seeking assistance from Christian or Jewish lawyers or physicians. Because of the inclusive nature of the Catholic Church, conservative Catholics have not been able to isolate in this way.

8. It appears that members of Victory Church had slightly higher levels of education and income than Evangelicals elsewhere in the United States, but were fairly representative of Evangelicals in California. According to a national survey conducted in 1992 by the Gallup Organization, Evangelicals constitute 36 percent of the U.S. population. They represent 28 percent of college graduates. Of Americans with incomes above $75,000, only 26 percent are Evangelical, while Evangelicals represent 27 percent of those with incomes between

$50,000 and $74,999, 37 percent of those with incomes between $20,000 and $49,999, and 44 percent of those with incomes under $20,000 (PRRC, April 1993). While demographic statistics for Evangelicals in California are not available, studies of other Evangelical churches can serve as a basis of comparison. According to a study conducted by Paul Kennedy (1992) of the Vineyard Christian fellowship, a growing Evangelical denomination in California, 54 percent of those surveyed declared their family income to be $40,000 or more and 46 percent had graduated from college. According to a study conducted by Donald Miller (1992) of Hope Chapel, a charismatic Evangelical denomination very similar to Victory Church, 28 percent of respondents earned more than $60,000 and 30 percent between $40,000 and $59,999; 46 percent were college graduates and another 40 percent had attended some college.

9. According to a recent Gallup poll, 25 percent of U.S. Catholics are college graduates and another 26 percent have attended at least some college; 28 percent of U.S. Catholics reported an annual household income of more than $50,000, 27 percent an income between $30,000 and 49,000, 25 percent an income between $15,000 and $29,000, and 20 percent an income under $15,000 (PRRC, September 1991). It thus appears that levels in income and education of the women at St. Joseph's were higher than for Catholics elsewhere in the United States; however, since salaries and cost of living are higher in California, it is likely that, as was true at Victory Church, they are fairly representative of white Catholics in California.

10. Demographic data on Orthodox Jews are difficult to come by, as most surveys do not break down education and income data by Jewish denomination. California state and national polls conducted in 1980–1982 and 1979 respectively indicate that 56 percent of U.S. Jews are college educated (measure does not specify what kind of degree was attained), while in California 35 percent have at least some college education, 23 percent have college degrees, and 23 percent have graduate degrees (Fisher and Tanaka 1986). These figures suggest that the relatively high level of education of the women at Beth Israel is typical of American Jews generally and California Jews in particular. The surveys also indicate that 29 percent of California Jews earned less than $20,000, 19 percent between $20,000 and $30,000, and 52 percent more than $30,000 (nationally, 50 percent of Jews earned less than $20,000 and 49 percent more than $20,000). Because of the level of inflation that has occurred over the last decade, it is not possible to compare these income data with those of Beth Israel; however, it is likely that high levels of education are accompanied by high levels of income. One of the few surveys of Orthodox Jews available is Heilman and Cohen's (1989) study which is based on surveys conducted in 1980 in various East coast cities. In their sample, 23 percent of Orthodox Jews earned less than $20,000, 41 percent between $20,000 and $40,000, and 36 percent above $40,000. Among the women in their sample, 50 percent had earned graduate degrees and 26 percent had a bachelor's degree. While inflation means that income figures from 1980 are not comparable with mine, the educational statistics are similar. Since Heilman and Cohen acknowledge that the levels of income and education of their sample was somewhat higher than those of other samples of Orthodox Jews in the New York area, it is likely that the women at Beth Israel were better educated and therefore earned more income than other Orthodox Jews.

11. For further discussion of this division, see Manning 1997.

Chapter 4   Feminists in Society

1. Charles Hall (1995) has shown that religious teaching about motherhood and homemaking as the ideal female role has only an indirect effect on labor force participation of conservative Protestant women, affecting women's ideals but not necessarily their behavior. By contrast, my research suggests that at least some women may be changing their ideals by reinterpreting religious teaching.

Chapter 5   Traditionalists in Church and Synagogue

1. This is an illustration of the advantages of qualitative research. Though it would be misleading to use these indicators in a survey, unstructured interviews coupled with direct observation allow the researcher to verify what the indicators mean.
2. The exception to this exemption rule are three women's mitzvot: *Hadlakat ner Shabbat* (kindling of Sabbath and festival lights), challah (preparing the Sabbath loaf), and *Taharat hamishpacha* (family purity laws).
3. Women have the option of performing mitzvot not required of them, except for the wearing of tallit and tefillin.
4. St. Joseph's allows wives of men who want to be deacons to attend the classes with their husbands but women cannot become deacons themselves.
5. The woman who heads St. Joseph's Hispanic outreach program told me that acceptance of change is more limited in the Hispanic community. "I find that the overall church here took [the changes in women's roles] very well. With the Hispanics it took longer, and it's still kind of a touchy subject. They're coming from old church. People who come from Mexico and South American and other Latin countries, they are reluctant to changes in women's role in the church. They're reluctant to see leadership of women in ministries." As leader of St. Joseph's Hispanic ministry as well as of Growth through Loss (a support group for Catholics who are mourning the death of a loved one), she herself has encountered resistance from Hispanic parishioners. However, she says, "I've seen it more with people from their own countries. They treat me a little different because I'm bilingual, and I'm here in the U.S., but with women from their own countries they seem to be more critical."

Chapter 6   But What About the Home?

1. I borrow this term from Susan Starr Sered's (1997) book, which contains an wonderful chapter on food preparation as a religious activity.
2. Some women even argue that male headship is not authentic Jewish teaching, describing it as a product of Eastern European culture or an adaptation to Christian society. Marcia, for example, asserted that "women are the central roles of the family—not men. I think that is kind of a secular or Christian model of the male being the head of the house." Michelle admitted that "there are some families in other [Orthodox] congregations where that [male headship] is the case…but they basically have an Eastern European mentality, and that's never going to change. They can treat their wives like doormats and the wives aren't going to mind, because their mothers were treated like doormats and that's the way life is….[But] I can't think of a single family I know of where you can look and you say, it fits the traditional patriarchal family."

3. For a description of what Orthodox Jewish domestic ritual entails, see Blu Greenberg 1983.
4. Abortion, for instance, may be permitted if pregnancy would endanger a woman's mental and physical health.
5. This belief has led to a degree of anti-intellectualism within Evangelicalism that scorns seminary training. While such disdain seems to be fading in larger conservative Protestant denominations, many Evangelicals (especially in charismatic congregations like Victory) believe that anyone called to preach can lead a congregation.
6. Many Evangelical leaders endorse the use of contraceptives so long as they are used by married people as part of family planning. Many Orthodox rabbis permit some forms of contraception (because the obligation to "not spill seed" falls only on the man, contraceptive devices such as the pill, which are employed by women and do not act as a barrier, are permitted). By contrast, the Catholic Church prohibits any form of artificial birth control. There are liberal Catholic theologians (e.g., Charles Curran) who dissent from this teaching, and their writing seems to have influenced some of the more liberal lay persons in the church.
7. It is in the nature of hierarchies, especially large ones, that decisions made at the top seem very far removed from the people at the bottom whom they affect, making it easier for the latter to ignore the rules. This may explain why Catholic women have a long history of ignoring church mandates (see Kenneally 1990).

Chapter 7   *Understanding Inconsistency*

1. For a comprehensive review of cognitive dissonance research since Festinger, see Brehm and Wicklund 1976 and Clemence 1991.

Chapter 8   *Profeminist or Antifeminist?*

1. Curiously, many of the women seemed to assume that the 1950s were a time when homemakers were revered and respected as much as lawyers or surgeons.
2. In the Catholic tradition, the highest life is one of consecrated virginity; however, conservative Catholic writings (especially the popular literature read by ordinary women) have emphasized motherhood and the nurturing qualities it fosters as the role in which most women can best serve God.
3. Their assumption that gender differences are important and their tendency to elevate feminine characteristics may help explain the opposition of conservative Protestant and Catholic profeminists in this study to abortion and homosexuality. Men and women are different, but they complement each other, and the qualities of both are needed to keep the world in balance and harmony. Homosexuality, to these women, seems a direct contradiction of this theory of complementarity. By the same token, abortion seems to deny women's unique contribution of bringing children into this world. Allowing reproductive choice elevates male values of competition over female values of nurturing.
4. For a good summary of radical feminism see Tong 1989.

Chapter 9　Conflict with Secular America— Abortion and Homosexuality

1. Quoted in Ingersoll 1993.
2. The women used the terms "diseased" and "sinful" interchangeably: society is diseased or sick because too many people have turned away from God and are engaging in sinful behavior.
3. Like any other violation of halacha, committing such a sin is an act that requires repentance and change of behavior. As in conservative Protestant communities, an individual who is openly homosexual or had several abortions would experience considerable social pressure to leave.

Chapter 10　Understanding the Differences

1. This also explains why so many Evangelicals are opposed to welfare: they believe that most poor women do not deserve our help because they have had children out of wedlock.
2. For an excellent history of fundamentalism and gender, see Bendroth 1993. Interesting perspectives are also provided by DeBerg 1990 and Hassey 1986.
3. Fundamentalism was distinct from Pentecostalism, which, in its early stages, did correlate with economic deprivation (see Anderson 1979).
4. Among the results of that reformation were the establishment of the National Association of Evangelicals, Fuller Seminary, and Christianity Today as centrist Evangelical institutions (Marsden 1987).
5. For a more detailed treatment of Evangelical politics, see Conover and Gray 1983, Jorstadt 1987, and Liebman and Wuthnow 1983.
6. Useful histories of Catholic women include Kenneally 1989 and 1990, and Weaver 1985, all of which attempt to correct for the institutional bias of Catholic history which tends to render lay people, women in particular, invisible.
7. Until recently, even religiously conservative Catholics have tended to be Democrats.
8. Contrary to stereotypes, middle-class Catholic women played an important role in progressive reform, especially temperance.
9. The reason for this may be that Protestants split into liberal and conservative denominations, allowing the former to reject Victorian womanhood while the latter retained that model.
10. Ironically, the Americanist controversy, which had been initiated by liberal Catholics, resulted in greater centralization of the church which in turn led to strong Catholic opposition to ERA when it was first proposed in 1922 (Kenneally 1989).
11. The long process of writing the Pastoral Letter on Women's Concerns illustrates this dilemma. For a detailed discussion of how these divisions affect both liberal and conservative Catholic women, see Manning 1997.
12. Unfortunately, no history of Orthodox Jewish women—as a religious group—exists. Histories of Jewish women (e.g., Baum 1976; Glenn 1990) tend to treat them as an ethnic group and do not differentiate between Reform and Orthodox Jews. We can assume, however, that most first generation immigrants in the late nineteenth and early twentieth century were Orthodox, so that even ethnic histories can provide some insight into the lives of women in Orthodox communities.
13. As in the case of Catholics and Protestants, the Victorian cult of domesticity

had the ironic effect of increasing middle-class Jewish women's public role in society—e.g., via involvement in Progressive reform efforts—but also in the synagogue—e.g., running charity events (Baum 1976).

14. All pre-industrial women economically supported their families but only in Jewish families was it considered appropriate for the wife to be the sole breadwinner (Baum 1976).

15. Although middle-class Reform Jews participated actively in the suffrage movement, most working immigrants, many of whom were Orthodox, did not. However, Glenn (1990) argues that the latter's union activity provided a model for U.S. feminists.

16. There are some interesting parallels between the socialist/labor leanings of immigrant Orthodox Jewish and Catholic women on the one hand, and middle-class Reform Jews and liberal Protestants and their attempts to "civilize" working-class immigrants on the other.

17. This is a good illustration of the tension between "women-focused" and "race/class-focused" feminism discussed in chapter 2. As for black women today, Jewish women's loyalty to their community conflicted with the woman-centered rhetoric of feminists. Just as racism among white feminists has contributed to the emergence of a black "womanist" movement today, so Protestant discrimination earlier this century caused Jews to form their own feminist movement.

18. Some conservative scholars advocate compartmentalization as the only way to avoid adaptation; others see compartmentalization as a sign of compromise (e.g., compare Heilman 1977 and Kaplan 1983). Either way, compartmentalization has become a common method of avoiding conflict.

Bibliography

Albanese, Catherine. 1981. *America: Religions and Religion.* Belmont, Calif.: Wadsworth.

Alexander, Kay. 1993. *Californian Catholicism.* The Religious Contours of California Series, vol. 1. Santa Barbara, Calif.: Fithian Press.

Alwin, Duane, et. al. 1983. "Causes and Consequences of Sex-Role Attitudes and Attitude Change." *American Sociological Review* 48:211–227.

Ammerman, Nancy. 1982. "Operationalizing Evangelicalism: An Amendment." *Sociological Analysis* 43, 2:170–171.

———. 1987. *Bible Believers: Fundamentalists in the Modern World.* New Brunswick, N.J.: Rutgers University Press.

Anderson, Robert M. 1979. *Vision of the Disinherited: The Making of American Pentecostalism.* New York: Oxford University Press.

Appleby, R. Scott. 1995. "What Difference Do They Make?" In *Being Right: Conservative Catholics in America,* edited by R. S. Appleby and M. J. Weaver. Bloomington: Indiana University Press.

Arnold, Patrick. 1987. "The Rise of Catholic Fundamentalism." *America,* 11 April:297–302.

Balmer, Randall. 1989. *Mine Eyes Have Seen the Glory: A Journey into the Evangelical Subculture in America.* New York: Oxford University Press.

Barfoot, Charles, and Gerald Sheppard. 1980. "Prophetic vs. Priestly Religion: The Changing Role of Women in Classical Pentecostal Churches." *Review of Religious Research* 22,1:2–17.

Baum, Charlotte, Paula Hyman, and Sonya Michel. 1976. *The Jewish Woman in America.* New York: Dial Press.

Bellah, Robert. 1967. "Civil Religion in America," *Daedalus* 96,1:1–9.

Bendroth, Margaret Lamberts. 1993. *Fundamentalism and Gender: 1875 to the Present.* New Haven, Conn.: Yale University Press.

Biale, Rachel. 1984. *Women and Jewish Law: An Exploration of Women's Issues in Halakhic Sources.* New York: Schocken Books.

Blau, Joseph. 1976. *Judaism in America: From Curiosity to Third Faith.* Chicago: University of Chicago Press.

Brehm, Jack, and Robert Wicklund. 1976. *Perspectives on Cognitive Dissonance.* Hillsdale, New Jersey: Lawrence Erlbaum Associates.

Brown, Ruth Murray. 1984. "In Defense of Traditional Values: The Anti-Feminist Movement." *Marriage and Family Review* 7,3/4:19–35.

Browne, J. Patrick, and Timothy Lukes. 1988. "Women Called Catholics: The Sources of Dissatisfaction Within the Church, Santa Clara County, California." *Journal for the Scientific Study of Religion* 27,2:284–290.

Bulka, Reuven, ed. 1983. *Dimensions of Orthodox Judaism*. New York: Ktav Publishing.

Bunim, Sarah. 1986. *Religious and Secular Factors of Role Strain in Orthodox Jewish Mothers*. Ph.D. diss., Yeshiva University.

Butler, Diana Hochstedt. 1993. "Between Two Worlds." *Christian Century*, 3 March:231–232.

Butman, Rabbi Shmuel. 1984. "The Fulfillment of the Jewish Woman." *The Jewish Press*, 28 December:8 B.

Campbell, Debra. 1989. "Reformers and Activists." In *American Catholic Women: A Historical Exploration*, edited by Karen Kennelly. New York: Mcmillan.

Campbell, Dwight. 1993. "The Value of Motherhood." *Hearth: Journal of the Authentic Catholic Woman*, Spring:17–22.

Capps, Walter. 1994. *The New Religious Right*. Columbia, South Carolina: University of South Carolina Press.

Carmody, Denise Lardner. 1986. *The Double Cross: Ordination, Abortion, and Catholic Feminism*. New York: Crossroad.

Carroll, Jackson, Barbara Hargrove, and Adair Lummis. 1981. *Women of the Cloth: A New Opportunity for the Churches*. San Francisco: Harper & Row.

Chaves, Mark. 1994. *Ordaining Women: Culture and Conflict in Religious Organizations*. Cambridge, Mass.: Harvard University Press.

Chervin, Rhonda, et. al. 1988. *Woman to Woman: Handing on our Experiences of the Joyful, Sorrowful, and Glorious Mysteries of Life*. San Francisco: Ignatius Press.

Christ, Carol, and Judith Plaskow, eds. 1979. *Womanspirit Rising: A Feminist Reader in Religion*. San Francisco: Harper & Row.

———. 1989. *Weaving the Visions: New Patterns in Feminist Spirituality*. San Francisco: Harper & Row.

Clamar, Aphrodite. 1979. "Torah True and Feminist Too: A Psychotherapist's View of the Conflict Between Orthodox Judaism and the Women's Movement." Paper presented at the annual meeting of the American Psychological Association, New York.

Clemence, Alain. 1991. "Theories of Cognitive Dissonance." *Social Science Information* 30,1:55–79.

Clouse, Bonnidell, and Robert Clouse, eds. 1989. *Women in Ministry: Four Views*. Downers Grove, Illinois: Intervarsity Press.

Cohen, Steven. 1980. "American Jewish Feminism." *American Behavioral Scientist* 23:519–558.

———. 1988. *American Assimilation or Jewish Revival?* Bloomington: Indiana University Press.

Cohen-Nusbacher, Ailene. 1977. *The Orthodox Professional Jewish Woman*. Masters thesis, Brooklyn College.

———. 1987. *Responses to Secular Influences Among Orthodox Jewish Women*. Ph.D. diss., New York University.

Cohler, Larry. 1985. "Angered Women Vow to Continue: Orthodox Rabbis' Responsa Condemns Women's Prayer Group." *Jewish World*, 15–21 February:12.

Conn, Joseph. 1993a. "Unholy Matrimony." *Church & State* 46,4:4.

———. 1993b. "Playing Broadway." *Church & State* 46,6:4.

Conover, Pamela Johnston, and Virginia Gray. 1983. *Feminism and the New Right: Conflict over the American Family*. New York: Praeger.

Coontz, Stephanie. 1992. *The Way We Never Were: American Families and the Nostalgia Trap*. New York: Basic Books.

Cross, Robert. 1958. *The Emergence of Liberal Catholicism in America*. Cambridge: Harvard University Press.

Cuneo, Michael. 1988. "Soldiers of Orthodoxy: Revivalist Catholicism in North America." *Studies in Religion/Sciences Religieuses* 17,3:347–363.

———. 1989. *Catholics Against the Church: Anti-Abortion Protest in Toronto, 1969–1985.* Toronto: University of Toronto Press.

Daly, Mary. 1968. *The Church and the Second Sex.* New York: Harper & Row.

D'Antonio, William, et. al. 1989. *American Catholic Laity in a Changing Church.* Kansas City, Missouri: Sheed & Ward.

Danzger, M. Herbert. 1989. *Returning to Tradition: The Contemporary Revival of Orthodox Judaism.* New Haven: Yale University Press.

Davidman, Lynn. 1991. *Tradition in a Rootless World: Women Turn to Orthodox Judaism.* Berkeley: University of California Press.

Davidman, Lynn, and Janet Stocks. 1995. "Varieties of Fundamentalist Experience." In *New World Hasidim: Ethnographic Studies of Hasidic Jews in America,* edited by J. Belcove-Shalin. New York: State University of New York Press.

Davidson, Haviva Krasner. 1993. "Why I'm Applying to Yeshiva University." *Moment,* December:54.

DeBerg, Betty. 1990. *Ungodly Rage: Gender and the First Wave of American Fundamentalism.* Minneapolis, Minn.: Fortress Press.

Demmit, Kevin. 1992. "Loosening the Ties that Bind: The Accommodation of Dual Earner Families in a Conservative Protestant Church." *Review of Religious Research* 34,1:3–19.

Dobson, James. 1982. *Marriage and Sexuality: Dr. Dobson Answers Your Questions.* Wheaton, Illinois: Tyndale House Publishers.

Dworkin, Andrea.1983. *Right Wing Women.* New York: Coward McCann.

Ernst, Eldon. 1993. *Pilgrim Procession: The Protestant Experience in California.* The Religious Contours of California Series, vol. 2. Santa Barbara, Calif.: Fithian Press.

Faludi, Susan. 1991. *Backlash: The Undeclared War against American Women.* New York: Crown.

Farrell, Susan. 1991. "'It's Our Church, Too!': Women's Position in the Catholic Church Today." In *The Social Construction of Gender,* edited by J. Lorber and S. Farrell. Newbury Park, Calif.: Sage Publications.

Festinger, Leon. 1957. *A Theory of Cognitive Dissonance.* Stanford, Calif.: Stanford University Press.

Fisher, Alan, and Curtis Tanaka. 1986. "California Jews: Data from the Field Polls." *American Jewish Yearbook*:196–218.

Fishman, Sylvia Barack. 1989. "The Impact of Feminism on American Jewish Life." *American Jewish Yearbook,* 3–62.

Fiorenza, Elizabeth Schuessler. 1983. *In Memory of Her: A Feminist Reconstruction of Christian Origins.* New York: Crossroad.

Flexner, Eleanor. 1975. *Century of Struggle: The Women's Rights Movement in the United States.* Cambridge: Harvard University Press.

Forman, Sheila Hoban. 1988. *The Effects of Being Raised and Educated Roman Catholic on Women's Self-Concept.* Ph.D. diss., University of San Francisco.

Fox-Genovese, Elizabeth. 1991. *Feminism Without Illusions: A Critique of Individualism.* Chapel Hill: University of North Carolina Press.

———. 1996. *Feminism Is Not the Story of My Life.* New York: Doubleday.

Fowler, Robert Booth. 1985. "The Feminist and Antifeminist Debate Within Evangelical Protestantism." *Women and Politics* 5,2/3:7–39.

Francome, Caroline, and Colin Francome. 1979. "Towards an Understanding of the American Abortion Rate." *Journal of Biosocial Science* 1,3:303–313.

Frankiel, Tamar. 1990. *The Voice of Sarah: Feminine Spirituality and Traditional Judaism*. San Francisco: Harper & Row.

Garfinkel, Harold. 1967. *Studies in Ethnomethodology*. Englewood Cliffs, New Jersey: Prentice Hall.

Gittleson, Natalie. 1984. "American Jews Rediscover Orthodoxy." *New York Times Magazine*, 30 September:40.

Glenn, Susan. 1990. *Daughters of the Shtetl: Life and Labor in the Immigrant Generation*. Ithaca, N.Y.: Cornell University Press.

Goldenberg, Naomi. 1987. "The Return of the Goddess." *Studies in Religion* 16,1:37–52.

Goldman, Ari. 1992. "Catholics at Odds with Bishops." *New York Times*, 19 June:A 8.

Greeley, Andrew. 1990. *The Catholic Myth: The Behavior and Beliefs of American Catholics*. New York: Charles Scribner's Sons.

———. 1991. "Who are the Catholic 'Conservatives'?" *America*, 21 September:158–162.

Greeley, Andrew, and Mary Durkin. 1984. *Angry Catholic Women*. Chicago: The Thomas Moore Press.

Greenberg, Blu. 1981. *On Women and Judaism: A View from Tradition*. Philadelphia: Jewish Publication Society of America.

———. 1983. *How to Run a Traditional Jewish Household*. Northvale, N.J. Jason Aaronson.

———. 1993. "Is Now the Time for Orthodox Women Rabbis?" *Moment*, December:50.

Griffith, R. Marie. 1997. *God's Daughters: Evangelical Women and the Power of Submission*. Berkeley: University of California Press.

Gundry, Patricia. 1977. *Woman Be Free!* Grand Rapids, Mich.: Zondervan.

Hall, Charles. 1995. "Entering the Labor Force." In *Work, Family, and Religion in Contemporary Society*, edited by W. C. Roof and N. T. Ammerman. New York: Routledge.

Hardesty, Nancy. 1984. *Women Called to Witness: Evangelical Feminism in the 19th Century*. Nashville, Tenn.: Abingdon Press.

Hargrove, Barbara, Jean Miller Schmidt, and Sheila Greeve Davaney. 1985. "Religion and the Changing Role of Women." *Annals*, AAPSS 480 (July):117–131.

Hassey, Janette. 1986. *No Time for Silence: Evangelical Women in Public Ministry around the Turn of the Century*. Grand Rapids, Michigan: Academie Books (Zondervan).

Hatch, Nathan. 1992. "Can Evangelicalism Survive its own Success?" *Christianity Today*, 5 October:20–31.

Haut, Rivka. 1992. "Women's Prayer Groups and the Orthodox Synagogue." In *Daughters of the King: Women and the American Synagogue*, edited by S. Grossman and R. Haut. Philadelphia: Jewish Publication Society.

Hegy, Pierre. 1993. "The End of American Catholicism? Another Look." *America*, 1 May:4.

Heilman, Samuel. 1976. *Synagogue Life: A Study in Symbolic Interaction*. Chicago: University of Chicago Press.

———. 1977. "Inner and Outer Identities: Sociological Ambivalence among Modern Orthodox Jews." *Jewish Social Studies* 39,3:227–240.

———. 1978. "Constructing Orthodoxy." *Society* 15,4:32–40.

Heilman, Samuel, and Steven Cohen. 1989. *Cosmopolitans & Parochials: Modern Orthodox Jews in America*. Chicago: University of Chicago Press.

Heritage, John. 1984. *Garfinkel and Ethnomethodology*. Cambridge, U.K.: Polity Press.

Heshel, Susannah. 1983. *On Being A Jewish Feminist: A Reader*. New York: Schocken Books.

Hirsch, Samson Raphel. 1959. *Judaism Eternal*. London: Soncino.

Hitchcock, Helen Hull, ed. 1992. *The Politics of Prayer: Feminist Language and the Worship of God*. San Francisco: Ignatius Press.

Hoge, Dean. 1981. *Converts, Dropouts, Returnees: A Study of Religious Change among Catholics*. New York: Pilgrim Press.

Hunter, James Davidson. 1981. "Operationalizing Evangelicalism: A Review, Critique and Proposal." *Sociological Analysis* 42,4:363–372.

———. 1987. *Evangelicalism: The Coming Generation*. Chicago: University of Chicago Press.

———. 1991. *Culture Wars: The Struggle to Define America*. New York: Basic Books.

Hyer, Marjorie. 1984. "Evangelical Women Seek to Reconcile Bible, Equality." *Washington Post*, 7 July:D 10.

———. 1986. "Conservative Catholics Act to Hold Up Jesuit's Appointment." *Washington Post*, 17 July:A 15.

———. 1988a. "Pro-Choice Nuns Face Expulsion." *Washington Post*, 21 January:A 8.

———. 1988b. "U.S. Catholic Bishops Label Sexism 'Sin': Pastoral Letter Urges More Women's Roles." *Washington Post*, 12 April:A 1.

Ingersoll, Julie. 1993. "From Right to Life to Anti-Gay Rights: Shifting Traditional Family Values." Paper presented at the annual meeting of the Society for the Scientific Study of Religion, Raleigh, North Carolina.

Jewett, Paul. 1975. *Man as Male and Female*. Grand Rapids, Mich.: Eerdmans.

Johnson, Paul. 1982. *Pope John Paul II and the Catholic Restoration*. London: Weidenfeld and Nicolson.

Jorstadt, Erling. 1987. *The New Christian Right, 1981–1988*. Lewiston, New York: Edwin Mellen Press.

Kaplan, Lawrence. 1983. "The Ambiguous Modern Orthodox Jew." In *Dimensions of Orthodox Judaism*, edited by R. Bulka. New York: Ktav Publishing.

Kantzer, Kenneth. 1992. "The Doctrine Wars." *Christianity Today*, 5 October:32–35.

Karrsen, Gien. 1987. *The Man Who Was Different*. Colorado Springs, Colo.: Nav Press.

Kaufman, Debra. 1991. *Rachel's Daughters: Newly Orthodox Jewish Women*. New Brunswick, N.J.: Rutgers University Press.

Kaufman, Michael. 1993. *The Woman in Jewish Law and Tradition*. Northvale, N.J.: Jason Aronson.

Kayfetz, Ben. 1985. "Jewish Feminists Called New 'Jezebels' by Rabbi." *The Jewish Week*, January:7.

Kelley, Dean. 1972. *Why Conservative Churches are Growing*. New York: Harper & Row.

Kenneally, James. 1989. "A Question of Equality." In *American Catholic Women: A Historical Exploration*, edited by K. Kennelly. New York: Mcmillan.

———. 1990. *The History of American Catholic Women*. New York: Crossroad.

Kennedy, Paul. 1992. "The Vineyard Christian Fellowship: Demographic Characteristics of Pastors and People." Paper presented at the annual meeting of the Society for the Scientific Study of Religion, Washington, D.C.

Kennelly, Karen, ed. 1989. *American Catholic Women: A Historical Exploration*. New York: Mcmillan.

Klatch, Rebecca. 1987. *Women of the New Right.* Philadelphia: Temple University Press.

Kolthun, Elizabeth, ed. 1976. *The Jewish Woman: New Perspectives.* New York: Schocken Books.

Kranzler, Gershon. 1983. "The Changing Orthodox Jewish Family." In *Dimensions of Orthodox Judaism,* edited by R. Bulka. New York: Ktav Publishing.

Krasner-Davidson, Haviva. 1993. "Why I'm Applying to Yeshiva U." *Moment,* December:54.

Kuzmack, Linda Gordon. 1990. *Woman's Cause: The Jewish Woman's Movement in England and the United States, 1881–1933.* Columbus: Ohio State University Press.

LaHaye, Beverly. 1976. *The Spirit-Controlled Woman.* Eugene, Oregon: Harvest House Publishers.

LaHaye, Tim. 1968. *How to Be Happy though Married.* Wheaton, Illinois: Tyndale House.

Lawless, Elaine. 1988. *Handmaidens of the Lord: Pentecostal Women Preachers and Traditional Religion.* Philadelphia: University of Pennsylvania Press.

Lehman, Edward. 1985. *Women Clergy: Breaking through Gender Barriers.* New Brunswick, N.J.: Transaction Books.

Lerner, Ann Lapidus. 1977. "'Who Hast Not Made Me a Man': The Movement for Equal Rights for Women in American Jewry." *American Jewish Yearbook:*3–38.

Levi, Leo. 1980. *Man and Woman: The Torah Perspective.* Jerusalem: Ezer Layeled.

Lifton, Robert Jay. 1993. *The Protean Self: Human Resilience in an Age of Fragmentation.* New York: Basic Books.

Liebman, Charles. 1983a. "Religion and the Chaos of Modernity." In *Take Judaism, for Example: Studies toward the Comparison of Religions,* edited by Jacob Neusner. Chicago: University of Chicago Press.

———. 1983b. "Orthodoxy in American Jewish Life." In *Dimensions of Orthodox Judaism,* edited by R. Bulka. New York: Ktav Publishing.

———. 1983c. "Orthodox Judaism Today." In *Dimensions of Orthodox Judaism,* edited by R. Bulka. New York: Ktav Publishing.

———. 1988. *Deceptive Images: Toward a Redefinition of American Judaism.* New Brunswick, New Jersey: Transaction Books.

Liebman, Robert, and Robert Wuthnow, eds. 1983. *The New Christian Right: Mobilization and Legitimation.* New York: Aldine Publishing.

Lienesh, Michael. 1993. *Redeeming America: Piety and Politics in the New Christian Right.* Chapel Hill: University of North Carolina Press.

Life Cycle Institute of America. 1994. *Overview and Profile of the Dioceses.* Washington, D.C.: Catholic University of America.

Lincoln, Bruce. 1989. *Discourse and the Construction of Society.* New York: Oxford University Press.

Luker, Kristin. 1984. *Abortion and the Politics of Motherhood.* Berkeley: University of California Press.

Malcolm, Kari Torjesen. 1982. *Women at the Crossroads.* Downers Grove, Ill.: Intervarsity Press.

Manning, Christel. 1997. "Women in a Divided Church: Liberal and Conservative Catholic Women Negotiate Changing Gender Roles." *Sociology of Religion* 58,4:375–390.

Marsden, George. 1980. *Fundamentalism and American Culture: The Shaping of Twentieth Century Evangelicalism, 1870–1925.* New York: Oxford University Press.

————. 1987. *Reforming Fundamentalism: Fuller Seminary and the New Evangelicalism*. Grand Rapids, Mich.: William B. Eerdmans.

Marty, Martin, and R. Scott Appleby. 1992. *The Glory and the Power: The Fundamentalist Challenge to the Modern World*. Boston: Beacon Press.

————, eds. 1995. *Fundamentalisms Comprehended*. The Fundamentalism Project, vol. 5. Chicago: University of Chicago Press.

Matthews, J. 1989. "Abortion Rights Win Follows Bishop's Rebuke: Catholic Democrat Wins California Senate Race." *Washington Post* , 7 December:A 1.

McBrien, Richard. 1981. *Catholicism*. Rev. ed. San Francisco: HarperCollins.

McDannell, Collen. 1989. "Catholic Domesticity, 1860–1960." In *American Catholic Women: A Historical Exploration*, edited by K. Kennelly. New York: Mcmillan.

McGlen, Nancy, and Karen O'Connor. 1983. *Women's Rights: The Struggle for Equality in the Nineteenth and Twentieth Centuries*. New York: Praeger.

McLaughlin, Steven, et. al. 1988. *The Changing Lives of American Women*. Chapel Hill: University of North Carolina Press.

McNamara, Patrick H. 1992. *Conscience First, Tradition Second*. Albany: State University of New York Press.

Meyer, John, and Brian Rowan. 1977. "Institutional Organizations: Formal Structure as Myth and Ceremony." *American Journal of Sociology* 83,2:340–363.

Miller, Donald. 1992. "Hope Chapel: Revisioning the Future of the Foursquare Gospel." Paper presented at the annual meeting of the Society for the Scientific Study of Religion, Washington, D.C.

Monson, Rela Geffen. 1992. "The Impact of the Jewish Women's Movement on the American Synagogue." In *Daughters of the King: Women and the American Synagogue*, edited by S. Grossman and R. Haut. Philadelphia: Jewish Publication Society.

Mueller, Carol. 1981. *Women's Issues and the Search for a "New" Religious Right: A Belief Systems Analysis, 1972–1980*. Wellesley, Mass.: Wellesley College Center for Research on Women.

National Conference of Catholic Bishops (NCCB). 1980. "Changing Roles of Women and Men." In *The Churches Speak on: Sex and Family Life*, edited by J. G. Melton. Detroit: Gale Research.

National Conference of Catholic Bishops, Ad Hoc Committee on Women's Concerns. 1992. "One in Christ Jesus: Toward a Pastoral Response to the Concerns of Women for Church and Society." *Origins* 22,29:490–508.

Neff, David. 1988. "Christian Feminists Regroup to Debate Future." *Christianity Today*, 2 September:43–44.

Neitz, Mary Jo. 1987. *Charisma and Community: A Study of Religious Commitment within the Charismatic Renewal*. New Brunswick, N.J.: Transaction Books.

Neumark, Rabbi Yosef. 1984. "Feminism vs. Judaism." *The Jewish Woman's Outlook*, April/May:13–17.

O'Connor, Cardinal John. 1986. "Addressing the Issues of Work and the Family." In *The Churches Speak on: Sex and Family Life*, edited by J. Gordon Melton. Detroit: Gale Research.

O'Leary, Dale. 1993. "The Authentic Catholic Woman." *Hearth: Journal of the Authentic Catholic Woman*, Spring:5–9.

Orsi, Robert. 1985. *The Madonna of 115th Street: Faith and Community in Italian Harlem, 1880–1950*. New Haven, Conn.: Yale University Press.

O'Sullivan, Gerry. 1993. "Catholicism's New Cold War: The Church Militant Lurches Rightward." *Humanist* 53,5:27.

Paloma, Margaret. 1982. *The Charismatic Movement: Is There a New Pentecost?* Boston: Twayne Publishers.

Parsons, Talcott, and Robert Bales. 1953. *Family, Socialization and Interaction Process.* New York: Free Press.

Perkins, H. Wesley, and Debra DeMeis. 1996. "Gender and Family Effects of the 'Second Shift' Domestic Activity on College-Educated Young Adults." *Gender & Society* 10,1:78–93.

Phillips, Bruce. 1986. "Los Angeles Jewry." *American Jewish Yearbook*:126–195.

Plaskow, Judith. 1990. *Standing Again at Sinai: Judaism from a Feminist Perspective.* San Francisco: Harper & Row.

Pope John Paul II. 1981. *On the Family.* Washington, D.C.: United States Catholic Conference.

————. 1988. "On the Dignity and Vocation of Women." *Origins* 18,17:262–283.

Poston, Dudley, and Kathryn Kramer. 1986. "Patterns of Childlessness among Catholic and Non-Catholic Women in the U.S." *Sociological Inquiry* 56,4:507–522.

Poupko, Chana, and Devorah Wohlgelernter. 1983. "Women's Liberation—An Orthodox Response." *Tradition* 15 (spring):45–52.

Powell, Walter, and Paul DiMaggio, eds. 1991. *The New Institutionalism in Organizational Analysis.* Chicago: University of Chicago Press.

Princeton Religious Research Center (PRRC). 1989–1993. *PRRC Emerging Trends* (monthly newsletter). Princeton, N.J.: Princeton University.

Quebedeaux, Richard. 1974. *The Young Evangelicals: Revolution in Orthodoxy.* New York: Harper & Row.

————. 1983. *The New Charismatics II.* San Francisco: Harper & Row.

Rackman, Emanuel. 1984. "Suggestions for Alternatives." *Judaism* 33 (winter):66–69.

————. 1992. "Not Set in Stone: Orthodox Legal System Must Have Room for Creative Innovation." *The Jewish Week*, 14–20 February:30.

Rader, Rosemary. 1989. "Catholic Feminism: Its Impact on U.S. Catholic Women." In *American Catholic Women: A Historical Exploration*, edited by K. Kennelly. New York: Mcmillan.

Raphael, Marc Lee. 1984. *Profiles in American Judaism: The Reform, Conservative, Orthodox, and Reconstructionist Traditions in Historical Perspective.* San Francisco: Harper & Row.

Rapoport, Gitelle. 1978. "Orthodox Rabbis Belatedly See Red over 'Get' Change." *The Jewish Week*, 12 February.

————. 1992. "Seminar Whets the Appetite of Women Yearning to Learn." *The Jewish Week*, 14–20 February:41.

Robbins, Thomas, and Dick Anthony, eds.1990. *In Gods We Trust*, 2d ed. New Brunswick, N.J.: Transaction.

Roof, Wade Clark. 1993. *A Generation of Seekers: The Spiritual Journeys of the Baby Boom Generation.* San Francisco: HarperCollins.

Roof, Wade Clark, and Christel Manning. 1994. "Cultural Conflicts and Identity: Second Generation Hispanic Catholics in the United States." *Social Compass* 41,1:171–184.

Roof, Wade Clark, and William McKinney.1987. *American Mainline Religion: Its Changing Shape and Future.* New Brunswick, N.J.: Rutgers University Press.

Rose, Susan.1987. "Women Warriors: The Negotiation of Gender in a Charismatic Community." *Sociological Analysis* 48,3:245–258.

Rosen, Gladys. 1979. "The Impact of the Women's Movement on the Jewish Family." *Judaism* 28 (spring):160–168.

Rousseau, Mary. 1991. "Pope John Paul II's Teaching on Women." In *The Catholic Woman,* edited by R. McInerny. San Francisco: Ignatius Press.

Ruether, Rosemary Radford. 1983. *Sexism and God-Talk: Toward a Feminist Theology.* Boston: Beacon Press.

Sandeen, Ernest. 1970. *The Roots of Fundamentalism.* Chicago: University of Chicago Press.

Sarna, Jonathan. 1987. "The Debate over Mixed Seating." In *The American Synagogue: A Sanctuary Transformed,* edited by J. Wertheimer. Cambridge, U.K.: Cambridge University Press.

Scanzoni, Letha. 1966. "Woman's Place: Silence or Service." *Eternity* 17 (February):14–16.

Scanzoni, Letha, and Nancy Hardesty. 1975. *All We're Meant to Be: A Biblical Approach to Women's Liberation.* Waco, Tex.: Word.

Schmalzbauer, John. 1993. "Evangelicals in the New Class: Class Versus Subcultural Predictors of Ideology." *Journal for the Scientific Study of Religion* 32,4:330–342.

Schnall, David. 1987. "Is Feminism Good for the Jews?" *The Jewish Times,* 25 December:7.

Schonfeld, Bella. 1989. *Orthodox Jewish Professional Women Who Return to School for Graduate Degrees during Their Midlife Years.* Ph.D. diss., Columbia University Teachers College.

Schwartz, Sharon. 1991. "Women and Depression: A Durkheimian Perspective" *Social Science and Medicine* 32,2:299–314.

Sered, Susan Starr. 1992. *Women as Ritual Experts: The Religious Lives of Elderly Jewish Women in Jerusalem.* New York: Oxford University Press.

Short, Russell. 1997. "Belief by the Numbers." *New York Times Magazine,* December 7:60–61.

Simon, Rita, and Gloria Danziger. 1991. *Women's Movements in America: Their Successes, Disappointments, and Aspirations.* New York: Praeger.

Small, Andrea. 1992. *Pious and Professional: Medicine as a Career Choice for Orthodox Jewish Women.* Ph.D. diss., Columbia University Teachers College.

Smidt, Corwin. 1989. "Praise the Lord Politics: A Comparative Analysis of the Social Characteristics and Political Views of American Evangelicals and Charismatic Christians." *Sociological Analysis* 50,1:53–72.

Smith, Janet. 1991. "Feminism, Motherhood, and the Church." In *The Catholic Woman,* edited by R. McInerny. San Francisco: Ignatius Press.

Smith-Rosenberg, Carroll. 1984. "Women and Religious Revivals." In *The Evangelical Tradition in America,* edited by L. Sweet. Macon, Georgia: Mercer University Press.

Sperling, Aliza. 1992. "Just Like Any Other Yeshiva—Except It's for Women." *Jewish World,* 4–10 September:15.

Spero, Moshe. 1973. "Negativism and Feminism." *Jewish Life* 40,3:22–25.

Stacey, Judith. 1990. *Brave New Families: Stories of Domestic Upheaval in Late Twentieth Century America.* New York: Basic Books.

Stacey, Judith, and Elizabeth Gerard. 1990. "'We Are Not Doormats': The Influence of Feminism on Contemporary Evangelicals in the United States." In *Uncertain Terms: Negotiating Gender in American Culture,* edited by F. Ginsburg and A. L. Tsing. Boston: Beacon Press.

Steichen, Donna. 1991. *Ungodly Rage: The Hidden Face of Catholic Feminism.* San Francisco: Ignatius Press.

Stuhlmueller, Carol, ed. 1978. *Women and Priesthood: Future Directions.* Collegeville, Minn.: Liturgical Press.

Szasz, Ferenc. 1982. *The Divided Mind of Protestant America, 1880–1930.* University: University of Alabama Press.

Tong, Rosemary. 1989. *Feminist Thought: A Comprehensive Introduction.* Boulder: Westview Press.

Trebbi, Diana. 1986. *Daughters in the Church Becoming Mothers in the Church: A Study of the Roman Catholic Women's Movement.* Ph.D. diss., City University of New York.

————. 1990. "Women-Church: Catholic Women Produce an Alternative Spirituality." In *In Gods We Trust,* 2d ed., edited by T. Robbins and D. Anthony. New Brunswick, New Jersey: Transaction.

Wallace, Ruth. 1988. "Catholic Women and the Creation of a New Social Reality." *Gender & Society* 2,1:24–38.

————. 1992. *They Call Her Pastor: A New Role for Catholic Women.* Albany: State University of New York Press.

Warner, R. Stephen. 1979. "Theoretical Barriers to the Understanding of Evangelical Christianity." *Sociological Analysis* 40,1:1–9.

Waxman, Chaim. 1992. "Are America's Jews Experiencing a Religious Revival?" *Qualitative Sociology* 15,2:203–211.

Weaver, Mary Jo. 1985. *New Catholic Women: A Contemporary Challenge to Traditional Religious Authority.* San Francisco: Harper & Row.

Weaver, Mary Jo, and R. Scott Appleby, eds. 1995. *Being Right: Conservative Catholics in America.* Bloomington: Indiana University Press.

Weissman, Deborah. 1976. "Bais Yaakov: A Historical Model for Jewish Feminists." In *The Jewish Woman: New Perspectives,* edited by E. Kolthun. New York: Schocken Books.

Weitzman, Leonore. 1985. *The Divorce Revolution: The Unexpected Social and Economic Consequences for Women and Children in America.* New York: The Free Press.

Wertheimer, Jack, ed. 1987. *The American Synagogue: A Sanctuary Transformed.* Cambridge, U.K.: Cambridge University Press.

————. 1989. "Recent Trends in American Judaism." *American Jewish Yearbook,* 63–162.

————. 1993. *A People Divided: Judaism in Contemporary America.* New York: Basic Books.

Westoff, Charles, and Elise Jones. 1977. "The Secularization of U.S. Catholic Birth Control Practices." *Family Planning Perspectives* 9,5:203–207.

Wilcox, Clyde. 1986. "Evangelicals and Fundamentalists in the New Christian Right: Religious Differences in the Ohio Moral Majority." *Journal for the Scientific Study of Religion* 25,3:355–363.

————. 1991. "Evangelicalism, Social Identity, and Gender Attitudes among Women." *American Politics Quarterly* 19,3:353–363.

Wilcox, Clyde, and Elizabeth Cook. 1989. "Evangelical Women and Feminism: Some Additional Evidence." *Women and Politics* 9,2:27–48.

Wilcox, Clyde, and Ted Jelen. 1991. "The Effects of Employment and Religion on Women's Feminist Attitudes." *International Journal for the Psychology of Religion* 1,3:161–171.

Willetts, Judith Bingman. 1993. *Role Satisfaction and Religiosity among Professional Women.* Ph.D. diss., Biola University.

Wolowelsky, Joel. 1986. "Modern Orthodoxy and Women's Changing Self-Perception." *Tradition* 22,1:65–81.

Women for Faith and Family (WFF). 1994. "Affirmation for Catholic Women." *Voices* 8,4:31.

Woodward, Kenneth. 1993. "What Evil Lurks in the Heart." *Newsweek* 122,6:4.

Wuthnow, Robert. 1981. "Two Traditions in the Study of Religion." *Journal for the Scientific Study of Religion* 20,1:16–32.

———. 1983. "The Political Rebirth of American Evangelicals." In *The New Christian Right: Mobilization and Legitimation*, edited by R. Liebman and R. Wuthnow. New York: Aldine Publishing.

———. 1988. *The Restructuring of American Religion: Society and Faith Since World War II*. Princeton, N.J.: Princeton University Press.

Zolty, Shoshana Pantel. 1993. *And All Your Children Shall Be Learned: Women and the Study of Torah in Jewish Law and History*. Northvale, N.J.: Jason Aronson.

Index

About the Author

Christel J. Manning is assistant professor of religious studies at Sacred Heart University in Fairfield, Connecticut. Born in southern California, she spent her teen years in Germany, received her B.A. from Tufts University in Boston, and earned her M.A. and Ph.D. in religious studies from the University of California at Santa Barbara. She has published articles in a variety of books and scholarly journals, examining the role of women in traditional and new religions and at the intersection of religion and politics. She is working on a study of religion and health.

Printed in the United States
130103LV00002B/21/A